MW00453357

# Autodesk® Revit® 2017 (R1) Architecture Review for Certification

## Official Certification Preparation

*Student Guide*
*Imperial - 1st Edition*

**AUTODESK.**
Authorized Publisher

# ASCENT - Center for Technical Knowledge®
## Autodesk® Revit® 2017 (R1) Architecture
## Review for Certification
Imperial - 1<sup>st</sup> Edition

Prepared and produced by:

ASCENT Center for Technical Knowledge
630 Peter Jefferson Parkway, Suite 175
Charlottesville, VA 22911

866-527-2368
www.ASCENTed.com

Lead Contributors: Martha Hollowell

ASCENT - Center for Technical Knowledge is a division of Rand Worldwide, Inc., providing custom developed knowledge products and services for leading engineering software applications. ASCENT is focused on specializing in the creation of education programs that incorporate the best of classroom learning and technology-based training offerings.

We welcome any comments you may have regarding this student guide, or any of our products. To contact us please email: feedback@ASCENTed.com.

© ASCENT - Center for Technical Knowledge, 2016

All rights reserved. No part of this guide may be reproduced in any form by any photographic, electronic, mechanical or other means or used in any information storage and retrieval system without the written permission of ASCENT, a division of Rand Worldwide, Inc.

The following are registered trademarks or trademarks of Autodesk, Inc., and/or its subsidiaries and/or affiliates in the USA and other countries: 123D, 3ds Max, Alias, ATC, AutoCAD LT, AutoCAD, Autodesk, the Autodesk logo, Autodesk 123D, Autodesk Homestyler, Autodesk Inventor, Autodesk MapGuide, Autodesk Streamline, AutoLISP, AutoSketch, AutoSnap, AutoTrack, Backburner, Backdraft, Beast, BIM 360, Burn, Buzzsaw, CADmep, CAiCE, CAMduct, Civil 3D, Combustion, Communication Specification, Configurator 360, Constructware, Content Explorer, Creative Bridge, Dancing Baby (image), DesignCenter, DesignKids, DesignStudio, Discreet, DWF, DWG, DWG (design/logo), DWG Extreme, DWG TrueConvert, DWG TrueView, DWGX, DXF, Ecotect, Ember, ESTmep, FABmep, Face Robot, FBX, Fempro, Fire, Flame, Flare, Flint, ForceEffect, FormIt 360, Freewheel, Fusion 360, Glue, Green Building Studio, Heidi, Homestyler, HumanIK, i-drop, ImageModeler, Incinerator, Inferno, InfraWorks, Instructables, Instructables (stylized robot design/logo), Inventor, Inventor HSM, Inventor LT, Lustre, Maya, Maya LT, MIMI, Mockup 360, Moldflow Plastics Advisers, Moldflow Plastics Insight, Moldflow, Moondust, MotionBuilder, Movimento, MPA (design/logo), MPA, MPI (design/logo), MPX (design/logo), MPX, Mudbox, Navisworks, ObjectARX, ObjectDBX, Opticore, P9, Pier 9, Pixlr, Pixlr-o-matic, Productstream, Publisher 360, RasterDWG, RealDWG, ReCap, ReCap 360, Remote, Revit LT, Revit, RiverCAD, Robot, Scaleform, Showcase, Showcase 360, SketchBook, Smoke, Socialcam, Softimage, Spark & Design, Spark Logo, Sparks, SteeringWheels, Stitcher, Stone, StormNET, TinkerBox, Tinkercad, Tinkerplay, ToolClip, Topobase, Toxik, TrustedDWG, T-Splines, ViewCube, Visual LISP, Visual, VRED, Wire, Wiretap, WiretapCentral, XSI.

NASTRAN is a registered trademark of the National Aeronautics Space Administration.

All other brand names, product names, or trademarks belong to their respective holders.

General Disclaimer:

Notwithstanding any language to the contrary, nothing contained herein constitutes nor is intended to constitute an offer, inducement, promise, or contract of any kind. The data contained herein is for informational purposes only and is not represented to be error free. ASCENT, its agents and employees, expressly disclaim any liability for any damages, losses or other expenses arising in connection with the use of its materials or in connection with any failure of performance, error, omission even if ASCENT, or its representatives, are advised of the possibility of such damages, losses or other expenses. No consequential damages can be sought against ASCENT or Rand Worldwide, Inc. for the use of these materials by any third parties or for any direct or indirect result of that use.

The information contained herein is intended to be of general interest to you and is provided "as is", and it does not address the circumstances of any particular individual or entity. Nothing herein constitutes professional advice, nor does it constitute a comprehensive or complete statement of the issues discussed thereto. ASCENT does not warrant that the document or information will be error free or will meet any particular criteria of performance or quality. In particular (but without limitation) information may be rendered inaccurate by changes made to the subject of the materials (i.e. applicable software). Rand Worldwide, Inc. specifically disclaims any warranty, either expressed or implied, including the warranty of fitness for a particular purpose.

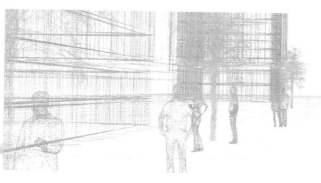

# Contents

© 2016, ASCENT - Center for Technical Knowledge®

© 2016, ASCENT - Center for Technical Knowledge®

© 2016, ASCENT - Center for Technical Knowledge®

# Preface

*Autodesk® Revit® 2017 (R1) Architecture: Review for Certification* is a comprehensive review guide to assist in preparing for the Autodesk Revit Architecture Certified Professional exam. It enables experienced users to review learning content from ASCENT that is related to the exam objectives.

New users of Autodesk® Revit® 2017 (R1) Architecture software should refer to the following ASCENT student guides:

- *Autodesk® Revit® 2017 (R1): Architecture: Fundamentals*

- *Autodesk® Revit® 2017 (R1): Architecture: Conceptual Design & Visualization*

- *Autodesk® Revit® 2017 (R1): Architecture: Site and Structural Design*

- *Autodesk® Revit® 2017 (R1): BIM Management: Template and Family Creation*

- *Autodesk® Revit® 2017 (R1): Collaboration Tools*

| Exam Topic | Exam Objectives | Chapter(s) |
|---|---|---|
| **Collaboration** | Copy and monitor elements in a linked file | • Ch 1 |
| | Use Worksharing | |
| | Import DWG and image file | |
| | Use Worksharing Visualization | |
| | Assess review warnings in Revit | |
| **Documentation** | Create and modify filled regions | • Ch 2 |
| | Place detail components and repeating details | |
| | Tag elements (doors, windows, etc.) by category | |
| | Use dimension strings | |
| | Set the colors used in a color scheme legend | |
| | Work with phases | |

| Exam Topic | Exam Objectives | Chapter(s) |
|---|---|---|
| **Elements and Families** | Change elements within a curtain wall (grids, panels, mullions) | • Ch 3 |
| | Create compound walls | |
| | Create a stacked wall | |
| | Differentiate system and component families | |
| | Work with family Parameters | |
| | Create a new family type | |
| | Use Family creation procedures | |
| **Modeling** | Create a building pad | • Ch 4 |
| | Define floors for a mass | |
| | Create a stair with a landing | |
| | Create elements such as a floors, ceilings, or roofs | |
| | Generate a toposurface | |
| | Model railings | |
| | Edit a model element's material (door, window, furniture) | |
| | Change a generic floor/ceiling/roof to a specific type | |
| | Attach walls to a roof or ceiling | |
| | Edit room-aware families | |
| **Views** | Define element properties in a schedule | • Ch 5 |
| | Control visibility | |
| | Use levels | |
| | Create a duplicate view for a plan, section, elevation, drafting view, etc. | |
| | Create and manage legends | |
| | Manage view position on sheets | |
| | Organize and sort items in a schedule | |

© 2016, ASCENT - Center for Technical Knowledge®

## Note on Software Setup

This review guide assumes a standard installation of the software using the default preferences during installation. Lectures and practices use the standard software templates and default options for the Content Libraries.

## Students and Educators can Access Free Autodesk Software and Resources

Autodesk challenges you to get started with free educational licenses for professional software and creativity apps used by millions of architects, engineers, designers, and hobbyists today. Bring Autodesk software into your classroom, studio, or workshop to learn, teach, and explore real-world design challenges the way professionals do.

Get started today - register at the Autodesk Education Community and download one of the many Autodesk software applications available.

Visit www.autodesk.com/joinedu/

*Note: Free products are subject to the terms and conditions of the end-user license and services agreement that accompanies the software. The software is for personal use for education purposes and is not intended for classroom or lab use.*

## Lead Contributor: Martha Hollowell

Martha incorporates her passion for architecture and education into all her projects, including the training guides she creates on Autodesk Revit for Architecture, MEP, and Structure. She started working with AutoCAD in the early 1990's, adding AutoCAD Architecture and Autodesk Revit as they came along.

After receiving a B.Sc. in Architecture from the University of Virginia, she worked in the architectural department of the Colonial Williamsburg Foundation and later in private practice, consulting with firms setting up AutoCAD in their offices.

Martha has over 20 years' experience as a trainer and instructional designer. She is skilled in leading individuals and small groups to understand and build on their potential. Martha is trained in Instructional Design and has achieved the Autodesk Certified Instructor (ACI) and Autodesk Certified Professional designations for Revit Architecture.

Martha Hollowell has been the Lead Contributor for the *Autodesk Revit Architecture: Review for Certification* since its initial release in 2013.

© 2016, ASCENT - Center for Technical Knowledge®

# In this Guide

The following images highlight some of the features that can be found in this Student Guide.

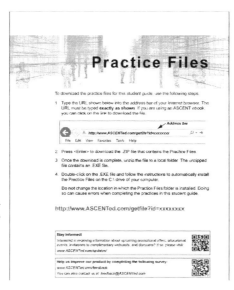

**Link for practice files**

***Practice Files***

The Practice Files page tells you how to download and install the practice files that are provided with this student guide.

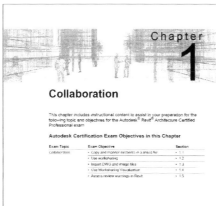

**Exam Topics and Objectives in the chapter**

***Chapters***

Each chapter begins with a list of the exam topics and objectives covered in the chapter.

## Instructional Content

Each chapter is split into a series of sections of instructional content on specific topics. These lectures include the descriptions, step-by-step procedures, figures, hints, and information you need to achieve the chapter's exam objectives.

## Side notes

Side notes are hints or additional information for the current topic.

## Practice Objectives

## Practices

Practices enable you to use the software to perform a hands-on review of a topic.

Some practices require you to use prepared practice files, which can be downloaded from the link found on the Practice Files page.

## Review Questions

Review questions, located at the end of this guide, enable you to self-evaluate your understanding of the key topics and objectives in this guide.

© 2016, ASCENT - Center for Technical Knowledge®

# Practice Files

To download the practice files for this student guide, use the following steps:

1. Type the URL shown below into the address bar of your Internet browser. The URL must be typed **exactly as shown**. If you are using an ASCENT ebook, you can click on the link to download the file.

*Address bar*

http://www.ASCENTed.com/getfile?id=ciconiiformes

File   Edit   View   Favorites   Tools   Help

2. Press <Enter> to download the .ZIP file that contains the Practice Files.

3. Once the download is complete, unzip the file to a local folder. The unzipped file contains an .EXE file.

4. Double-click on the .EXE file and follow the instructions to automatically install the Practice Files on the C:\ drive of your computer.

   **Do not** change the location in which the Practice Files folder is installed. Doing so can cause errors when completing the practices in this student guide.

## http://www.ASCENTed.com/getfile?id=ciconiiformes

---

**Stay Informed!**

Interested in receiving information about upcoming promotional offers, educational events, invitations to complimentary webcasts, and discounts? If so, please visit:

*www.ASCENTed.com/updates/*

---

**Help us improve our product by completing the following survey:**

*www.ASCENTed.com/feedback*

You can also contact us at: *feedback@ASCENTed.com*

---

© 2016, ASCENT - Center for Technical Knowledge®

# Collaboration

This chapter includes instructional content to assist in your preparation for the following topic and objectives for the Autodesk® Revit® Architecture Certified Professional exam.

## Autodesk Certification Exam Objectives in this Chapter

| Exam Topic | Exam Objective | Section |
|---|---|---|
| Collaboration | • Copy and monitor elements in a linked file | • 1.1 |
| | • Use worksharing | • 1.2 |
| | • Import DWG and image files | • 1.3 |
| | • Use Worksharing Visualization | • 1.4 |
| | • Assess review warnings in Revit | • 1.5 |

# 1.1 Copy and Monitor Elements in a Linked File

When working with linked files, such as an architectural model linked into a structural or MEP project, you can coordinate information between the files using the **Copy/Monitor** tool. When you monitor an item in the linked file with an identical or similar one in the host project, the program tracks these two items, looking for changes in location, existence, height, etc. It always requires two elements to compare.

Items that are monitored display the ⌷ icon when selected, as shown in Figure 1–1.

*Copy/Monitor works with grids, levels, columns, walls, and floors, as well as MEP fixtures in the same file or in a linked file.*

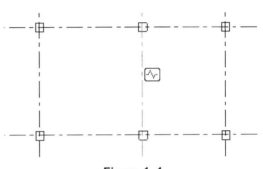

**Figure 1–1**

- **Monitor:** Compares two elements of the same type (in the same project or in a project and a linked model) to ensure that the correct relationship between them is maintained. For example, you can monitor two grid lines in the project that you want to keep a specific distance apart or an architectural level in a linked model and the T.O. Steel level in the structural host project.

- **Copy:** Duplicates elements from the linked model into the host project and monitors those elements against the linked model. For example, you may want to copy and monitor plumbing fixtures from the linked architectural model into the MEP host project.

© 2016, ASCENT - Center for Technical Knowledge®

## What is Typically Copied/Monitored:

- **Architects:** The **Copy/Monitor** tool is not heavily used by architects, although they might on occasion monitor elements in their project. For some projects they might use the structural engineer's linked model to control the grids and column locations or the plumbing engineer's linked model to control the location of the plumbing fixtures.

- **Structural:** Structural consultants copy/monitor levels, grids, columns, floors, and bearing walls from the architectural project.

- **MEP:** Mechanical consultants monitor levels and grids from the architectural model. They also copy/monitor some elements including plumbing and lighting fixtures.

- It is especially important to agree who controls datum elements, such as levels and grids, and not to modify them without explicit communication with others using that project as a link.

## How To: Monitor Elements

1. In the *Collaborate* tab>Coordinate panel, expand ![icon] (Copy/Monitor) and click ![icon] (Use Current Project) or ![icon] (Select Link).

2. In the *Copy/Monitor* tab>Tools panel, click ![icon] (Monitor).
3. Pick the first element to monitor and then the corresponding element to monitor.
4. The ![icon] icon displays on the first element of the selected pair.
5. If you want to monitor other pairs you can continue selecting the element to monitor and then the corresponding element.
6. When you have finished selecting elements, click  (Finish).

- If you move or otherwise modify one of the monitored elements, the related elements highlight and a warning displays alerting you of the change as shown in Figure 1–2.

Figure 1–2

## How To: Copy Elements from a Linked File into a Host File

1. Have a linked file in the host drawing.
2. In the *Collaborate* tab>Coordinate panel, expand  (Copy/Monitor) and click  (Select Link).
3. In the project, select the linked file.
4. In the *Copy/Monitor* tab>Tools panel, click  (Copy).
5. Pick the elements that you want to copy into the host project.
   - Click on them one at a time.
   - Select **Multiple** in the Options Bar, select all of the elements you need, and click **Finish**.
6. When you have finished selecting elements to copy into the host project, in the *Copy/Monitor* tab>Copy/Monitor panel, click  (Finish).
7. The elements become part of your host drawing and you can manipulate them, as required. The originals remain in the linked file with a monitoring watch set between them.

© 2016, ASCENT - Center for Technical Knowledge®

## Copy/Monitor Options

Before starting the copy/monitor process, you can modify settings for the types of elements. In the *Copy/Monitor* tab>Tools panel, click 🔧 (Options). In the Copy/Monitor Options dialog box, select the tab for the type of element that you want to copy: *Levels*, *Grids*, *Columns*, *Walls*, or *Floors*, as shown in Figure 1–3.

*Tabs display for the categories that exist in the linked project.*

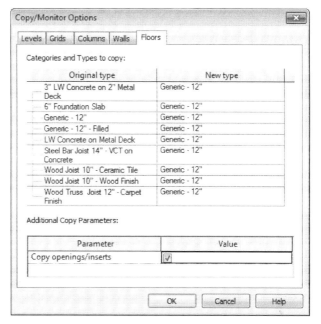

**Figure 1–3**

- By default, hosted elements such as shaft openings in floors and door, and window openings in walls (as shown in Figure 1–4) are automatically copied with their host elements. You can change this response in the Copy/Monitor Options dialog box, in the *Floors* tab *Additional Copy Parameters* area, as shown in Figure 1–3.

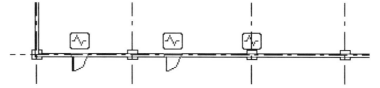

**Figure 1–4**

- MEP projects have additional options for Coordination Settings where you specify the copy and mapping behavior for different HVAC, Plumbing, Electrical equipment and fixtures, and other related devices, as shown in Figure 1–5. These elements can also be batch copied into the host project from the linked model.

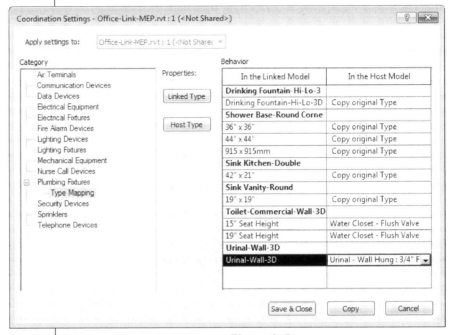

**Figure 1–5**

## Working with Copy/Monitor Elements

- When you open a project with a linked file that includes changes to elements that are monitored, the warning dialog box opens as shown in Figure 1–6.

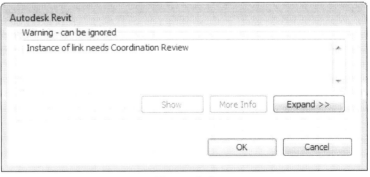

**Figure 1–6**

© 2016, ASCENT - Center for Technical Knowledge®

- When you work in a host project and move an element that is copied into the host file, you see a warning as shown in Figure 1–7. This does not prevent you from making the change, but alerts you that this is a monitored element that requires further coordination with the other disciplines involved.

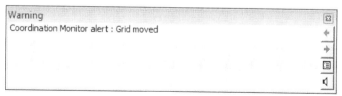

**Figure 1–7**

- If you make a change to a monitored host element, such as adding a door in a wall, a warning opens as shown in Figure 1–8.

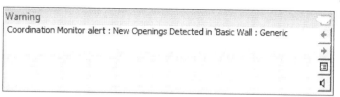

**Figure 1–8**

- If you no longer want an element to be monitored, select it and in the associated *Modify* tab>Monitor panel, click

 (Stop Monitoring).

# Practice 1a
# Copy and Monitor Elements in a Linked File

### Practice Objective

- Copy and monitor elements.

In this practice you will start a new structural project and link in an architectural model. You will then Copy/Monitor the grids, setup Column options to use structural columns, and Copy/Monitor in the columns, as shown in Figure 1–9.

*Estimated time of completion: 15minutes*

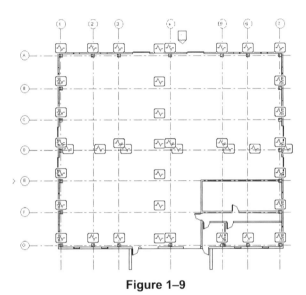

**Figure 1–9**

### Task 1 - Link a file and copy/monitor elements

1. Start a new project based on the Structural template and save the project as **Warehouse-Structural.rvt**.

2. Open the **Structural Plans: Level 1** view.

3. In the *Insert* tab>Link panel, click  (Link Revit).

© 2016, ASCENT - Center for Technical Knowledge®

4. In the Import/Link RVT dialog box, navigate to the practice files folder and select **Warehouse-A.rvt**. Verify that the *Positioning* is set to **Auto - Origin to Origin** and click **Open**.

5. The columns and grids of the linked model, and the doors and foundation elements display, while the walls do not because they are not structural.

6. In the Project Browser, right-click on the **Structural Plans: Level 1** view and select **Apply Template Properties...**.

7. In the Apply View Template dialog box, select **Architectural Plan** and click **OK**.

8. In the *Collaborate* tab>Coordinate panel, expand (Copy/Monitor) and click (Select Link).

9. Select the linked warehouse model.

10. In the *Copy/Monitor* tab>Tools panel, click (Copy).

11. In the Options Bar, select **Multiple**. Select all of the grids using any selection method, such as that shown in Figure 1–10. Hold <Ctrl> and select additional grids, as required. In the Options Bar, click **Finish**.

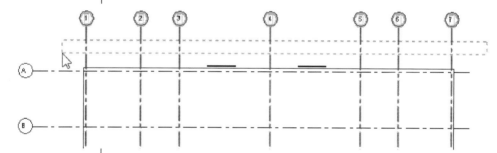

**Figure 1–10**

12. The grids are copied into the host project and monitored in place, as shown in Figure 1–11.

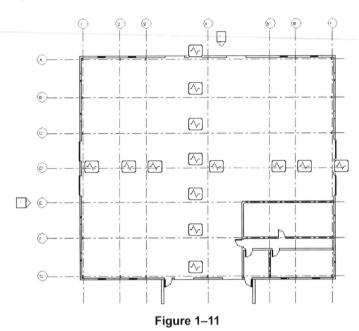

**Figure 1–11**

13. Click ▷ (Modify) to release the grids.

14. Return to the *Copy/Monitor* tab. In the Tools panel, click 🔧 (Options).

15. In the Copy/Monitor Options dialog box, select the *Columns* tab. The types of columns in the linked file are listed on the left. Verify that the architectural columns are set to a structural column type. For the *Pipe-Column*, select **Copy original Type** as shown in Figure 1–12.

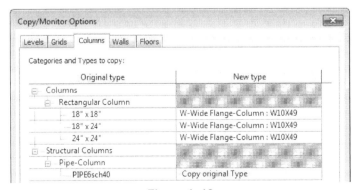

**Figure 1–12**

© 2016, ASCENT - Center for Technical Knowledge®

16. Click **OK**.

17. In the *Copy/Monitor* tab>Tools panel, click 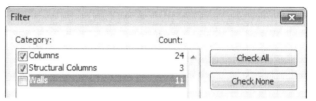 (Copy).

18. In the Options Bar, select **Multiple**.

19. Create a window around the entire building to select everything but the grids.

20. In the Status Bar or Options Bar, click ▼ (Filter).

21. In the Filter dialog box, select **Columns** and **Structural Columns**. Clear **Walls** as shown in Figure 1–13 and click **OK**.

**Figure 1–13**

22. In the Options Bar, click **Finish**.

23. The columns are copied into the project as shown in Figure 1–14.

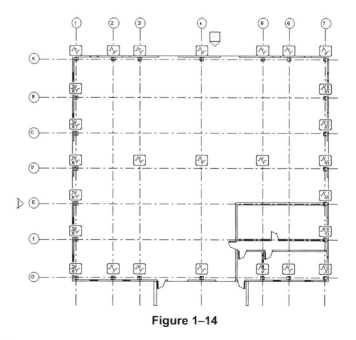

**Figure 1–14**

24. In the *Copy/Monitor* tab, click ✓ (Finish).

25. Zoom into the columns. There should be structural columns at the location of the square architectural columns, as shown in Figure 1–15, and pipe columns in the center of the building.

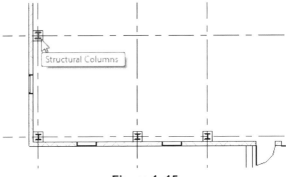

**Figure 1–15**

26. Save and close the project.

© 2016, ASCENT - Center for Technical Knowledge®

# 1.2 Use Worksharing

When a project becomes too big for one person, it needs to be subdivided so that a team of people can work on it. Since Autodesk® Revit® projects include the entire building model in one file, the file needs to be separated into logical components (as shown in Figure 1–16), without losing the connection to the whole. This process is called "worksharing" and its main component is worksets.

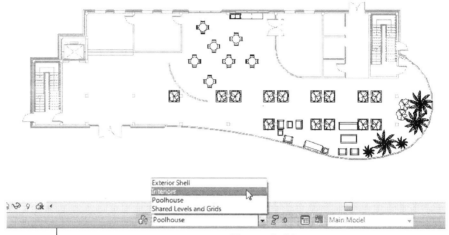

Figure 1–16

When worksets are established in a project, there is one **central file** and as many **local files** as required for each person on the team to have a file, as shown in Figure 1–17. All local files are saved back to the central file, and updates to the central file are sent out to the local files. This way, all changes remain in one file and all parts of the project, model views, and sheets are automatically updated.

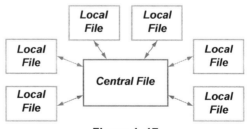

Figure 1–17

- The central file is created by the BIM Manager, Project Manager, or Project Lead, and stored on a server, enabling multiple user access.

# Workset Definitions

**Workset:** A collection of related elements in a project. Each user-created workset matches a part of the project that an individual team member would work on (such as the exterior shell, site, or interior partitions). There are also worksets created automatically for Families, Project Standards (such as materials and line styles), and Views. Worksets can be checked out so that others cannot modify them without permission.

**Central File:** The main file that holds all of the worksets. This is the file to which everyone saves their changes. Typically, the file is not edited directly.

**Local File:** A copy of the central file that is saved to your local computer. This is the file that you modify. You then save the file locally and synchronize it with the central file.

**Element borrowing:** Refers to the process of modifying items in the project that are not part of the workset you have checked out. This either happens automatically (if no one else has checked out a workset), or specifically, when you request to have control of the elements (if someone else has a workset checked out).

## General Process of Using Worksets

1. Create a local file from the central file that is set up by the project manager.
2. Open the local file and select the worksets on which you need to work.
3. Set a workset active. This is the workset on which any new elements are placed.
4. Add and modify elements, as required.
   - You may need to request access to elements in worksets that are currently checked out by other project team members.
5. Save the local file frequently as you would save any other project.
6. Synchronize the local file with the central file several times a day or as required by company policy or project status.
   - This reloads any changes from the central file to your local file and vice versa.
7. Save the local file every time you save to the central file.

*Close any worksets to which you do not need access. This saves system memory and frees up elements for other project team members to edit.*

© 2016, ASCENT - Center for Technical Knowledge®

# Opening and Saving Workset-Related Projects

The first step in using a workset-related project is to create a local file. This is the file you use to add and modify any of the elements in a project. Once you have a local file created, you can open it with only specific worksets opened. Local files are saved directly to your computer. You can also synchronize the local file with the central file.

## How To: Create a Local File

*Some people recommend that you create a new local file every morning to ensure that you have the most up-to-date information.*

1. Open the central file. This is typically on a server and might have "Central" in its name. Do not work in this file.
2. In the Open dialog box, when a central file is selected, use the option **Create New Local**, as shown in Figure 1–18.
3. Verify that it is selected and click **Open**.

**Figure 1–18**

4. A copy of the project is created. It has the same name as the central file with Autodesk Revit *User Name* added to the end.

5. In the Quick Access Toolbar, click  (Save) if you want to use the default filename (*Central File Name-Local*.rvt). Alternatively, in the Application Menu, select **File>Save As> Project** and name the file according to your office standard. It can include "Local" in the name to indicate that it is saved on your local computer or that you are the only one working with that copy of the file.
6. Click **Save**.

## Hint: Setting the Username and Default File Location

The Autodesk Revit software checks the current *Username* to assign the local file name and determine which worksets are available for you to open after you create a local file. By default, it uses the login name you provided when you entered the operating system. You can change the *Username* in the Options dialog box (**Application Menu>Options**) in the *General* pane, as shown in Figure 1–19.

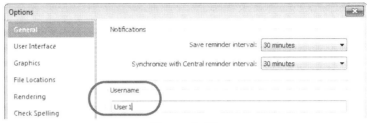

**Figure 1–19**

- This pane is also where you can set reminders to save and synchronize the local file with the central file.

In the *File Locations* pane, set the *Default path for user files*, as shown in Figure 1–20.

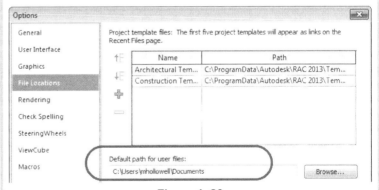

**Figure 1–20**

- This pane is also where you set location for project template files, family template files, and point cloud files.

© 2016, ASCENT - Center for Technical Knowledge®

## How To: Open a Local File with Specific Worksets Editable

Once you have created a local file, you can open it with specific worksets editable.

1. Start the  (Open) command.
2. In the Open dialog box, select the local file set up on your computer.

3. Click ▾ beside **Open** and select which worksets you want to open, as shown in Figure 1–21.

File name: Condo-Project-local.rvt

Files of type: All Supported Files (*.rvt, *.rfa, *.rte, *.adsk)

Worksharing

☐ Audit  ☐ Detach from Central  ☐ Create New Local  Open ▾  Cancel

Workset:

All

Editable

✓ Last Viewed

Specify...

**Figure 1–21**

4. Click **Open**.

## Open Worksets Options

| All | Opens all worksets. |
|---|---|
| Editable | Opens all worksets that are editable (not checked out by someone else). |
| Last Viewed | Opens the worksets that were viewed last time you saved the local file. This is the default after the local file has been saved once. |
| Specify | Opens the Opening Worksets dialog box (once you click **Open**) where you select the worksets you want opened or closed. |

**Enhanced** in 2017

- A rarely used option, **Detach from Central**, opens the file and detaches it from the central file. The new file name automatically has "detached" appended to the end of the name. You can either detach and preserve worksets, which you can then save as a different central file, or detach and discard worksets and all the related elements which removes all worksharing options from the file.

## How To: Specify Opened or Closed Worksets

If you select **Specify...** when you open a workset-related file, it opens the Opening Worksets dialog box.

1. In the Opening Worksets dialog box (shown in Figure 1–22), select the name of the workset you want to open or close.

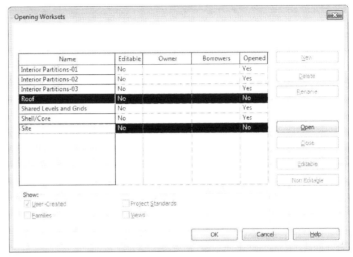

**Figure 1–22**

2. Click **Close** if a workset is opened and you want to close it. Click **Open** if a workset is closed and you want to open it.
3. Click **OK** to finish.

- You can select more than one workset by holding <Ctrl> or <Shift>. To select all of the worksets, press <Ctrl>+A.

## Notes on Local Files

- When you open a local file, select only those worksets you need to open. Limiting the number of worksets speeds up the process of opening and saving the file.

- Only the user who created a local file should work on it, although others can open it. If you do open someone else's file, an alert box displays recommending that you change the user name or stop working on the file.

- If you try to save a file listed in someone else's name, you are alerted that it cannot be saved.

© 2016, ASCENT - Center for Technical Knowledge®

# Saving Workset Related Files

To save workset-related files, you save them to your local machine as you would any other file. You also synchronize the file with the central file periodically and at the end of the day.

- Save the local file frequently (every 15-30 minutes). In the Quick Access Toolbar, click ![Save icon] (Save) to save the local file as you would any other project.

- Synchronize to the central file periodically (every hour or two) or after you have made major changes to the project.

## Synchronizing to the Central File

There are two methods for synchronizing to the central file.

**Synchronize Now:** Updates the central file and then the local file with any changes to the central file since the last synchronization without prompting you for any settings. It automatically relinquishes elements borrowed from any workset but retains worksets used by the current user.

*The last used command is active if you click the top level icon.*

- In the Quick Access Toolbar or *Collaborate* tab>Synchronize panel, expand ![icon] (Synchronize and Modify Settings or Synchronize with Central), and click ![icon] (Synchronize Now).

**Synchronize and Modify Settings:** Opens the Synchronize with Central dialog box, as shown in Figure 1–23, where you can set the location of the central file, add comments, save the file locally before and after synchronization, and set the options for relinquishing worksets and elements.

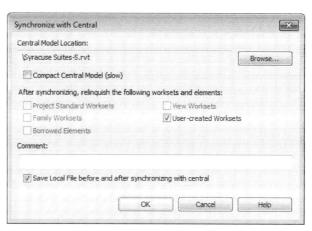

**Figure 1–23**

- In the Quick Access Toolbar or *Collaborate* tab>Synchronize panel, expand (Synchronize and Modify Settings or Synchronize with Central), and click (Synchronize and Modify Settings).

- Always save the local file after you have synchronized the file with central. Changes from the central file might have been copied into your file.

- When you close a local file without saving to the central file you are prompted to do so as shown in Figure 1–24.

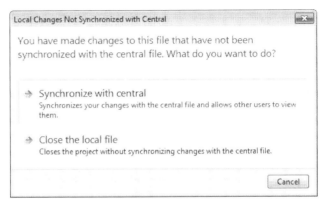

**Figure 1–24**

### Hint: Save As Options

If you want to save the central file as a new central file, use **Save As**. In the Save As dialog box, click **Options....** In the File Save Options dialog box, select the **Make this a Central File after save** option, as shown in Figure 1–25. This option is toggled off by default because you typically create local files from the central file.

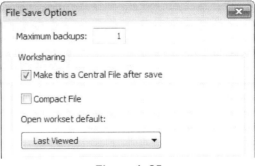

**Figure 1–25**

© 2016, ASCENT - Center for Technical Knowledge®

# Working in Workset-Related Projects

Most of the work you do in a workset is no different to working in any other project. You draw and modify elements. You create views, sheets, and schedules. You even create families and modify family types, if you have permissions to do so.

Several workset-specific methods and tools can increase your effectiveness as you work. You can edit elements in worksets that you have not checked out, check out worksets, request and receive editing permissions, and save the worksets locally and to the central file.

- Once you are in a workset-related project, select the *Collaborate* tab, as shown in Figure 1–26. The workset-related tools are in the Worksets and Synchronize panels.

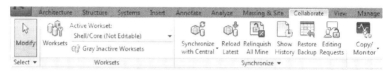

**Figure 1–26**

## Setting the Active Workset

When new elements are added to the project, they are placed on the active workset. It is therefore important to set the active workset correctly before adding new elements. Not doing so can result in visibility and permissions-related issues.

### How To: Set the Active Workset

1. Open your local file.
2. In the Status Bar, expand the *Active Workset* list and select a workset, as shown in Figure 1–27.

*You can also set the active workset in the Collaborate tab>Manage Collaboration panel.*

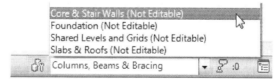

**Figure 1–27**

- It does not matter if the workset says (**Not Editable**); you can still add elements to it. **Not Editable** means that you have not checked out the workset but are working on the basis of borrowing elements.

- You can gray out inactive worksets in a view to easily distinguish between active and inactive worksets, as shown in Figure 1–28. In the *Collaborate* tab>Manage Collaboration panel, toggle 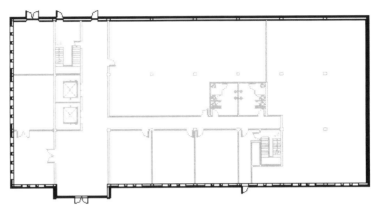 (Gray Inactive Workset Graphics) on. You can also select **Gray Inactive Workset Graphics** in the Worksets dialog box.

**Figure 1–28**

## Editing Elements in Worksets

There are two different ways to edit elements in worksets:

1. Borrow elements: If you *borrow* the elements as you make changes, no one has to wait for permission to make modifications even if someone else is working on the same workset. This can speed up the work if you have a fairly small group of people working on the project, especially when there is some overlap between the purposes of the users or when the project has only been divided into a few worksets.

2. Check out a workset: When you *check out* a specific workset and make it editable, no one else can modify elements in that workset without expressed permission.

*Check with your project coordinator to see which method your office uses.*

© 2016, ASCENT - Center for Technical Knowledge®

## Borrowing Elements

When you select an element and see the **Make element editable** icon, as shown in Figure 1–29, it means you have not checked out that particular workset or that you are not currently borrowing the element.

*It is not necessary to click the icon; simply proceed to edit the element as required.*

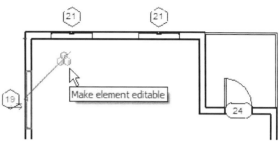

**Figure 1–29**

- If you modify the element and it enables you to do so, then no one else has that workset checked out and you were given automatic permission to modify this element.

- If someone else has borrowed the element or checked out the workset to which it belongs, you are prompted to request permission to edit the element.

## How To: Check Out Worksets

1. In the *Collaborate* tab>Manage Collaboration panel, click (Worksets).

*You can also open the Worksets dialog box from the Status Bar.*

2. In the Worksets dialog box, select **Yes** in the *Editable* column next to the workset name that you want to checkout and edit, as shown in Figure 1–30. More than one workset can be checked out and made editable at a time, but ensure that you only check out those that you really need.

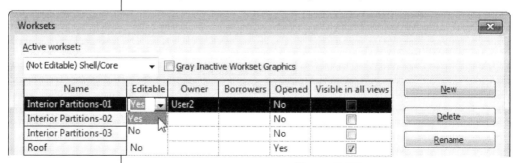

**Figure 1–30**

3. Select **Active workset** in the menu. You can also set the active workset from the list in the Manage Collaboration panel and Status Bar.
4. Click **OK**.

- When editing elements, you can control which ones can be picked by selecting the **Editable Only** option in the Options Bar, as shown in Figure 1–31. If **Editable Only** is selected, you can only select items that are available in the editable worksets or those which you borrowed. If it is cleared, you can select anything.

**Figure 1–31**

## Permissions to Edit

If you try to edit an element that is being used by someone else, an alert box opens stating that you cannot edit the element without their permission, as shown in Figure 1–32. First, you must request an edit. Second, the owner of the workset either grants or denies the request. If the request is granted, you can update your local file and have control of the element until you relinquish it.

**Figure 1–32**

© 2016, ASCENT - Center for Technical Knowledge®

## How To: Request an Edit

1. When the alert box opens stating that you need to have permission to modify an element, click **Place Request** to ask to borrow the element.
2. An alert box opens, stating the request has been made, as shown in Figure 1–33. If you expect a quick reply, leave the message in place. If you want to continue working, click **Close** and cancel out of the alert box. The request is still active.

**Figure 1–33**

## How To: Grant or Deny an Editing Request

1. When a user sends an editing request for an element you are currently borrowing or which belongs to a workset which you have checked out (editable), an alert displays as shown in Figure 1–34.

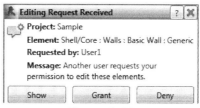

**Figure 1–34**

2. In the Editing Request Received dialog box, click **Show** to zoom into the element requested, **Grant** to allow the other user to modify the element, or **Deny** to stop the other user from modifying the element.

3. If you do not respond right away to the editing request, you can always access it again. In the *Collaborate* tab> Synchronize panel, click  (Editing Requests) or in the Status Bar, click (Editing Request). The information on the Status Bar includes the number of requests outstanding, as shown in Figure 1–35.

**Figure 1–35**

4. In the Editing Requests dialog box, as shown in Figure 1–36, select the pending request. Click on the date.

**Figure 1–36**

- When you select the editing request date, the elements included in the request are highlighted in the project. Click **Show** to zoom in on the elements if required.

5. Click **Grant** to enable the other user to make the changes or **Deny/Retract** to deny the request. (The original user can also retract the request with this button.) You can also grant the request by saving the entire workset back to the central file and relinquishing the items.

## Applying an Editing Request

When an editing request is granted, a confirmation alert box opens in the program of the user who requested it, as shown in Figure 1–37. Close the alert box.

*Once a request is granted, you can make modifications to the element again without having to request to edit the feature, although the icon still displays.*

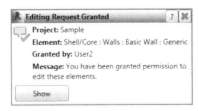

**Figure 1–37**

© 2016, ASCENT - Center for Technical Knowledge®

- If the requesting user canceled out of the Error dialog box, when they are notified that they have permission, click

  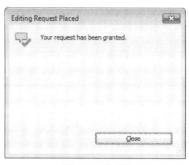 (Reload Latest) or type **RL** to make the ownership modification.

- If the Error dialog box is still open, the Editing Request Placed dialog box displays that the request has been granted, as shown in Figure 1–38. Click **Close** and the element is modified.

*An additional note "Reload Latest is required to edit the elements" might display in the dialog box depending on what the other user did with the borrowed elements.*

**Figure 1–38**

### Editing Request Frequency

To control the frequency of updates to editing requests (and worksharing display modes), in the Options dialog box, in the *General* tab, move the slider bar between *Less Frequent* and *More Frequent*, as shown in Figure 1–39.

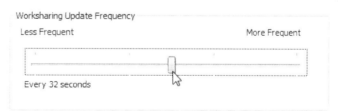

**Figure 1–39**

- If the bar is moved to the far side of *Less Frequent*, it changes to manual and updates only when you borrow elements or synchronize with the central file. This can improve the performance of the program but also causes the other user to wait until you receive the request.

# Relinquishing Worksets

After you have been working with borrowed elements or have checked out worksets, you should return them to the central file when you are finished. In the Quick Access Toolbar or

*Collaborate* tab>Synchronize panel, click 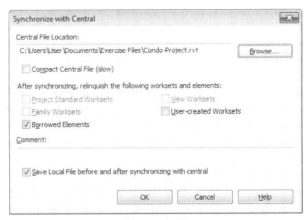 (Synchronize and Modify Settings). The Synchronize with Central dialog box displays, as shown in Figure 1–40. In this dialog box, select the worksets and/or elements you want to relinquish. Only those of which you have ownership are available.

**Figure 1–40**

## Synchronize with Central Options

- The **Borrowed Elements** option is selected by default. This relinquishes any elements you borrowed from another workset.

- Select the **Save the Local File before and after synchronizing with central** option to save extra steps.

- If the central file location changes, select the new central file using **Browse...**.

- Periodically, use the **Compact Central File (slow)** option when you save to the central file. This reduces the file size, but also increases the time required to save.

© 2016, ASCENT - Center for Technical Knowledge®

*Adding comments at key points and for significant changes in the project is useful in case the project backup needs to be restored in the future.*

- You can add comments to the central file for others to see. To view the comments, in the *Collaborate* tab>Synchronize panel, click 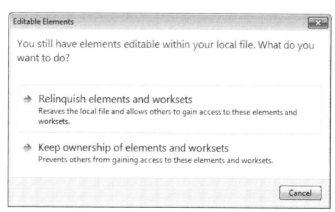 (Show History), and select the central file whose history you want to view. The History dialog box displays with the *Date/Time Stamp*, *Modified by*, and *Comments* columns populated with information, as shown in Figure 1–41.

### History

Click on a column heading to sort by that column.

| Date/Time Stamp | Modified by | Comments |
|---|---|---|
| 7/17/2013 11:29:21 AM | User1 | |
| 7/17/2013 11:19:44 AM | User1 | |
| 7/17/2013 11:19:36 AM | User2 | |
| 7/17/2013 11:18:52 AM | User1 | |
| 7/17/2013 11:18:35 AM | User2 | |

Close  Export...  Help

**Figure 1–41**

# Ending the Day Using Worksets

**IMPORTANT:** When you have finished working on the project for the day, you need to save to the central file and relinquish all user-created editable worksets. Then, you must save your local file before exiting the Autodesk Revit software. This way, the two files are in sync and you are able to save to the central file next time you work on the local file.

- If you close a project, but have not relinquished all worksets when you saved to the central file, the alert shown in Figure 1–42 displays.

*If you are working on a project with other people, you need to relinquish all your worksets when closing a project so they can edit them. This is correct worksharing etiquette.*

### Editable Elements

You still have elements editable within your local file. What do you want to do?

→ Relinquish elements and worksets
Resaves the local file and allows others to gain access to these elements and worksets.

→ Keep ownership of elements and worksets
Prevents others from gaining access to these elements and worksets.

Cancel

**Figure 1–42**

© 2016, ASCENT - Center for Technical Knowledge®

- To relinquish worksets without saving to the central file, in the *Collaborate* tab>Synchronize panel, click 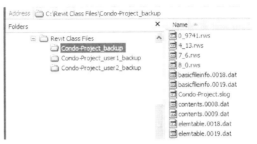 (Relinquish All Mine)

*Do not delete any files in these directories.*

- The backup directory for central and local files, as shown in Figure 1–43, holds information about the editability of worksets, borrowed elements, and workset/element ownership. If required, you can restore the backup directory. In the *Collaboration* tab>Synchronize panel, click (Restore Backup).

**Figure 1–43**

## Visibility and Display Options with Worksharing

While using worksets, there are certain display tools to help you as you work. Worksets can be toggled off and on in the Visibility/Graphics dialog box. You can use the Worksharing Display settings to graphically show by color information, such as the Owners of different elements and the elements that need to be updated.

© 2016, ASCENT - Center for Technical Knowledge®

# Controlling Workset Visibility

Not all worksets need to be visible in every view. For example, the exterior shell of a building should display in most views, but interior walls or the site features only need to be displayed in related views. The default workset visibility is controlled when the workset is first created, but can be managed in the Visibility/Graphics dialog box, as shown in Figure 1–44.

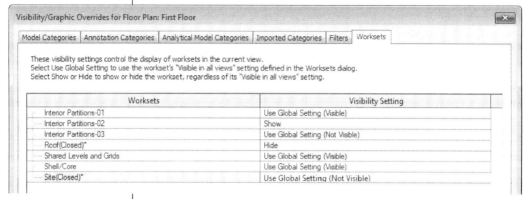

**Figure 1–44**

## How To: Change the Visibility of Worksets

1. Type **VV** or **VG** to open the Visibility/Graphics dialog box.
2. Select the *Worksets* tab. Modify the *Visibility Setting* for each workset, as required. Changing the setting to **Show** or **Hide** only impacts the current view.
3. Click **OK** to close the dialog box.

- Worksets marked with an asterisk (*) have not been opened in this session of the Autodesk Revit software and are therefore not visible in any view.

- Closing worksets toggles off element visibility in all views. It also saves more computer memory than just toggling off the display of worksets.

- The *Worksets* tab in the Visibility/Graphics dialog box is only available if worksets have been enabled.

- These overrides can also be setup in a view template.

# Worksharing Display Options

A handy way to view the status of elements in worksharing is to set the Worksharing Display. For example, when you set the Worksharing Display to Worksets, as shown in Figure 1–45, the elements in each workset are highlighted in a different color.

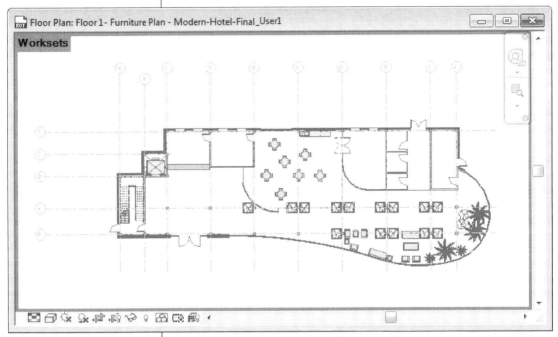

**Figure 1–45**

There are several type of Worksharing displays: Checkout Status, Owners, Model Updates, and Worksets. You can access those in the Status Bar, as shown in Figure 1–46.

**Figure 1–46**

© 2016, ASCENT - Center for Technical Knowledge®

- As you hover the cursor over elements in a view, with Worksharing Display selected, information about the element displays, depending on the type you selected, as shown in Figure 1–47.

*Toggling on Gray Inactive Worksets while using Worksharing Display might change the display status of elements in two tones of the same color.*

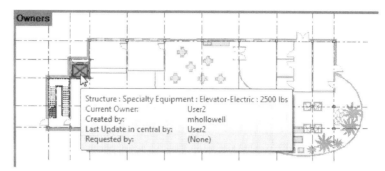

**Figure 1–47**

- You can modify the colors in the Worksharing Display Settings, as well as select which items you want to display, as shown in Figure 1–48.

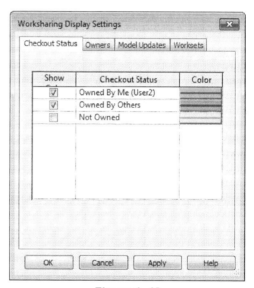

**Figure 1–48**

# Practice 1b

# Using Worksharing I

## Practice Objectives

- Set up two copies of the Autodesk Revit software with different user names.
- Update an existing central file for use in the practice.
- Create a local file of the central file from each copy of the software.

*Estimated time for completion: 10 minutes*

In this practice you create two local files using two different copies of the Autodesk Revit software. You open the local files and select specific worksets to open in each project, as shown in Figure 1–49.

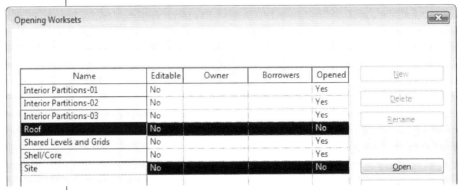

**Figure 1–49**

This practice uses a project that has been subdivided into worksets. To simulate a worksharing environment, you will open two sessions of the Autodesk Revit software and change the *Username* to **User1** and **User2**.

- **User1** focuses on the interiors of the condo units.

- **User2** focuses on the Exterior and Core.

## Task 1 - Setup Two Copies of Autodesk Revit Using Different User Names.

1. Start the first copy of the Autodesk Revit software. You do not need to be in a project.

2. In the Application Menu, click **Options**.

3. In the Options dialog box, in the *General* tab, sign out of Autodesk® A360 if required, and change the *Username* to **User1**, as shown in Figure 1–50.

© 2016, ASCENT - Center for Technical Knowledge®

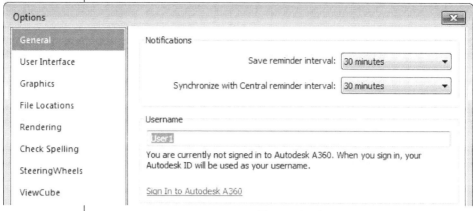

**Figure 1–50**

- Write down the existing name before you change it, so that you can return it to the original name at the end of these practices.

4. In the *File Locations* tab, change the *Default path for user files* to the practice files folder.

5. Click **OK** to close the dialog box.

6. Open a second copy of Autodesk Revit and repeat the steps above changing the *User Name* to **User 2**.

**Task 2 - Update the Central File.**

1. Working in the **User1** copy of Autodesk Revit, in the Quick Access Toolbar, click ☞ (Open). In the practice files folder, open **Condo-Project-A.rvt**.

2. Alert boxes about a Copied Central Model display. Read and then close the alert boxes.

3. In the Application Menu, expand 💾 (Save As) and click ▣ (Project).

4. In the Save As dialog box, click **Options**....

5. In the File Save Options dialog box, select **Make this a Central File after save** and then click **OK**.

6. Verify that the name is still set to **Condo-Project-A.rvt**, and then click **Save**.

*A central file needs to be repathed if it has been relocated. This typically does not happen in an office environment, but does in the training environment, depending on where the central file is saved.*

7. When the Workset File Already Exists dialog box displays, click **Yes** to replace the existing file.

8. Close the project.

## Task 3 - Create the Local File for User1.

1. Continue working in the **User1** copy of Autodesk Revit. In the Quick Access Toolbar, click 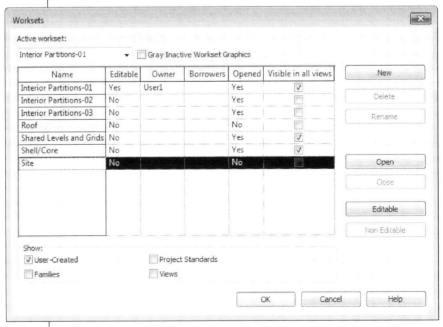 (Open). In the practice files folder, open **Condo-Project-A.rvt**.

   - Do not select central files from the startup screen, as that opens the central file itself. Instead, use the **Open** command to create a new local file.

2. Verify that **Create New Local** is selected and click **Open**. A file with the name **Condo-Project-A_User1.rvt** is opened.

3. In the *Collaborate* tab>Manage Collaboration panel, click (Worksets) or in the Status Bar, click (Worksets).

4. In the Worksets dialog box, make **Interior Partitions-01** the Active Worksets. Set *Editable* to **Yes** and select **Visible in all views** for this workset. Select the worksets **Roof** and **Site**. Click **Close** so that the worksets are not open in this session, as shown in Figure 1–51.

**Worksets**

Active workset:

Interior Partitions-01    ▼    ☐ Gray Inactive Workset Graphics

| Name | Editable | Owner | Borrowers | Opened | Visible in all views | |
|------|----------|-------|-----------|--------|---------------------|---|
| Interior Partitions-01 | Yes | User1 | | Yes | ☑ | New |
| Interior Partitions-02 | No | | | Yes | ☐ | Delete |
| Interior Partitions-03 | No | | | Yes | ☐ | Rename |
| Roof | No | | | No | ☐ | |
| Shared Levels and Grids | No | | | Yes | ☑ | |
| Shell/Core | No | | | Yes | ☑ | |
| Site | No | | | No | ☐ | Open |
| | | | | | | Close |
| | | | | | | Editable |
| | | | | | | Non Editable |

Show:
☑ User-Created          ☐ Project Standards
☐ Families              ☐ Views

[ OK ]   [ Cancel ]   [ Help ]

**Figure 1–51**

© 2016, ASCENT - Center for Technical Knowledge®

5. Click **OK** to finish.

6. In the Quick Access Toolbar, click 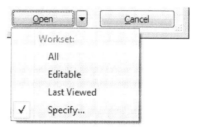 (Save) to save the local file.

### Task 4 - Create the Local File for User2.

1. Work in the **User2** copy of Autodesk Revit.

2. In the Quick Access Toolbar, click 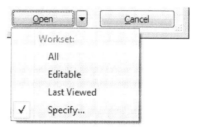 (Open) and select the file **Condo-Project-A.rvt**. Verify that **Create New Local** is selected, click the arrow next to **Open**, and select **Specify...** in the drop-down list, as shown in Figure 1–52.

**Figure 1–52**

3. Click **Open** to open the project.

4. In the Opening Worksets dialog box, select the three **Interior Partition** worksets and click **Close** so that these worksets are not opened in this session, as shown in Figure 1–53.

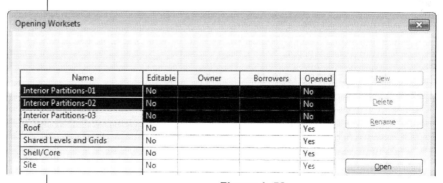

**Figure 1–53**

5. Click **OK** to finish. The file is opened and automatically named **Condo-Project-A_User2.rvt**.

6. Save the local file.

7. Leave both copies of the Autodesk Revit software open for the next practices.

---

# Practice 1c | Using Worksharing II

## Practice Objectives

- Add and Modify Elements in Worksets.
- Request and grant permissions to edit.
- Save, synchronize, and reload files to display the changes made by each user.

*Estimated time for completion: 20 minutes*

In this practice you will work with two different sessions of the Autodesk Revit software. In the first session, you will make worksets visible and add, modify elements in worksets without having to get permission. You will then switch to a different user and make a workset editable. The first user requests an edit to the workset owned by the second user. Permission will be granted and the first user will make the change. You save the local file, save to central file, and reload the latest file. An example of Worksets dialog box used in this practice is shown in Figure 1–54.

| Name | Editable | Owner | Borrowers | Opened | Visible in all views |
|------|----------|-------|-----------|--------|----------------------|
| Interior Partitions-01 | Yes | User1 | | Yes | ☑ |
| Interior Partitions-02 | No | | | Yes | ☐ |
| Interior Partitions-03 | No | | | Yes | ☐ |
| Roof | No | | | No | ☐ |
| Shared Levels and Grids | No | | | Yes | ☑ |
| Shell/Core | No | User2 | user1 | Yes | ☑ |
| Site | No | | | No | ☐ |

**Figure 1–54**

- You must complete **Practice 1b: Using Worksharing I** before beginning this practice.

© 2016, ASCENT - Center for Technical Knowledge®

**Task 1 - Add and Modify Elements in Worksets.**

1. Working as **User1** in the file **Condo-Project-A_User1.rvt**, verify that you are in the **Floor Plans: First Floor** view.

2. Zoom in on Unit 1C, and add several walls using an interior wall type with the *Height* set to **Second Floor**. Include one that butts up against an existing window, as shown in Figure 1–55. A warning displays, noting that the Insert conflicts with the joined wall.

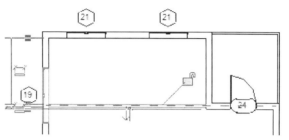

**Figure 1–55**

3. Close the warning.

4. Click ▷ (Modify) and select the window. It has an icon connected to it (as shown in Figure 1–56), indicating that it belongs to another workset. Click the **Make element editable** icon.

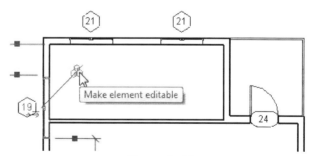

**Figure 1–56**

© 2016, ASCENT - Center for Technical Knowledge®

5. Move the window so it does not conflict with the wall.

6. Open the Worksets dialog box. **User1** is noted as the *Owner* of the **Interior Partitions-01** workset and a *Borrower* of **Shell/Core** workset, as shown in Figure 1–57.

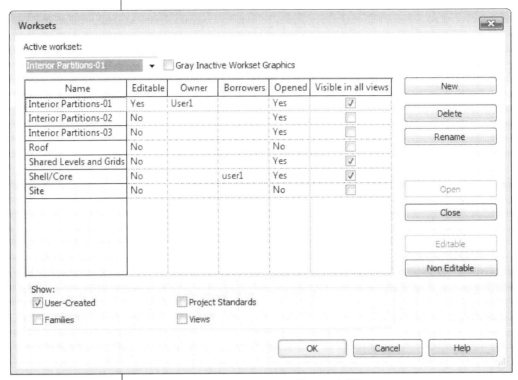

**Figure 1–57**

7. Click **OK** to close the dialog box.

8. In the *Collaborate* tab>Synchronize panel or in the Quick Access Toolbar, click  (Synchronize and Modify Settings) to open the Synchronize with Central dialog box, as shown in Figure 1–58. The **Borrowed Elements** option should be selected. Add a comment about moving the window and select the **Save Local File before and after synchronizing with central** option.

© 2016, ASCENT - Center for Technical Knowledge®

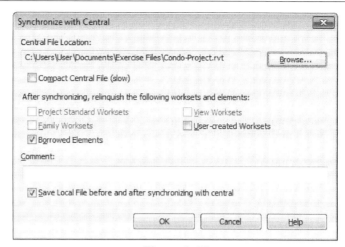

**Figure 1–58**

9. Click **OK**.

## Task 2 - Check out a Workset.

1. Open the session of the Autodesk Revit software used by **User2** and open the **Floor Plans: First Floor** view if it is not already open. None of the changes show in the local file.

2. In the *Collaborate* tab>Synchronize panel, click 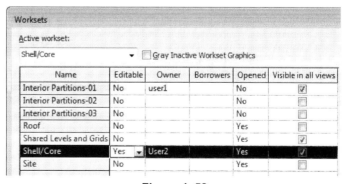 (Reload Latest or type **RL**. The window location changes but you do not see the new walls because that workset is not open.

3. Click (Worksets) to open the dialog box.

4. Select **Shell/Core** in the *Active workset* drop-down list and make it editable (select **Yes** in the *Editable* column). The *Owner* should display **User 2**, as shown in Figure 1–59.

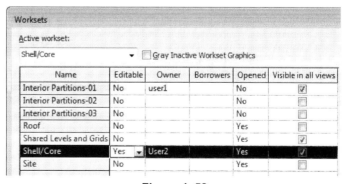

**Figure 1–59**

5. Click **OK** to close the dialog box.

6. Move door number 5 in Unit 1A down in the wall so that it is no longer opposite to door number 6.

7. In the Quick Access Toolbar, click 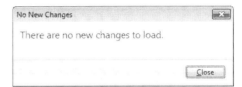 (Save) to save the local file.

8. Switch to the **User1** session and type **RL** (Reload Latest). There are no new changes to load, as shown in Figure 1–60, because User 2 has not saved back to the central file. Close the dialog box.

| No New Changes | ✕ |
| --- | --- |
| There are no new changes to load. | |
| | Close |

**Figure 1–60**

9. Switch to the **User2** session and click 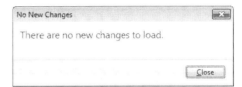 (Synchronize Now). This saves the changes to the central file without relinquishing the Shell/Core workset.

## Task 3 - Request Permission to Edit.

1. Switch to the **User1** session and type **RL** (Reload Latest) again. This time, the door moves in response to the change made in the central file.

2. Try to move the door back where it was. This time, an error message displays that cannot be ignored, as shown in Figure 1–61. **User2** has made the Shell/Core workset editable. Therefore, anyone else cannot edit elements in it without permission.

**Figure 1–61**

© 2016, ASCENT - Center for Technical Knowledge®

3. Click **Place Request**. The Editing Request Placed dialog box opens. Close the dialog boxes.

4. Switch to the **User2** session. An alert box displays, as shown in Figure 1–62.

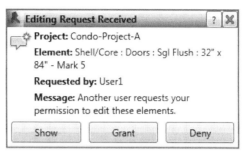

**Figure 1–62**

5. Hover the cursor over the **Show** button to highlight the door. Move the dialog box out of the way if required, to see the door.

6. The other user can have permission to modify the placement of this door. Click **Grant**. By doing this, you enable the other user full control over this one element in the workset.

7. Switch to the **User1** session. The Editing Request is granted, as shown in Figure 1–63.

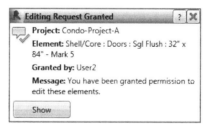

**Figure 1–63**

8. Close the Editing Request Granted dialog box. Your request was granted and the door moves.

9. Move the door again to exactly where you want it. This time, you are not prompted to ask to move the door because you are still borrowing it.

10. Try to move another door. You do not have permission to move this door. Click **Cancel** rather than place the request. The door returns to its original location.

11. In the View Control Bar, expand the Worksharing display and click 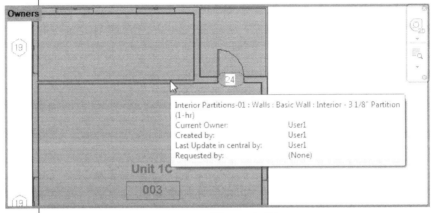 (Owners). Different colors highlight the elements and their respective owners. Hover the cursor over one of the walls to display information about the owner, as shown in Figure 1–64.

**Figure 1–64**

- The color on your display might be different.

12. Zoom out so you can see the full floor plan.

13. Click  (Synchronize and Modify Settings) and relinquish **User created Worksets** and **Borrowed Elements.**

14. The new interior walls once displayed as owned by **User1** are now not in color and the door that was borrowed returns to the original owner User 2.

15. Toggle the Worksharing Display off.

16. Save the local file.

17. Switch to the **User2** session.

18. Click  (Synchronize Now). The door moves to the location where **User1** moved it. When you save to the central file, it also reloads the latest changes.

© 2016, ASCENT - Center for Technical Knowledge®

19. Close the project. When the Editable Elements dialog box opens, as shown in Figure 1–65, click **Relinquish elements and worksets**.

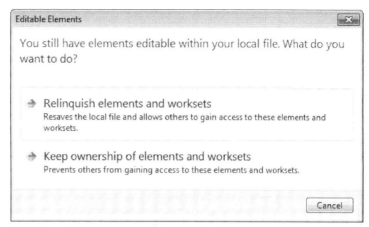

**Figure 1–65**

20. Close the **User2** session of the Autodesk Revit software.

21. In the **User1** session of the Autodesk Revit software, return the *Username* to the original name at the start of this set of practices.

22. Close the project and synchronize with central if required.

# 1.3 Import DWG and Image Files

Many firms have legacy drawings from vector-based CAD programs and could be working with consultants that use them. For example, you may want to link a DWG plan into your project, as shown in the Link CAD Formats dialog box in Figure 1–66, that you would then trace over using Autodesk Revit tools. Other non-CAD specific file formats including ADSK, IFC. Point clouds can also be opened or linked into Autodesk Revit projects.

*You can print a hybrid drawing - part Autodesk Revit project and part imported/linked drawing.*

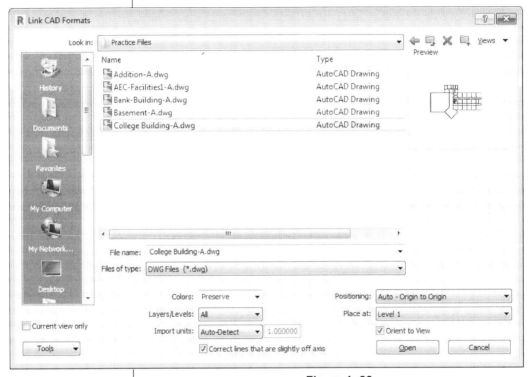

**Figure 1–66**

CAD Files can be either linked or imported into a project.

- **Link:** A connection is maintained with the original file and the link updates if the original file is updated.
- **Import:** No connection is maintained with the original file. It becomes a separate element in the Autodesk Revit model.
- CAD file formats that can be imported or linked include: AutoCAD® (DWG and DXF), MicroStation (DGN), 3D ACIS modeling kernel (SAT), and SketchUp (SKP).

© 2016, ASCENT - Center for Technical Knowledge®

## How To: Import or Link a CAD File

1. In the *Insert* tab>Import panel, click  (Import CAD), or in the *Insert* tab>Link panel, click (Link CAD).
2. Fill out the Import CAD (or Link CAD) dialog box. The top part of the dialog box holds the standard select file options. The bottom outlines the various options for importing or linking, as shown in Figure 1–67.

**Figure 1–67**

3. Click **Open**.
4. Depending on the selected Positioning method, the file is automatically placed or you can place it with the cursor.

## Import/Link Options

| | |
|---|---|
| **Current view only** | If selected, the file is imported/linked into the current view and not into other views. You might want to enable this option if you are just working on a floor plan and do not want the objects to display in 3D and other views. |
| **Colors** | The Autodesk Revit software works mainly with black lines of different weights on a white background to describe elements, but both AutoCAD and MicroStation use a variety of colors. To make the move into the Autodesk Revit software easier, you can select to turn all colors to Black and White, Preserve colors, or Invert colors |
| **Layers** | You can select which layers from the original drawing are imported/linked. The options are All, Visible (those that are not off or frozen), and Select. Select opens a list of layers or levels from which you can select when you import the drawing file. |
| **Import units** | Autodesk Revit software can auto-detect the units in the imported/linked file. You can also specify the units that you want to use from a list of typical Imperial and Metric units or set a Custom scale factor. |
| **Correct lines that are slightly off axis** | Corrects lines that are less than 0.1 degree of axis so that any elements based on those line are created correctly. It is on by default. Toggle it off if you are working with site plans. |

| Positioning | Select from the methods to place the imported/linked file in the Autodesk Revit host project. 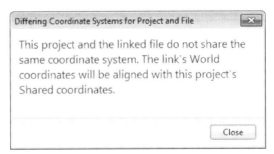 |
|---|---|
| **Place at:** | Select a level in the drop-down list to specify the vertical positioning for the file. This is grayed out if you have selected Current view only. |
| **Orient to View** | Select this to place the file at the same orientation as the current view. |

- The default positioning is **Auto - Origin to Origin**. The software remembers the most recently used positioning type as long as you are in the same session of Autodesk Revit. (The CAD Links dialog box remembers the last positioning used separately from the RVT Links dialog box.)

- If you are linking a file, an additional Positioning option, **Auto-By Shared Coordinates**, is available. It is typically used with linked Autodesk Revit files. If you use it with a CAD file, an alert box opens, as shown in Figure 1–68, containing information about the coordinate systems and what the Autodesk Revit software does.

Differing Coordinate Systems for Project and File

This project and the linked file do not share the same coordinate system. The link's World coordinates will be aligned with this project's Shared coordinates.

Close

**Figure 1–68**

- When you link a drawing that includes reference files (XREFS), only the top level drawing is linked in and excludes any of the reference files. You need to bind the reference files to the main drawing before linking them into the project or you can link in each one separately.

- When you import a drawing that includes references (XREFS), the references come in as well.

© 2016, ASCENT - Center for Technical Knowledge®

## Importing Raster Image Files

Raster images are made up of pixels or dots in a file that create a picture. For example, a raster file is created when you scan a blueprint. A logo used in a title block is often a raster image made in a graphics program, as shown in Figure 1–69. You can add raster images to any 2D view, including sheet files. They can be used as a background view or as part of the final drawing. Imported images are placed behind model objects and annotation.

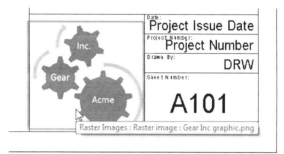

**Figure 1–69**

### How To: Import a Raster Image

1. On the *Insert* tab>Import panel, click ⬛ (Image).
2. In the Open dialog box, select the image you want to insert. You can insert bmp, jpg, jpeg, png, and tif files.
3. Click **Open**. Four blue dots and an "x" illustrate the default size of the image file, as shown on the left in Figure 1–70. Click on the screen to place the image. It displays with the shape handles still visible, as shown on the right in Figure 1–70.

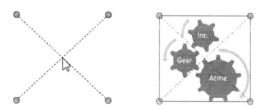

**Figure 1–70**

4. Drag the shape handles to resize the graphic, as required.

## Editing Raster Files

Select an image to make changes. Once it is selected, you can resize the image as you did when you first inserted it or in Properties, specify *Width* and *Height* values.

- Select **Lock Proportions** in the Options Bar to ensure that the length and width resize proportionally to each other when you adjust the size of an image.

- Use the standard modification tools to **Move**, **Copy**, **Rotate**, **Mirror**, **Array**, and **Scale** images. Images can also be grouped together into Detail Groups

- Use the *Arrange* tools, as shown in Figure 1–71, to move images to the front or back of other images or objects.

*You can also set the Foreground/Background status in the Options Bar and in Properties.*

- You can snap to edges of images, as shown in Figure 1–72.

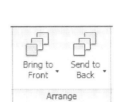

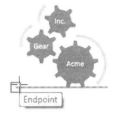

**Figure 1–71**                    **Figure 1–72**

- In the *Insert* tab>Import panel, click 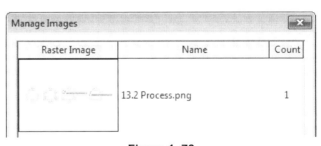 (Manage Images) to open the Manage Images dialog box, as shown in Figure 1–73. In this dialog box, you can delete images from your file. If you have several instances, it deletes all of them.

*You can also select an image and delete it. This removes that instance of the image, but does not remove it from the images associated with the project.*

| Raster Image | Name | Count |
|---|---|---|
|  | 13.2 Process.png | 1 |

Manage Images

**Figure 1–73**

© 2016, ASCENT - Center for Technical Knowledge®

# Practice 1d | Import DWG and Image Files

### Practice Objectives

- Import an AutoCAD file into an Autodesk Revit project and use it as a basis to add elements for a hybrid drawing.
- Query elements in the imported file and delete extraneous layers as well as explode and delete elements.
- Create a sheet and add a rendered raster image to the sheet.

In this practice you will create a hybrid CAD/Autodesk Revit project for an addition to an existing building. You will import an AutoCAD file into a project and add some Autodesk Revit elements, as shown in Figure 1–74. You will then query elements in an imported file, toggle off layers, and delete layers from the file. You will explode the imported file so that you can remove items that are not required. Finally, you will set up a sheet with a copy of the floor plan and add a rendered image of the new entrance.

*Estimated time for completion: 15 minutes*

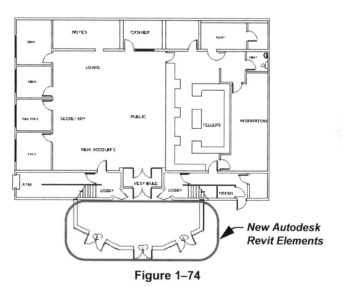

**Figure 1–74**

## Task 1 - Import a CAD file.

1. Start a new project based on the Architectural template.

2. Verify that you are in the **Floor Plans: Level 1** view.

*The CAD file is not going to change. So you can Import rather than link this file.*

3. In the *Insert* tab>Import panel, click 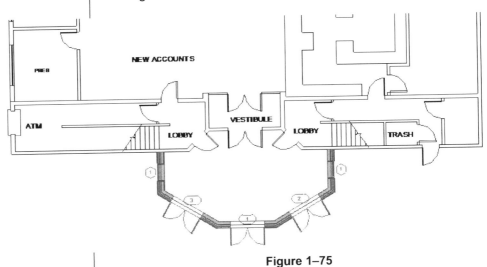 (Import CAD).

4. In the Import CAD dialog box, in the practice files folder, select the AutoCAD drawing file **Bank-Existing.dwg** and set the following options:

   - Select **Current View Only**.
   - *Colors*: **Black and White**
   - *Layers*: **All**
   - *Import Units*: **Auto-Detect**
   - Select **Correct lines that are slightly off axis**.
   - *Positioning*: **Auto-Center to Center**

5. Click **Open**.

6. Switch to an elevation view. No elements are in that view—the imported information is 2D only.

7. Switch back to the **Floor Plans: Level 1** view.

8. Use the outline to draw walls (with a Height to Level 2). Add doors and windows in front of the existing entrance of the building as a new entrance, similar to that shown in Figure 1–75.

NEW ACCOUNTS

PREB

ATM

VESTIBULE

LOBBY

LOBBY

TRASH

**Figure 1–75**

© 2016, ASCENT - Center for Technical Knowledge®

9. Switch to the **Elevations (Building Elevations): South** view. You should see the Autodesk Revit objects in the view.

10. Save the project as **Bank Addition Architectural.rvt**.

---

**Task 2 - Query Elements in an Imported File.**

---

1. Return to the **Floor Plans: Level 1** view.

2. Select the imported file. In the *Modify | Bank-Exisiting.dwg* tab>Import Instance panel, click 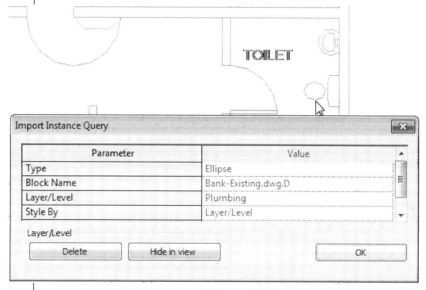 (Query).

3. Select one of the objects in the toilet room. It is a block from AutoCAD on the layer **Plumbing**, as shown in Figure 1–76.

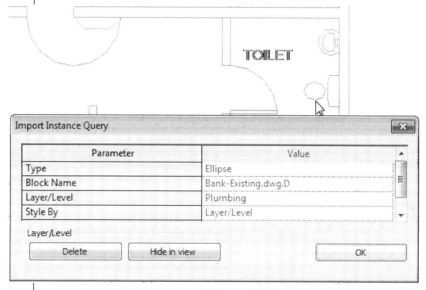

| Parameter | Value |
|-----------|-------|
| Type | Ellipse |
| Block Name | Bank-Existing.dwg.D |
| Layer/Level | Plumbing |
| Style By | Layer/Level |

Layer/Level

| Delete | Hide in view | | OK |

Figure 1–76

4. Click H**ide in View**. This and the other block are removed from the view.

5. Press <Esc> to end the query.

## Task 3 - Modify the Visibility of Graphics in an Imported File.

1. Type **VG** to open the Visibility/Graphic Overrides dialog box. Switch to the *Imported Categories* tab.

2. Click the "+" next to **Bank-Existing.dwg** to expand the layers. Toggle off the layers **Text** and **Furniture**. Click **OK**.

3. The cabinetwork of the tellers' booths is toggled off but the text still remains, as shown in Figure 1–77.

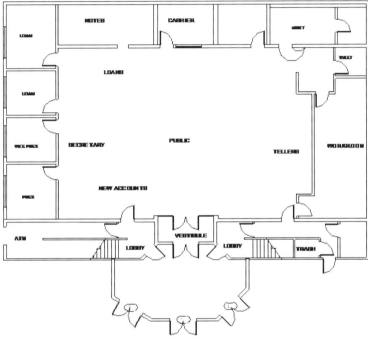

**Figure 1–77**

- The text in the AutoCAD drawing was not placed on the layer **Text**.

## Task 4 - Delete Objects in an Imported File.

1. Elements on several layers are not required for this project. Select the imported file in the drawing. In the Import Instance panel, click 🗑 (Delete Layers).

2. Select the layers **Header**, **Furniture**, and **Plumbing** in the dialog box, as shown in Figure 1–78, and click **OK**.

© 2016, ASCENT - Center for Technical Knowledge®

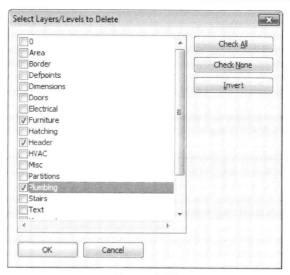

**Figure 1–78**

3. The text that you thought would be on one layer is on a different layer. Use  (Query) to find out which layer it is on.

   - Because the text is on a layer with other elements, you cannot delete it without impacting the rest of the drawing. Therefore, you need to explode the imported instance.

4. Press <Esc> twice to end the Query and exit the command.

5. Select the file. In the Import Instance panel, click  (Partial Explode). The file is exploded.

6. Move the cursor over elements in the project, as shown in Figure 1–79.

*Most elements in the imported file become detail lines, but the text becomes Autodesk Revit text objects and can be modified. The doors are imported symbols because they were blocks.*

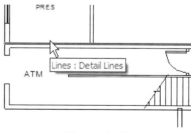

**Figure 1–79**

7. Delete the text. (Select everything and use  (Filter) to select only the Text Notes.)

8. Save the project.

### Task 5 - Importing Raster Files.

1. In the Floor Plans: **Level 1** view, toggle off the elevation markers so that they do not display when the view is placed on a sheet.

2. Create a new sheet using the default title block.

3. Drag and drop the **Level 1** view onto the sheet, leaving room for other information.

4. In the *Insert* tab>Import panel, click 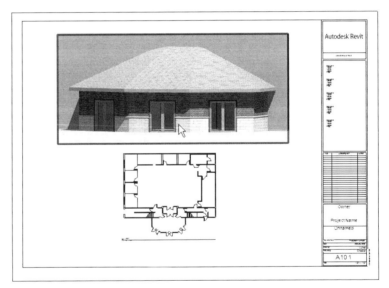 (Image). Select the image file **Entrance.jpg** (from your practice files folder) and place it on the sheet.

5. Move and resize it so that it fits on the sheet, as shown in Figure 1–80.

*The design of the rendered image might not match the design of the walls you created earlier.*

**Figure 1–80**

6. Save the project.

© 2016, ASCENT - Center for Technical Knowledge®

# 1.4 Use Worksharing Visualization

The content that is recommended to review for the Use Worksharing Visualization certification objective is covered in the following section:

- *Section 1.2 Use Worksharing*

# 1.5 Assess Review Warnings in Revit

When working with stairs and other elements, Warnings (such as the one shown in Figure 1–81), display when something is wrong, but you can keep on working. In many cases you can close the dialog box and fix the issue or wait and do it later.

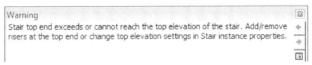

**Figure 1–81**

Sometimes Errors display where you must take action. These force you to stop and fix the situation.

When you select an element for which there has been a warning

⚠ (Show Related Warnings) displays in the Ribbon. It opens a dialog box in which you can review the warning(s) related to the selected element. You can also display a list of all of the

warnings in the project by clicking 📇 (Review Warnings) in the *Manage* tab>Inquiry panel.

© 2016, ASCENT - Center for Technical Knowledge®

# Documentation

This chapter includes instructional content to assist in your preparation for the following topic and objectives for the Autodesk® Revit® Architecture Certified Professional exam.

## Autodesk Certification Exam Objectives in this Chapter

| Exam Topic | Exam Objective | Section |
|---|---|---|
| Documentation | • Create and modify filled regions | • 2.1 |
| | • Place detail components and repeating details | • 2.2 |
| | • Tag elements (doors, windows, etc.) by category | • 2.3 |
| | • Use dimension strings | • 2.4 |
| | • Set the colors used in a color scheme legend | • 2.5 |
| | • Work with Phases | • 2.6 |

# 2.1 Create and Modify Filled Regions

Many elements include material information that displays in plan and section views, while other elements need such details to be added. For example, the concrete wall shown in Figure 2–1 includes material information, while the earth to the left of the wall needs to be added using the **Filled Region** command.

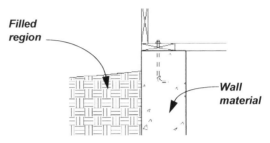

**Figure 2–1**

The patterns used in details are *drafting patterns*. They are scaled to the view scale and update if you modify it. You can also add full-size *model patterns*, such as a Flemish Bond brick pattern, to the surface of some elements.

- Fill patterns can be applied to all surfaces in a model. If the surface is warped, the patterns display as planar surfaces to keep the visual integrity of the geometry.

## How To: Add a Filled Region

1. In the *Annotate* tab>Detail panel, expand  (Region) and click  (Filled Region).
2. Create a closed boundary using the Draw tools.
3. In the Line Style panel, select the line style for the outside edge of the boundary. If you do not want the boundary to display, select the <Invisible lines> style.
4. In the Type Selector, select the fill type, as shown in Figure 2–2.

© 2016, ASCENT - Center for Technical Knowledge®

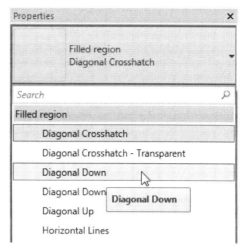

**Figure 2–2**

5. Click ✓ (Finish Edit Mode).

- You can modify a region by changing the fill type in the Type Selector or by editing the sketch.

- Double-click on the edge of the filled region to edit the sketch.

  If you have the Selection option set to ⬚ (Select elements by face) you can select the pattern.

# 2.2 Place Detail Components and Repeating Details

Autodesk Revit elements, such as the casework section shown on the left in Figure 2–3, typically require additional information to ensure that they are constructed correctly. To create details such as the one shown on the right in Figure 2–3, you add detail components, detail lines, and various annotation elements. These elements are not directly connected to the model, even if model elements display in the view.

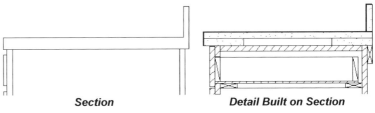

*Section*                    *Detail Built on Section*

**Figure 2–3**

## Detail Components

Detail components are families made of 2D and annotation elements. Over 500 detail components organized by CSI format are found in the *Detail Items* folder of the library, as shown in Figure 2–4.

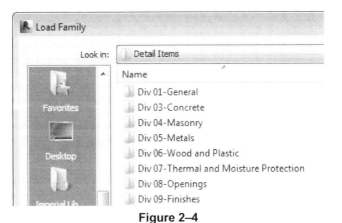

**Figure 2–4**

© 2016, ASCENT - Center for Technical Knowledge®

## How To: Add a Detail Component

1. In the *Annotate* tab>Detail panel, expand 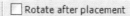 (Component) and click (Detail Component).
2. In the Type Selector, select the detail component type. You can load additional types from the Library.
3. Many detail components can be rotated as you insert them by pressing <Spacebar>. Alternatively, select the **Rotate after placement** option in the Options Bar, as shown in Figure 2–5.

☐ Rotate after placement

**Figure 2–5**

4. Place the component in the drawing. Rotate it if needed.

## Adding Break Lines

The Break Line is a detail component found in the *Detail Items\ Div 01-General* folder. It consists of a rectangular area (shown highlighted in Figure 2–6) which is used to block out elements behind it. You can modify the size of the area that is covered and change the size of the cut line using the controls.

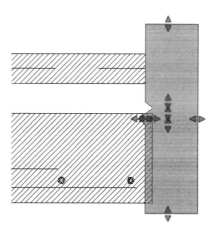

**Figure 2–6**

### Hint: Working with the Draw Order of Details

When you select detail elements in a view, you can change the draw order of the elements in the *Modify | Detail Items* tab> Arrange panel. You can bring elements in front of other elements or place them behind elements, as shown in Figure 2–7.

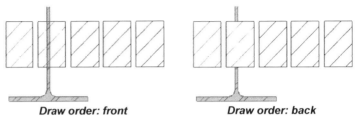

Draw order: front      Draw order: back

**Figure 2–7**

- 🗗 **(Bring to Front):** Places element in front of all other elements.

- 🗗 **(Send to Back):** Places element behind all other elements.

- 🗗 **(Bring Forward):** Moves element one step to the front.

- 🗗 **(Send Backward):** Moves element one step to the back.

- You can select multiple detail elements and change the draw order of all of them in one step. They keep the relative order of the original selection.

## Repeating Details

Instead of having to insert a component multiple times (such as with a brick or concrete block), you can use ⁞ (Repeating Detail Component) and draw a string of components, as shown in Figure 2–8.

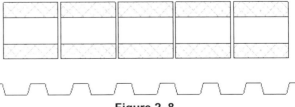

**Figure 2–8**

© 2016, ASCENT - Center for Technical Knowledge®

## How To: Insert a Repeating Detail Component

1.  In the *Annotate* tab>Detail panel, expand 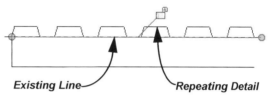 (Component) and click (Repeating Detail Component).
2.  In the Type Selector, select the detail you want to use.
3.  In the Draw panel, click (Line) or (Pick Lines).
4.  In the Options Bar, type a value for the *Offset* if needed.
5.  The components repeat as required to fit the length of the sketched or selected line, as shown in Figure 2–9. You can lock the components to the line.

**Existing Line** — **Repeating Detail**

**Figure 2–9**

---

### Hint: (Insulation)

Adding batt insulation is similar to adding a repeating detail component, but instead of a series of bricks or other elements, it creates the linear batting pattern, shown in Figure 2–10.

**Figure 2–10**

Before you place the insulation in the drawing, specify the *Width* and other options in the Options Bar, as shown in Figure 2–11.

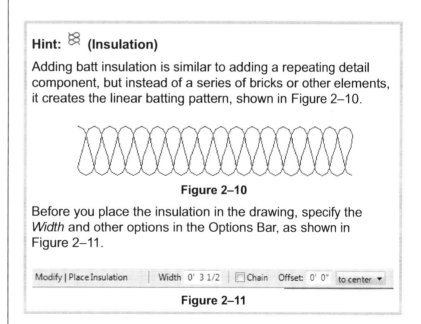

Modify | Place Insulation     Width  0' 3 1/2    ☐ Chain   Offset:  0' 0"   to center ▼

**Figure 2–11**

# Practice 2a | Create Details

### Practice Objective

- Create and annotate details.

In this practice you will create a window sill detail and a structural detail, and then annotate them. The following tasks are designed to be completed without detailed steps. Refer to the earlier topics and practice for assistance, as required. You can also use keynotes instead of text notes if required.

*Estimated time of completion: 30 minutes*

- Use the **Modern-Hotel-Detailing.rvt** project as the base file for these tasks.

### Task 1 - Create a window sill detail.

In this task you will create a window sill detail, as shown in Figure 2–12.

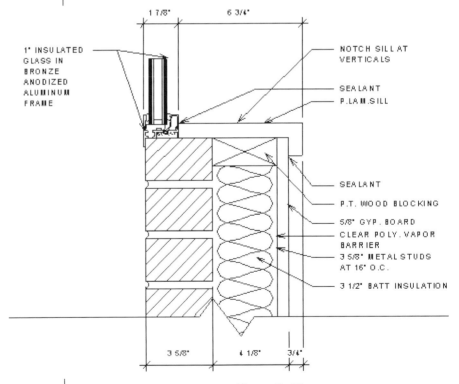

**Figure 2–12**

- Use detail components from the Library, detail lines, patterning, text, and dimensions to create the window sill.

© 2016, ASCENT - Center for Technical Knowledge®

## Task 2 - Add structural detail.

In this task you will create a structural detail, as shown in Figure 2–13.

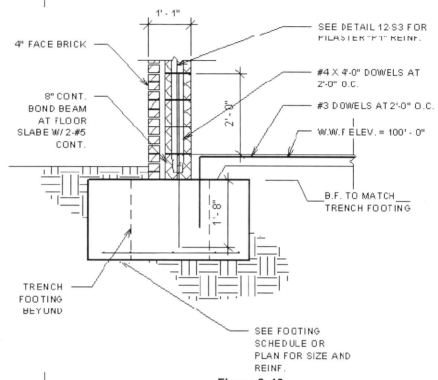

**Figure 2–13**

- Create a new drafting view and draw the structural detail using the various sketching tools and structural detail components.

- Use the **Invisible lines** line type when you draw the lines for the fill boundary. The curved lines are made with splines.

- Create the Earth pattern type by duplicating an existing type and assigning a new drafting pattern to it.

# 2.3 Tag Elements (Doors, Windows, etc.) by Category

Tags identify elements that are listed in schedules. Door and window tags are inserted automatically if you use the **Tag on Placement** option when inserting the door or window or other elements. You can also add them later to specific views as required. Many other types of tags are available in the Autodesk® Revit® software, such as wall tags and furniture tags, as shown in Figure 2–14.

*Additional tags are stored in the Library in the Annotations folder.*

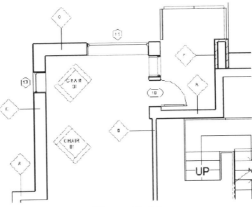

**Figure 2–14**

- The **Tag by Category** command works for most elements, except for a few that have separate commands.

- Tags can be letters, numbers, or a combination of the two.

You can place three types of tags, as follows:

- (Tag by Category): Tags according to the category of the element. It places door tags on doors and wall tags on walls.

- (Multi-Category): Tags elements belonging to multiple categories. The tags display information from parameters that they have in common.

- (Material): Tags that display the type of material. They are typically used in detailing.

© 2016, ASCENT - Center for Technical Knowledge®

### How To: Add Tags

1. In the *Annotate* tab>Tag panel, click ⌐① (Tag by Category),

   ⌐① (Multi-Category), or ⌐① (Material Tag) depending on the
   type of tag you want to place.
2. In the Options Bar, set the options as required, as shown in
   Figure 2–15.

**Figure 2–15**

3. Select the element you want to tag. If a tag for the selected
   element is not loaded, you are prompted to load it from the
   Library.

### Tag Options

* You can set tag options for leaders and tag rotation, as
  shown in Figure 2–16. You can also press <Spacebar> to
  toggle the orientation while placing or modifying the tag.

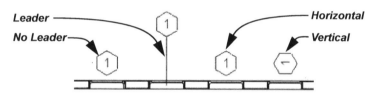

**Figure 2–16**

* Leaders can have an **Attached End** or a **Free End**, as
  shown in Figure 2–17. The attached end must be connected
  to the element being tagged. A free end has an additional
  drag control where the leader touches the element.

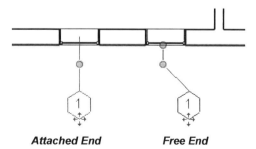

**Figure 2–17**

- The **Length** option specifies the length of the leader in plotting units. It is grayed out if the **Leader** option is not selected or if a **Free End** leader is defined.

- If a tag is not loaded a warning box opens as shown in Figure 2–18. Click **Yes** to open the Load Family dialog box in which you can select the appropriate tag.

No Tag Loaded

There is no tag loaded for Railings. Do you want to load one now?

Yes    No

Figure 2–18

## How To: Add Multiple Tags

1. In the *Annotate* tab>Tag panel, click (Tag All).
2. In the Tag All Not Tagged dialog box (shown in Figure 2–19), select one or more categories to tag,

*To tag only some elements, select them before starting this command. In the Tag All Not Tagged dialog box, select the **Only selected objects in current view** option.*

Tag All Not Tagged

Select at least one Category and Tag or Symbol Family to annotate non-annotated objects:

◉ All objects in current view
○ Only selected objects in current view
☐ Include elements from linked files

| Category | Loaded Tags |
| --- | --- |
| Casework Tags | Casework Tag : Boxed |
| Door Tags | Door Tag |
| Room Tags | Room Tag |
| Span Direction Symbol | Span Direction : One Way Slab |
| Stair Landing Tags | Stair Landing Tag |
| Stair Run Tags | Stair Run Tag : Standard |
| Stair Support Tags | Stair Support Tag |
| Stair Tags | Stair Tag : Standard |
| Structural Framing Tags | Structural Framing Tag : Boxed |
| View Titles | View Title |

☐ Leader    Leader Length: 1/2"

Tag Orientation: Horizontal ▼

OK    Cancel    Apply    Help

Figure 2–19

© 2016, ASCENT - Center for Technical Knowledge®

3. Set the *Leader* and *Tag Orientation* as required.
4. Click **Apply** to apply the tags and stay in the dialog box. Click **OK** to apply the tags and close the dialog box.

**New**
in 2017

- When you select a tag, the properties of that tag display. To display the properties of the tagged element, in the

  *Modify | <contextual>* tab>Host panel click 🗔 (Select Host).

### How To: Load Tags

1. In the *Annotate* tab, expand the Tag panel and click

   🗔 (Loaded Tags And Symbols) or, when a Tag command is active, in the Options Bar click **Tags...**
2. In the Loaded Tags And Symbols dialog box (shown in Figure 2–20), click **Load Family...**

**Figure 2–20**

3. In the Load Family dialog box, navigate to the appropriate *Annotations* folder, select the tag(s) needed and click **Open**.
4. The tag is added to the category in the dialog box. Click **OK**.

## Instance vs. Type Based Tags

Doors are tagged in a numbered sequence, with each instance of the door having a separate tag number. Other elements (such as windows and walls) are tagged by type, as shown in Figure 2–21. Changing the information in one tag changes all instances of that element.

*An additional window tag (**Window Tag-Number.rfa**) is stored in the Annotations> Architectural folder in the Library. It tags windows using sequential numbers.*

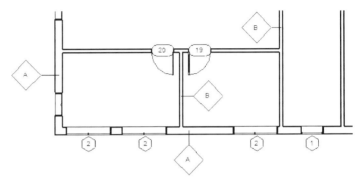

Figure 2–21

- To modify the number of an instance tag (such as a door or room), double-click directly on the number in the tag and modify it, or, you can modify the *Mark* property as shown in Figure 2–22. Only that one instance updates.

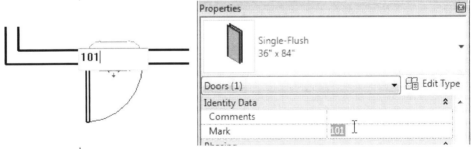

Figure 2–22

© 2016, ASCENT - Center for Technical Knowledge®

- To modify the number of a type tag (such as a window or wall), you can either double-click directly on the number in the tag and modify it, or select the element and, in Properties,

  click 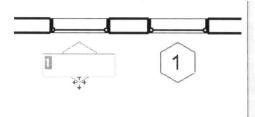 (Edit Type). In the Type Properties dialog box, in the *Identity Data* area, modify the *Type Mark*, as shown in Figure 2–23. All instances of this element then update.

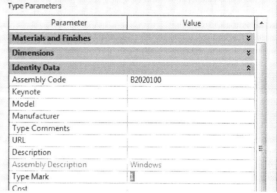

**Figure 2–23**

- When you change a type tag, an alert box opens to warn you that changing a type parameter affects other elements. If you want this tag to modify all other elements of this type, click **Yes**.

- If a type tag displays with a question mark, it means that no Type Mark has been assigned yet.

## Tagging in 3D Views

You can add tags (and some dimensions) to 3D views, as shown in Figure 2–24, as long as the views are locked first. You can only add tags in isometric views.

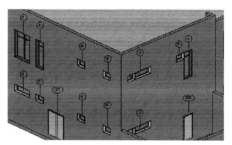

**Figure 2–24**

## How To: Lock a 3D View

1. Open a 3D view and set it up as you want it to display.

2. In the View Control Bar, expand 🧊 (Unlocked 3D View) and click 🧊 (Save Orientation and Lock View).

- If you are using the default 3D view and it has not been saved, you are prompted to name and save the view first.

- You can modify the orientation of the view, expand 🧊 (Locked 3D View) and click 🧊 (Unlock View). This also removes any tags you have applied.

- To return to the previous locked view, expand 🧊 (Unlocked 3D View) and click 🧊 (Restore Orientation and Lock View).

© 2016, ASCENT - Center for Technical Knowledge®

### Hint: Stair and Railing Tags

**Tag by Category** can be used to tag the overall stair, stair runs, landings, and railings, as shown in Figure 2–25. An additional type of tag, **Stair Tread/Riser Number**, creates a sequence of numbers for each tread or riser.

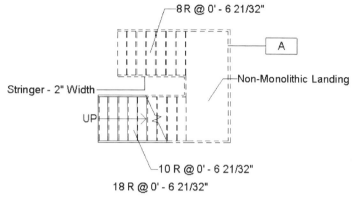

**Figure 2–25**

## How To: Add Tread/Riser Number Tags to Stairs

1. Open a plan, elevation, or section view.

2. In the *Annotate* tab>Tag panel, click 🖋 (Stair Tread/Riser Number).

3. In Properties setup the *Tag Type*, *Display Rule* and other parameters. These remain active for the project.

4. Select a reference line of a stair to place the numbers, as shown in Figure 2–26.

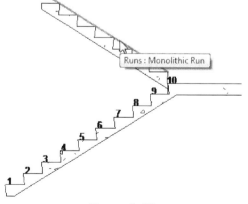

**Figure 2–26**

5. Continue selecting runs as required.

# Practice 2b

# Tag Elements (Doors, Windows, etc.) by Category

### Practice Objectives

- Add tags to a model.
- Use the Tag All Not Tagged dialog box.
- Set the Type Mark parameter for tags.

*Estimated time for completion: 10 minutes*

In this practice you will add wall tags in a floor plan and modify the Type Mark numbers for the walls. You will also tag all of the walls using the Tag All Not Tagged dialog box, as shown in Figure 2–27.

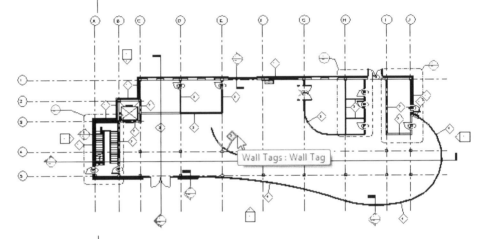

**Figure 2–27**

### Task 1 - Add tags to a floor plan.

1. Open the project **Modern-Hotel-Tags.rvt**.

2. In the **Floor Plans: Floor 1** view, zoom into the elevator and stair area near the left side of the building.

3. In the *Annotate* tab>Tag panel, click 📐 (Tag by Category). In the Options Bar, select **Leader** and verify that the **Attached End** option is selected.

© 2016, ASCENT - Center for Technical Knowledge®

4. Select the exterior wall, as shown in Figure 2–28.

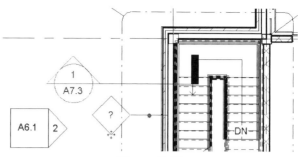

**Figure 2–28**

5. The tag comes in with a question mark because the wall does not have a *Type Mark* set yet. Click on the **?** in the tag and change the tag number to **1** and press <Enter>.

6. When alerted that you are changing a type parameter, click **Yes** to continue.

7. You are still in the **Tag** command. Add a tag to another exterior wall. This time, the tag number 1 comes in automatically as it is the same wall type as the first one.

8. Click ⬈ (Modify).

9. Select the masonry wall dividing the stairs from the lobby.

10. In Properties, click ⊞ (Edit Type).

11. In the Type Properties dialog box, in *Identity Data* area, set *Type Mark* to **2**, as shown in Figure 2–29. Click **OK**.

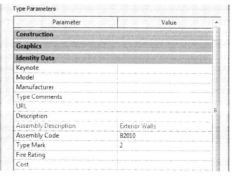

**Figure 2–29**

12. Select one of the interior partitions and set the *Type Mark* to **3**.

13. Use  (Tag By Category) to tag one of each of the wall types. The Type Mark displays as set in the Type Properties.

14. Zoom out to display the entire floor plan.

15. Save the project.

**Task 2 - Tag all the rest of the walls and modify tag locations.**

1. In the *Annotate* tab>Tag panel, click (Tag All).

2. In the Tag All Not Tagged dialog box, set the *Wall Tags* category to the **1/2"** tag type and select **Leader** as shown in Figure 2–30.

**Figure 2–30**

© 2016, ASCENT - Center for Technical Knowledge®

3. Click **OK** to add wall tags where they have not already been added.

4. Many of the tags overlap other annotation objects. Use the controls to move the tags and/or leaders to a more visible location, as shown in Figure 2–31.

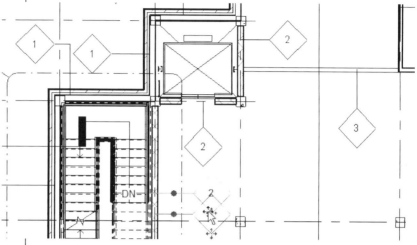

**Figure 2–31**

5. Update the tag for the main curtain wall to type number **4**.

6. Delete the wall tags that identify the storefront (inset) curtain walls along the back of the building and at the entrance. Delete any other wall tags you do not need to fully annotate the floor plan.

7. Save the project.

# 2.4 Use Dimension Strings

You can create permanent dimensions using aligned, linear, angular, radial, diameter, and arc length dimensions. These can be individual or a string of dimensions, as shown in Figure 2–32. With aligned dimensions, you can also dimension entire walls with openings, grid lines, and/or intersecting walls.

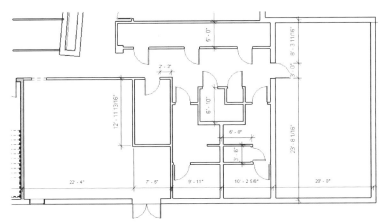

**Figure 2–32**

- Dimensions referencing model elements must be drawn on a model in an active view. You can dimension on sheets, but only to items drawn directly on the sheets.

- Dimensions are available in the *Annotate* tab>Dimension panel and the *Modify* tab>Measure panel, as shown in Figure 2–33.

*(Aligned) is also located in the Quick Access Toolbar.*

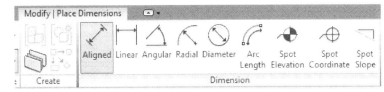

**Figure 2–33**

## How To: Add Aligned Dimensions

1. Start the ↗ (Aligned) command or type **DI.**
2. In the Type Selector, select a dimension style.

© 2016, ASCENT - Center for Technical Knowledge®

3. In the Options Bar, select the location line of the wall to dimension from, as shown in Figure 2–34.

   • This option can be changed as you add dimensions.

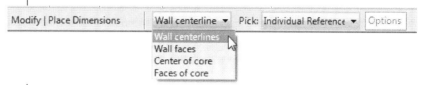

**Figure 2–34**

4. In the Options Bar, select your preference from the *Pick* drop-down list:

   • **Individual References**: Select the elements in order (as shown in Figure 2–35) and then click in empty space to position the dimension string.

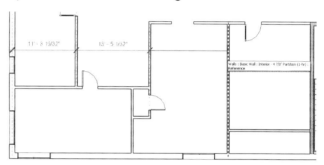

**Figure 2–35**

   • **Entire Walls**: Select the wall you want to dimension and then click the cursor to position the dimension string, as shown in Figure 2–36.

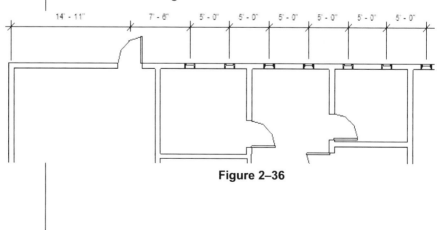

**Figure 2–36**

- When dimensioning entire walls you can specify how you want *Openings*, *Intersecting Walls*, and *Intersecting Grids* to be treated by the dimension string. In the Options Bar, click **Options**. In the Auto Dimension Options dialog box (shown in Figure 2–37), select the references you want to have automatically dimensioned.

*If the **Entire Wall** option is selected without additional options, it places an overall wall dimension.*

**Figure 2–37**

## How To: Add Other Types of Dimensions

*When the **Dimension** command is active, the dimension methods are also accessible in the Modify | Place Dimensions tab> Dimension panel.*

1. In the *Annotate* tab>Dimension panel, select a dimension method.

| | | |
|---|---|---|
| | **Aligned** | Most commonly used dimension type. Select individual elements or entire walls to dimension. |
| | **Linear** | Used when you need to specify certain points on elements. |
| | **Angular** | Used to dimension the angle between two elements. |
| | **Radial** | Used to dimension the radius of circular elements. |
| | **Diameter** | Used to dimension the diameter of circular elements. |
| | **Arc Length** | Used to dimension the length of the arc of circular elements. |

2. In the Type Selector, select the dimension type.
3. Follow the prompts for the selected method.

© 2016, ASCENT - Center for Technical Knowledge®

# Modifying Dimensions

When you move elements that are dimensioned, the dimensions automatically update. You can also modify dimensions by selecting a dimension or dimension string and making changes, as shown in Figure 2–38.

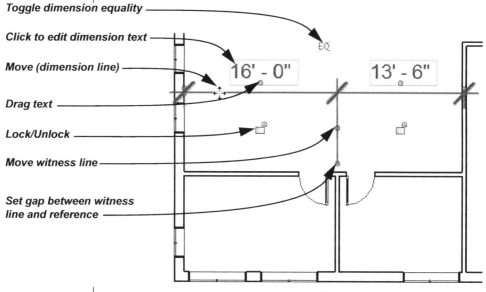

Toggle dimension equality

Click to edit dimension text

Move (dimension line)

Drag text

Lock/Unlock

Move witness line

Set gap between witness line and reference

**Figure 2–38**

- To move the dimension text, select the **Drag text** control under the text and drag it to a new location. It automatically creates a leader from the dimension line if you drag it away. The style of the leader (arc or line) depends on the dimension style.

- To move the dimension line (the line parallel to the element being dimensioned) simply drag the line to a new location or select the dimension and drag the ⊹ (Move) control.

- To change the gap between the witness line and the element being dimensioned, drag the control at the end of the witness line.

- To move the witness line (the line perpendicular to the element being dimensioned) to a different element or face of a wall, use the **Move Witness Line** control in the middle of the witness line. Click repeatedly to cycle through the various options. You can also drag this control to move the witness line to a different element, or right-click on the control and select **Move Witness Line**.

## Adding and Deleting Dimensions in a String

- To add a witness line to a string of dimensions, select the dimension and, in the *Modify | Dimensions* tab>Witness Lines panel, click 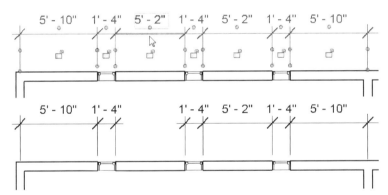 (Edit Witness Lines). Select the element(s) you want to add to the dimension. Click in space to finish.

- To delete a witness line, drag the **Move Witness Line** control to a nearby element. Alternatively, you can hover the cursor over the control, right-click, and select **Delete Witness Line**.

- To delete one dimension in a string and break the string into two separate dimensions, select the string, hover over the dimension that you want to delete, and press <Tab>. When it highlights (as shown on top in Figure 2–39), pick it and press <Delete>. The selected dimension is deleted and the dimension string is separated into two elements as shown on the bottom in Figure 2–39.

**Figure 2–39**

## Modifying the Dimension Text

Because the Autodesk® Revit® software is parametric, changing the dimension text without changing the elements dimensioned would cause problems throughout the project. These issues could cause problems beyond the model if you use the project model to estimate materials or work with other disciplines.

You can append the text with prefixes and suffixes (as shown in Figure 2–40), which can help you in renovation projects.

© 2016, ASCENT - Center for Technical Knowledge®

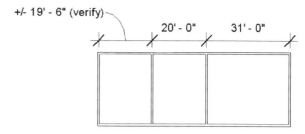

**Figure 2–40**

Double-click on the dimension text to open the Dimension Text dialog box, as shown in Figure 2–41, and make modifications as required.

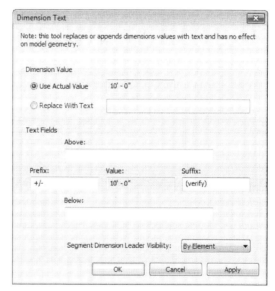

**Figure 2–41**

## Setting Constraints

The two types of constraints that work with dimensions are locks and equal settings, as shown in Figure 2–42.

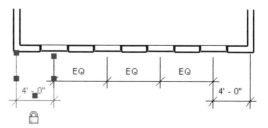

**Figure 2–42**

- When you lock a dimension, the value is set and you cannot make a change between it and the referenced elements. If it is unlocked, you can move it and change its value.

- For a string of dimensions, select the **EQ** symbol to constrain the elements to be at an equal distance apart. This actually moves the elements that are dimensioned.

- The equality text display can be changed in Properties as shown in Figure 2–43. The style for each of the display types is set in the dimension type.

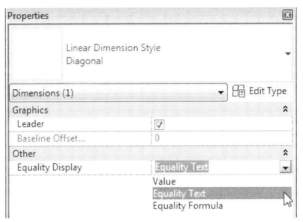

**Figure 2–43**

- To find out which elements have constraints applied to them, in the View Control Bar click  (Reveal Constraints). Constraints display as shown in Figure 2–44.

**New**
**in 2016**

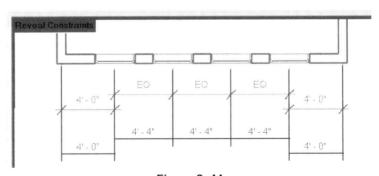

**Figure 2–44**

© 2016, ASCENT - Center for Technical Knowledge®

# Practice 2c | Use Dimension Strings

### Practice Objectives

- Add a string of dimensions.
- Dimension using the **Entire Walls** option.
- Edit the witness lines of dimensions.

*Estimated time for completion: 10 minutes*

In this practice you will add dimensions using several different methods to a floor plan view, as shown on the sheet in Figure 2–45. You will also modify the dimensions so that they show what you are expecting. Note that some additional elements including storefront curtain walls and windows have been added at the back of the building.

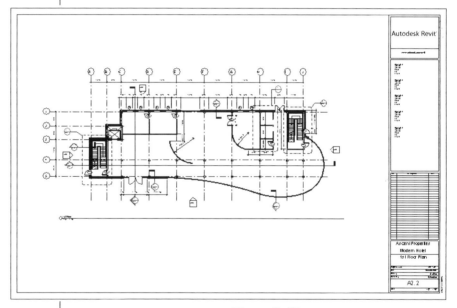

**Figure 2–45**

### Task 1 - Add dimensions to the column grid.

1. Open the project **Modern-Hotel-Dimensions.rvt**.

2. In the Project Browser, duplicate the **Floor Plans: Floor 1** view (without detailing so that the door and window tags do not display),

3. Rename the new view to **Floor 1-Dimensioned Plan**.

4. Move the location of the grid bubbles so that there is enough room for dimensioning.

5. In the Quick Access Toolbar, click ✗ (Aligned).

6. Dimension the column grid lines in each direction, as shown in Figure 2–46.

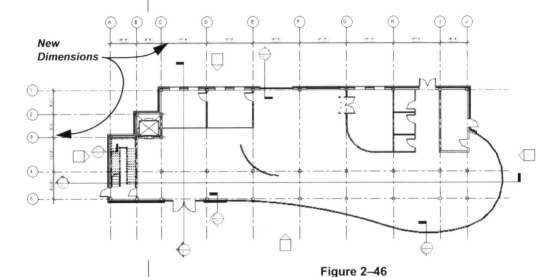

**New Dimensions**

**Figure 2–46**

---

### Task 2 - Dimension the exterior and interior walls.

---

1. Click ✗ (Aligned).

2. In the Options Bar, select **Wall faces** and set *Pick* to **Entire Walls**.

3. Click **Options** and set the *Openings* to **Widths** (as shown in Figure 2–47). Click **OK**.

**Figure 2–47**

© 2016, ASCENT - Center for Technical Knowledge®

4. Select the back wall and place the dimension above it.

5. Zoom in on the upper left corner of the building. Use the **Move Witness Line** control to relocate the line from the end of the wall (as shown in Figure 2–48), to Grid Line C, the closest grid line on the right that passes through the corner column.

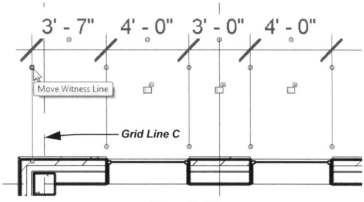

**Figure 2–48**

6. Click   (Modify)

7. In the same wall, pan over to the right between Grid Lines E, F, and G where the storefront openings are displayed. These were not dimensioned automatically.

8. Select the wall dimension line. In the *Modify | Dimensions* tab> Witness Lines panel, click   (Edit Witness Lines).

9. Select the outside edges of each side of the storefront openings to add the witness lines and then click in empty space to apply the changes. The modified dimension string displays as shown in Figure 2–49.

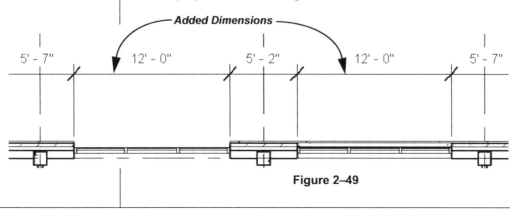

**Figure 2–49**

10. Move the elevation and section markers as well as the dimension line to keep the dimensions clear. You might also want to move the dimension text away from the grid lines.

11. Use the various dimensioning commands and methods to dimension the interior spaces, as shown in Figure 2–50. (Hint: don't forget to change from **Pick: Entire Walls** to **Pick: Individual References**.) The dimensions might not be exactly as shown.

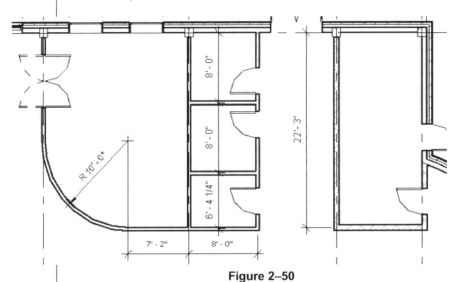

**Figure 2–50**

12. Save the project.

13. If time permits, dimension the **Floor Plans: Typical Guest Room - Dimension Plan** view. Make adjustments as required to the locations of the walls and doors.

© 2016, ASCENT - Center for Technical Knowledge®

# 2.5 Set the Colors Used in a Color Scheme Legend

Color Schemes added to views show information about rooms and areas. For example, if you add data to the room properties, such as Department or Occupancy, you can create a color scheme showing the groups using rooms. If you are using areas, you can identify the area types on an area plan, as shown in Figure 2–51.

Rentable Area Legend

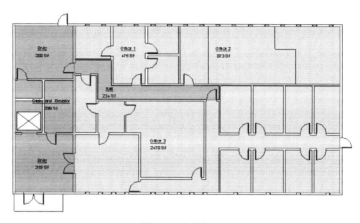

**Figure 2–51**

## How To: Set Up a Color Scheme in a View

1. Create or duplicate a view for the color scheme.

2. In the *Annotate* tab>Color Fill panel, click ⚏ (Color Fill Legend) and place the legend in the view.

3. In the dialog box, select the *Space Type* and *Color Scheme*, as shown in Figure 2–52, and click **OK.** The color scheme is applied to the view, as shown in Figure 2–53.

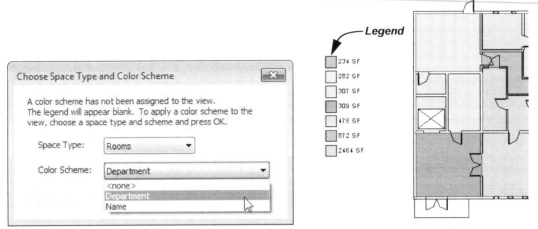

**Figure 2–52**                    **Figure 2–53**

- You can also select a Color Scheme and place the legend later. In Properties, click the button next to the *Color Scheme*, as shown in Figure 2–54. Then, in the Edit Color Scheme dialog box *Schemes* area, select the *Category* **Rooms** and an existing scheme.

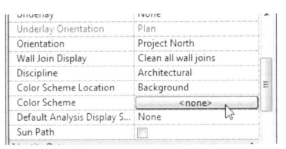

**Figure 2–54**

- If you change the **Color Scheme** in the View Properties dialog box, it also updates the associated legend.

- You can edit the color scheme through properties or select the **Color Fill Legend** and, in the *Modify | Color Fill Legend* tab>Scheme panel, click ✏ (Edit Scheme).

© 2016, ASCENT - Center for Technical Knowledge®

- The color fill of the scheme can display in background or the foreground of the view, as shown in Figure 2–55. This impacts how components display as well as whether or not the color fill stops at the walls.

*In Properties, set the Color Scheme Location.*

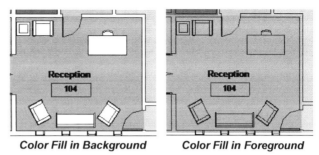

**Color Fill in Background**          **Color Fill in Foreground**

**Figure 2–55**

## How To: Define a Color Scheme

1. In View Properties, click the button next to the *Color Scheme* parameter, or in the *Architecture* tab>Room & Area panel, expand the panel title and click 🖾 (Color Schemes).
2. In the Edit Color Scheme dialog box, *Schemes* area, select a *Category*: **Areas (Gross Building)**, **Areas (Rentable)**, or **Rooms**, as shown in Figure 2–56.

**Figure 2–56**

- Additional options for MEP related elements may also be available, including: Ducts, HVAC Zones, Pipes, and Spaces.

3. Select an existing scheme and click 🗈 (Duplicate).
4. In the New color scheme dialog box, enter a new name and click **OK**.
5. In the Edit Color Scheme dialog box, in the *Scheme Definition* area, enter a name for the *Title* of the color scheme. This displays when the legend is placed in the view.

6. In the Color drop-down list, select an option, as shown in Figure 2–57. The available parameters depend on the type of scheme you are creating.

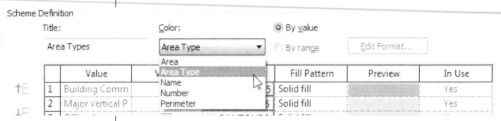

**Figure 2–57**

7. Select the **By value** or **By range** option to set how the color scheme displays.

8. Click ✛ (Add Value) to add more rows to the scheme, as shown in Figure 2–58. Modify the visibility (*Visible* column), *Color*, and *Fill Pattern* as required.

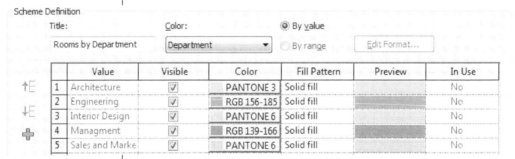

**Figure 2–58**

9. In the *Options* area, select **Include elements from linked files** if you are using linked files.
10. Click **OK** to finish.

- Click ⬆E (Move Rows Up) or ⬇E (Move Rows Down) to change the order of rows in the list.

- To remove a row, select it and click ▬ (Remove Value). This option is only available if the parameter data is not being used in the room or area elements in the project.

© 2016, ASCENT - Center for Technical Knowledge®

## Color Schemes By Value

If you select the **By value** option, you can modify the visibility, color, and fill pattern of the scheme. The value is assigned by the parameter data in the room or area object.

- Values are automatically updated when you add data to the parameters used in the color scheme. For example, if you create a color by room *Name* and then add another room name in the project, it is also added to the color scheme.

## Color Schemes By Range

If you select the **By range** option, you can modify the *At Least* variable and the *Caption*, as well as the visibility, color, and fill pattern, as shown in Figure 2–59.

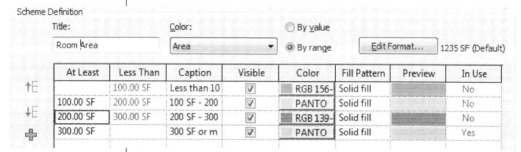

**Figure 2–59**

- Only the **Area** and **Perimeter** parameters can be set by range.

- Click **Edit Format...** to modify the units display format.

- When you add rows, the new row increments according to the previous distances set or double the value of the first row.

---

# Practice 2d

# Set the Colors Used in a Color Scheme Legend

## Practice Objectives

- Apply a color scheme to a view.
- Add a color scheme legend.
- Create **By value** and **By range** color schemes

*Estimated time for completion: 10 minutes*

In this practice, you will add an existing color scheme and a legend to a view, as shown in Figure 2–60. You will also create and apply color schemes By value for Room Names and By range for rentable area sizes.

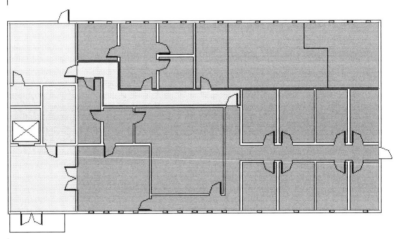

**Figure 2–60**

## Task 1 - Apply a color scheme.

1. In the practice files folder, open **Medical-Office-Colors.rvt**.

2. Duplicate the **Area Plans (Rentable)***:* **Level 1** view and name it **Level 1 - Rentable Area**.

3. In the *Annotate tab*>Color Fill panel, click ▪≡ (Color Fill Legend) and click to the left of the building to place the legend.

© 2016, ASCENT - Center for Technical Knowledge®

4. In the Choose Space Type and Color Scheme dialog boxes, set the *Space Type* to **Areas (Rentable)** and the *Color Scheme* to **Rentable Area**. Click **OK**.

5. The Legend and floor plan are set to the appropriate color fill, as shown in Figure 2–60.

6. Save the project.

---

**Task 2 - Create a Color Scheme**

---

1. Duplicate with detailing the **Area Plans (Rentable)***:* **Level 1 - Rentable Area** view and name it **Level 1 - Rentable Area by Size**.

2. Select the legend and in the *Modify | Color Fill Legends* tab> Scheme panel, click ▨✎ (Edit Scheme).

3. Click 🗋 (Duplicate) to create a copy of the existing area color scheme and name it **Rentable Area by Size**.

*Any time a warning about colors not being preserved displays. Click OK.*

4. In the *Scheme Definition* area, enter **Rentable Area by Size** for the *Title* and select **Area** in the Color drop-down list.

5. Select **By range**. The default ranges display as shown in Figure 2–61.

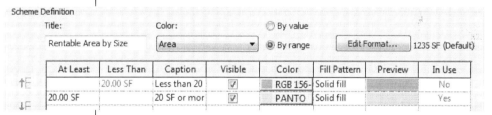

**Figure 2–61**

6. Set the value of the default *At Least* variable to **200 SF**.

7. Click ➕ (Add Value). This should create a value of 400 SF.

8. Select **400 SF** and click  (Add Value) again. Continue working down the menu until you have **1000 SF** in the *At Least* value list, as shown in Figure 2–62.

Scheme Definition

| Title: | | Color: | | ○ By value | | | |
|---|---|---|---|---|---|---|---|
| Rentable Area by Size | | Area ▼ | | ● By range | Edit Format... | | 1235 SF (Default) |

| | At Least | Less Than | Caption | Visible | Color | Fill Pattern | Preview | In Use |
|---|---|---|---|---|---|---|---|---|
| ↑E | | 200.00 SF | Less than 20 | ✓ | RGB 156- | Solid fill | | No |
| ↓E | 200.00 SF | 400.00 SF | 200 SF - 400 | ✓ | PANTO | Solid fill | | Yes |
| | 400.00 SF | 600.00 SF | 400 SF - 600 | ✓ | PANTO | Solid fill | | Yes |
| ✚ | 600.00 SF | 800.00 SF | 600 SF - 800 | ✓ | RGB 139- | Solid fill | | No |
| | 800.00 SF | 1000.00 SF | 800 SF - 1000 | ✓ | PANTO | Solid fill | | Yes |
| ▭ | 1000.00 SF | | 1000 SF or m | ✓ | RGB 096- | Solid fill | | Yes |

**Figure 2–62**

9. Modify any colors or fills as required.

10. Click **OK** to close the dialog box. The new color scheme is applied to the view, as shown in Figure 2–63.

Rentable Area by Size

Less than 200 SF
200 SF - 400 SF
400 SF - 600 SF
600 SF - 800 SF
800 SF - 1000 SF
1000 SF or more

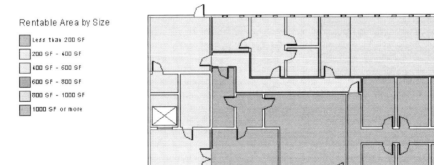

**Figure 2–63**

11. Save the project.

## Task 3 - Create a Room Color Scheme

1. In the *Architecture* tab>Room & Area panel, expand the panel title and select 🗺 (Color Schemes).

2. In the Edit Color Scheme dialog box, set the *Category* to **Rooms**.

© 2016, ASCENT - Center for Technical Knowledge®

3. Click (Duplicate) to create a copy of the existing room color scheme and name it **Room Names**.

4. In the *Scheme Definition* area, enter **Room Names** for the *Title* and select **Name** in the Color drop-down list.

5. The values are automatically applied according to the room names used in the project, as shown in part in Figure 2–64.

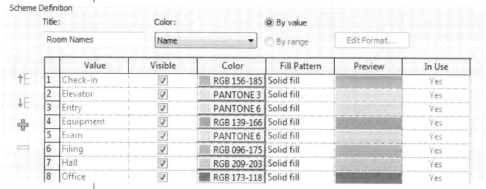

Figure 2–64

6. Click (Add Value) and create a new value named **Lab**. The new Lab value is set to **No** in the *In Use* column, as shown in Figure 2–65.

Figure 2–65

7. Modify the colors or fill patterns for the scheme as required.

8. Click **OK**. The scheme is not applied to the current view when you create it this way.

9. Open the **Floor Plans: Level 1 - Rooms** view.

10. In Properties, select the **Color Scheme** button.

11. In the Edit Color Scheme dialog box, set the *Category* to **Rooms** and select the new **Room Names** color scheme and click **OK**.

12. In the *Annotate* tab>Color Fill panel, click (Color Fill Legend).

13. Place the legend to the side of the building. It automatically displays using the current color scheme, as shown in Figure 2–66Figure 2–66.

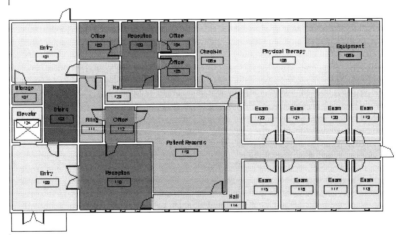

**Figure 2–66**

14. Change the name of one of the offices to **Lab**. The color updates to match the Lab value you added to the color scheme.

© 2016, ASCENT - Center for Technical Knowledge®

15. Change the name of one of the exam rooms to **Mechanical**. A new value is automatically added to the color scheme, as shown in Figure 2–67.

Room Names

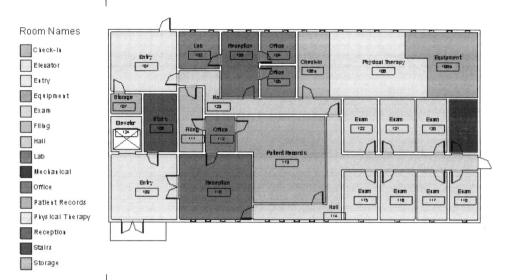

**Figure 2–67**

16. Save the project.

# 2.6 Work with Phases

Phases show distinct stages in a project's life. They are typically used with renovations and additions, as shown in Figure 2–68, or when a project involves several phases for its completion.

*Phases are applied to elements. The phases you see are controlled by views.*

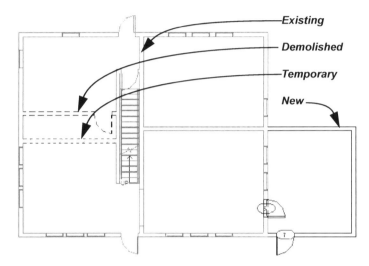

**Figure 2–68**

All construction elements have two phase properties, *Phase Created* and *Phase Demolished.* This creates four potential status conditions for each element regardless of how many phases you have in your project:

- **Existing:** Created in an earlier phase and exists in the current phase.

- **New:** Created in the current phase.

- **Demolished:** Created in an earlier phase and demolished in the current phase.

- **Temporary:** Created in the current phase and demolished in the current phase.

There are two default phases included in the template files: **Existing** and **New Construction**. Many projects can be completed just using these two options but you can also create additional phases for more complex projects.

© 2016, ASCENT - Center for Technical Knowledge®

When you add new elements in a view, they take on the phase set in the current view. In Properties, under the *Phasing* heading, select the *Phase* from the list, as shown in Figure 2–69.

**Figure 2–69**

- If you are working on a renovation project, start by modeling the building with the *Phase* set to **Existing**.

You can also move elements to a different phase. Select the element(s) and, in Properties, change the *Phase Created* as shown in Figure 2–70.

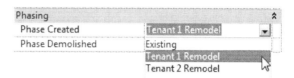

**Figure 2–70**

To demolish elements, select them and, in Properties, change the *Phase Demolished*. Or, in the *Modify* tab>Geometry panel,

click (Demolish) and select the elements that you want to demolish in the current phase.

- Demolishing a wall also demolishes any doors or windows associated with that wall.

- To change an element so that it is no longer demolished, set the *Phase Demolished* to **None**.

### Hint: Elements that do not have phases

Annotations (tags, text, or dimensions), view elements (elevations, sections, and callout views), and datum elements (grids and levels) do not have phases.

Curtain walls and beam systems include sub-elements that do not have phases. You need to select the primary curtain wall or beam system to change the phase.

When selecting multiple elements to apply a phase, click

 (Filter) in the Status Bar and clear the check next to any annotations and curtain wall sub-elements, as shown in Figure 2–71, before modifying the phase in the properties.

Figure 2–71

- Non-phase elements can be hidden in views where you do not want them to show. For example, in Figure 2–72, hide (by element) grids 5-8 and then modify the length of grids A-C (change the 3D icon to 2D so the change only shows in the current view.) You could also change the crop region of the view.

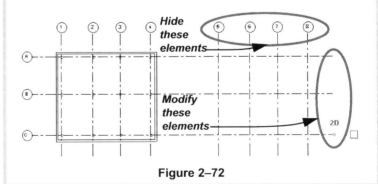

Figure 2–72

© 2016, ASCENT - Center for Technical Knowledge®

# Phases and Views

*The look of the elements is determined by graphic overrides assigned to each phase filter.*

Duplicate a view for each phase you want to display. For example, you might want to show only the existing and demolished items in one view and the existing and new items, without the demolished items, in another view. You may also want to show the completed project without any of the previous phases, as shown in Figure 2–73.

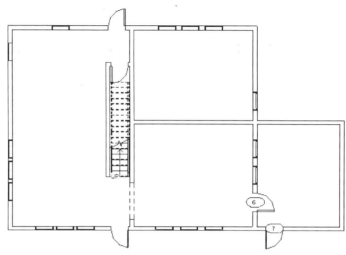

**Figure 2–73**

The *Phase Filter* determines which phases are displayed in the view relative to the current phase:

- **None:** Displays all elements regardless of the current phase.

- **Show All:** Displays all phases up to the current phase, with all except the current phase, which is grayed out.

- **Show Complete:** Displays all construction up to the current phase.

- **Show Demo + New:** Displays the current phase and any demolished elements.

- **Show New:** Displays only elements created in the current view.

- **Show Previous + Demo:** Displays elements created in previous phases and any demolished elements from the current phase.

- **Show Previous + New:** Displays elements created in the previous phase and any new elements created in the current phase.

- **Show Previous Phase:** Displays elements created in any previous phases.

## Creating Phases

When you create new phases, you can specify the names and time sequence, set up phase filters, and specify graphic overrides for each phase.

### How To: Create New Phases

1. In the *Manage* tab>Phasing panel, click 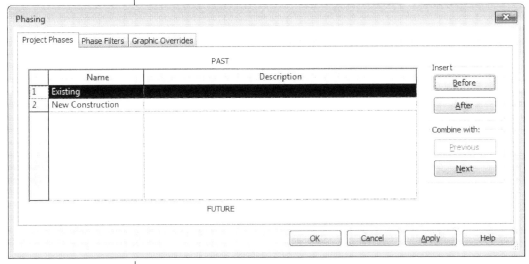 (Phases).
2. In the Phasing dialog box, *Project Phases* tab, the existing phases display. Two phases, **Existing** and **New Construction**, come with most templates, as shown in Figure 2–74.

**Figure 2–74**

- The default phases can be renamed in this dialog box.
3. In the *Project Phases* tab, select a phase in the list. In the *Insert* area, click **Before** or **After**, as required. You cannot change the order and need to be careful as you insert phases.
   - New phases are numbered (Phase 1, Phase 2, etc.). Select the name to change it. You can also add a description for each phase.
   - You can combine phases, as required. Click **Previous** or **Next**. The elements on the combined phases take on the phase properties of the phase with which they were combined.

*You need to add the phase in the correct time sequence. Past and Future notations are at the top and bottom of the dialog box.*

© 2016, ASCENT - Center for Technical Knowledge®

4. Select the *Phase Filters* tab, as shown in Figure 2–75. Several phase filters are supplied with the program and you can add more. Once you have a new phase filter, you define which of the phases are displayed. If listed as **Overridden**, the graphic overrides display for the phase.

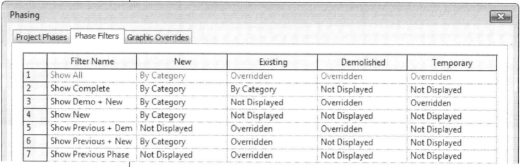

**Figure 2–75**

5. Select the *Graphic Overrides* tab, as shown in Figure 2–76. Set up the overrides, as required.

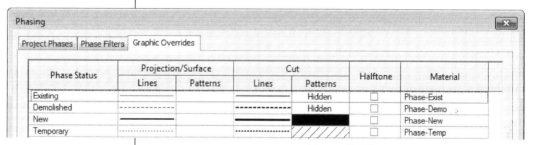

**Figure 2–76**

6. Click **OK** to close the dialog box.

# Practice 2e | Work with Phases

## Practice Objectives

- Set custom phases in a project.
- Apply phases to elements.
- Apply phases to views.

In this practice you will create several new phases and view the changes with the phase filters. You will also add some new elements in the existing building, as shown in Figure 2–77.

*Estimated time for completion: 10 minutes*

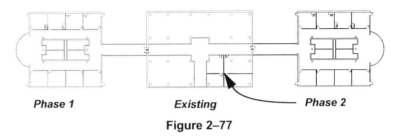

**Phase 1**          **Existing**          **Phase 2**

**Figure 2–77**

---

### Task 1 - Set up Phases.

1. In the practice files folder, open **Office-Phases-A.rvt**.

2. In the *Manage* tab>Phasing panel, click (Phases).

3. In the Phasing dialog box, in the *Project Phases* tab, rename the phase *New Construction* as **Phase 1** and add the description: **West Wing Addition**.

4. Insert an additional phase after the last one and accept the default name of **Phase 2**. Add the description: **East Wing Addition**, as shown in Figure 2–78.

**Figure 2–78**

5. Click **OK** to close the dialog box.

---

© 2016, ASCENT - Center for Technical Knowledge®

### Task 2 - Apply Phases to Views and Elements.

1. Duplicate three new views of **Level 1**. Rename them: **Level 1 - Existing**, **Level 1 - Phase 1**, and **Level 1 - Phase 2**.

2. Open the **Level 1- Existing** view.

3. Select all elements in the middle building, as shown in Figure 2–79. Filter out any annotation elements, such as tags, views, and elevations.

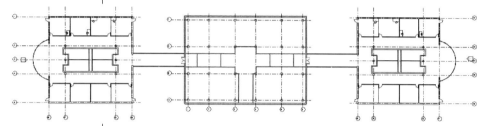

**Figure 2–79**

4. In Properties, change the *Phase Created* for these elements to **Existing**.

5. Click in the view to release the selection. The building elements should turn gray when you clear the selection.

6. In Properties (with no elements selected), scroll down and set *Phase Filter* to **Show Complete** and *Phase* to **Existing**, as shown in Figure 2–80.

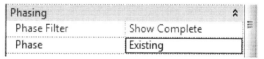

**Figure 2–80**

7. Click in the view. Only the central building is displayed but the grids on either side still display. Resize the crop region so only the main building displays as shown in Figure 2–81.

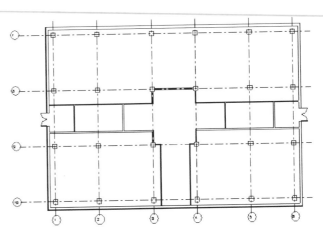

**Figure 2–81**

8. Open the **Level 1 - Phase 1** view.

9. Select the elements in the right (east) wing, filter out any views and tags, and change the *Phase Created* of these elements to **Phase 2**. In this case, the elements are removed from the view. Resize the crop region so the east wing grids do not display, as shown in Figure 2–82.

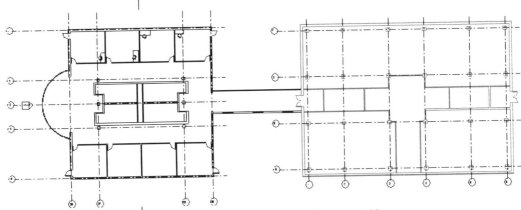

**Figure 2–82**

© 2016, ASCENT - Center for Technical Knowledge®

10. Without any elements selected, verify that the *Phase Filter* is set to **Show All** and the *Phase* is set to **Phase 1**.

11. In the *Modify* tab>Geometry panel, click ![hammer] (Demolish). Select the four walls in the center building that cross the long horizontal hallways, as shown in Figure 2–83.

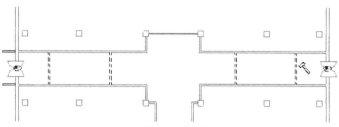

**Figure 2–83**

12. Click ![cursor] (Modify) and select one of the demolished walls. In Properties, scroll down to the *Phasing* area. Ensure that the *Phase Created* is set to **Existing** and *Phase Demolished* is set to **Phase 1**.

13. Open the view **Level 1 - Phase 2**.

14. In Properties set the *Phase Filter* to **Show All** and the *Phase* to **Phase 2**.

15. In Properties, set the *Phase Filter* to **Show All** and change the *Phase* to **Phase 2**. The East Wing is added and the demolished walls are removed, while the elements in the previous two phases are grayed out, as shown in Figure 2–84.

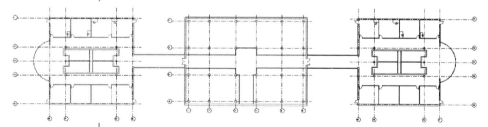

**Figure 2–84**

16. Modify the crop region so that it shows all of Phase 2 and part of the existing building. Hide the grids in the existing building, as shown in Figure 2–85.

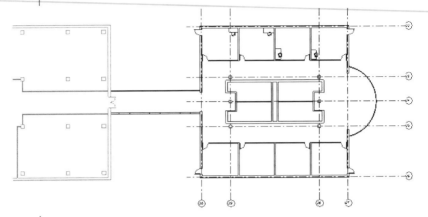

**Figure 2–85**

17. In the existing building add several walls and doors with some of the doors along the existing walls, as shown in Figure 2–86.

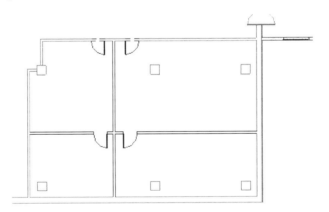

**Figure 2–86**

18. Save the project.

© 2016, ASCENT - Center for Technical Knowledge®

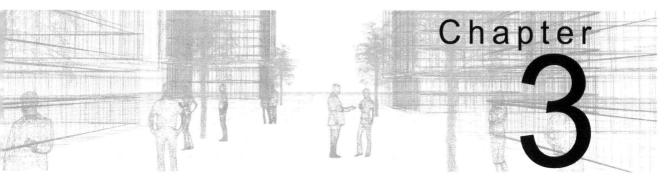

# Elements and Families

This chapter includes instructional content to assist in your preparation for the following topic and objectives for the Autodesk® Revit® Architecture Certified Professional exam.

## Autodesk Certification Exam Objectives in this Chapter

| Exam Topic | Exam Objective | Section |
|---|---|---|
| Elements and Families | • Change elements within a curtain wall (grids, panels, mullions) | • 3.1 |
| | • Create compound walls | • 3.2 |
| | • Create a stacked wall | • 3.3 |
| | • Differentiate system and component families | • 3.4 |
| | • Work with family Parameters | • 3.5 |
| | • Create a new family type | • 3.6 |
| | • Use Family creation procedures | • 3.7 |

# 3.1 Change Elements Within a Curtain Wall (Grids, Panels, Mullions)

Curtain walls are non-bearing walls consisting of panels laid out in a grid pattern. They can encase an entire building like a membrane or, as shown in Figure 3–1, fill a cutout in a standard wall, often called a storefront.

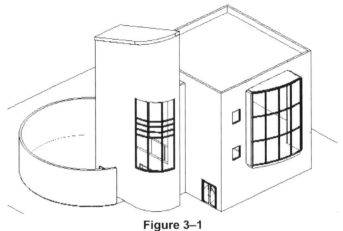

**Figure 3–1**

## How To: Create a Curtain Wall.

1. In a plan view, draw a wall using a curtain wall type.
2. In an elevation or 3D view, add grids to the curtain wall.
3. Modify the panels of the curtain wall. Panels can be a specific material (such as glass or stone) or can incorporate doors, windows, or other wall types.
4. Add mullions to separate the panels.

© 2016, ASCENT - Center for Technical Knowledge®

The components of a curtain wall are shown in Figure 3–2.

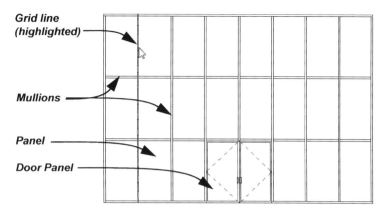

**Figure 3–2**

- The simplest way to create a curtain wall is to use a curtain wall type with a preset uniform grid already applied to it, such as **Curtain Wall:Exterior Glazing** or **Curtain Wall: Storefront**, which come with the software, as shown in Figure 3–3.

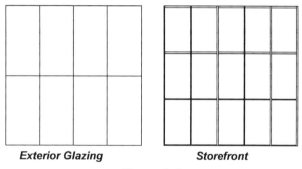

**Figure 3–3**

- The Autodesk® Revit® software also comes with a standard curtain wall type, **Curtain Wall 1**, that creates a single glass panel to which you can apply a grid in any pattern.

- Many curtain walls do not have a uniform pattern of exact distances between grids, as shown in Figure 3–4. Therefore, you need to create these designs directly on the curtain wall. You can start with a curtain wall type that has a basic uniform grid, if applicable.

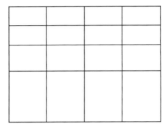

Figure 3–4

## Creating Storefronts

Storefronts are a special type of curtain wall that can be embedded into other walls, as shown in Figure 3–5. They can also be used to create what looks like a complex set of windows. Some curtain wall types, such as the **Storefront** wall type, are designed to be embedded in another wall.

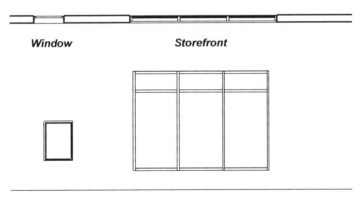

Figure 3–5

© 2016, ASCENT - Center for Technical Knowledge®

## How To: Add a Storefront Wall in an Existing Wall

1. In the *Architecture* tab>Build panel, click  (Wall).
2. In the Type Selector, select the curtain wall type you want to use. In Properties, set the *Base Constraint, Top Constraint,* and *Offsets* as required.The height can be less than the height of the wall in which you are embedding.
3. Select a point on the existing wall, as shown in Figure 3–6.

**Figure 3–6**

4. Select the second point along the wall. (Hint: Press <Tab> to cycle from the default Horizontal and Nearest snap to the dynamic dimension and then type the distance for the embedded curtain wall.) The wall displays as shown in Figure 3–7.

**Figure 3–7**

5. Open the appropriate elevation view. Select the outside edge of the curtain wall and use the shape handles and dynamic dimensions, as shown in Figure 3–8, to place the storefront in the wall as required.

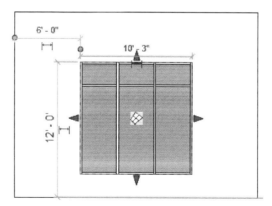

**Figure 3–8**

# Adding Curtain Grids

Once you have a curtain wall in place with at least one panel, you need to separate it into multiple panels for the design. Each grid line divides a panel into two or more smaller panels, as shown in Figure 3–9.

**Figure 3–9**

## How To: Create a Curtain Grid

1. After you have drawn the base curtain wall in a plan view, switch to an elevation or 3D view.

2. In the *Architecture* tab>Build panel, click (Curtain Grid).

3. In the *Modify | Place Curtain Grid* tab>Placement panel, select an insertion method, as described below.

| | |
|---|---|
| (All Segments) | Creates a grid line through the entire curtain wall height or width. |
| (One Segment) | Creates a grid line between only the selection point and the next line. The entire grid line is established, but only one segment displays. You can add other segments later. |
| (All Except Picked) | Creates a grid line through the entire grid and permits you to go back and remove segments of the grid line. The removed segment displays as a dashed line until you draw another grid line or start another command. |

© 2016, ASCENT - Center for Technical Knowledge®

4. Move the cursor over an edge of the curtain wall or an existing grid line. Dynamic dimensions are displayed, as shown in Figure 3–10. The new grid line is perpendicular to the edge at the point you select. Click at the required location.

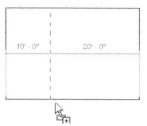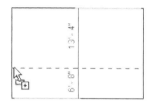

**Figure 3–10**

- Curtain grids automatically snap to the midpoint or 1/3 point of the panel. They also snap to levels, column grids, and reference planes.

- You can use 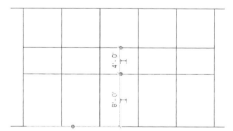 (Copy) and (Array) on the curtain grid lines. This method can be the fastest way of creating grids across the length of a wall.

- You can add additional grids to curtain wall types that include grids when they are created.

**Modifying Curtain Grids**

Once you have placed the grid lines, they might not be exactly where you want them or overlap other lines where you do not want them to overlap. You can modify the location of lines in the grid and add or remove segments from the lines, as shown in Figure 3–11.

**Figure 3–11**

- To modify the grid, you must select a grid line, not a wall or the mullion. Press <Tab> to cycle through elements.

- To move a grid line, select it and use dynamic dimensions or
   (Move).

**Enhanced**
in 2017

- If you select a grid line that was created using a curtain wall type, (Prevent or allow change of element position) is displayed, indicating that the element is constrained to a host element. Click on the icon to enable you to move the line.

### How To: Add or Remove Segments of Curtain Grids

1. Select a grid line to modify.
2. In the *Modify |Curtain Wall Grids* tab>Curtain Grid panel, click
   (Add/Remove Segments).
3. Click on the part of the grid that you want to add or remove. The line displays as dashed when you click to remove a segment, as shown in Figure 3–12. You must select grid lines one at a time with this command.

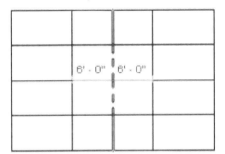  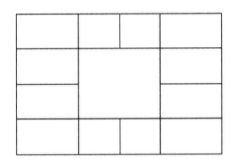

**Figure 3–12**

4. Click in empty space to finish the command.

- You can create non-rectangular panels by removing individual grid segments.

---

**Hint: Aligning and Locking**

When you use the **Align** command, you can also lock the lines together so if one moves, the other does as well. However, locking also causes the software to slow down. Therefore, be careful how much you use the **Lock** option and apply it only when you expect to make a lot of modifications.

---

   © 2016, ASCENT - Center for Technical Knowledge®

## Working with Curtain Wall Panels

The default panel for a curtain wall is typically a glazed panel. As you create the curtain grid and refine the wall design, you might want to use other materials for some of the panels, as shown in Figure 3–13. You can select the existing panels and in the Type Selector, select a panel type with the material you want to use. The panel type also controls the thickness and can define a door or window for the panel.

*To select all of the panels, select the edge of the curtain wall, right-click, and select **Select Panels on Host**.*

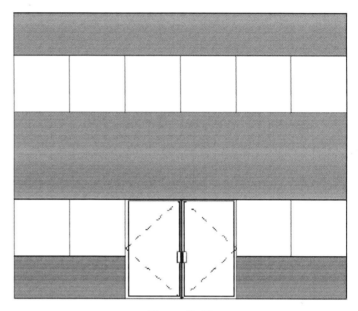

**Figure 3–13**

- To select a panel, move the cursor over its edge, press <Tab> until it highlights, and then click to select it. If 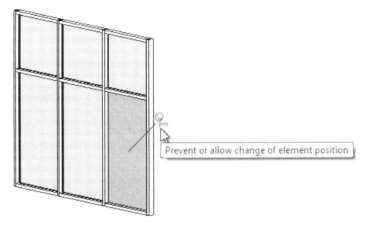 (Prevent or allow change of element position) displays (as shown in Figure 3–14), it indicates that the panel is locked and that changes to the element are not permitted. Click the icon to turn off the lock and modify the panel.

- To unpin multiple panels, select them and type **UP** (for **Unpin**).

Prevent or allow change of element position

**Figure 3–14**

## Default Panel Types

Three panel types come with the default project template:

| | |
|---|---|
| **Empty Panel** | You cannot delete a panel in a curtain wall, but you can change the panel type to an empty panel. |
| **Glazed Panel** | A typical panel type with glass as its material. |
| **Solid Panel** | A panel type using a solid material. You can create variations of this type with other materials. |

- You can use any other wall type (including other curtain wall types) to fill in a panel.

- Door and window panels are available through the Library. Similar to other panel types, door and window panels fill the size of the panel to which they are applied. Adjust the curtain grid for the correct sizes.

© 2016, ASCENT - Center for Technical Knowledge®

**Hint: Placing Doors in Curtain Walls**

You can place doors in curtain wall panels, as shown in Figure 3–15. You first need to have a door type that can be used as a curtain wall panel (the software comes with several). Then, ensure the size of the opening in the curtain wall matches the size of the door you want to use. The door type expands to fill the grid opening.

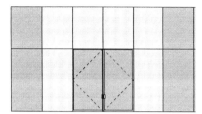

**Figure 3–15**

- When you tag a curtain wall panel door, you need to add the number to the tag. It does not automatically increment.

- You can also use a standard wall type as a panel. Then you can add a door into the panel using the standard **Door** command.

## Creating a Curtain Wall Panel

While you can create curtain wall panels in many complex ways, a basic technique is to specify a material for a flat system panel, as shown in Figure 3–16.

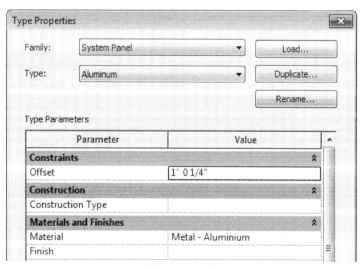

**Figure 3–16**

## How To: Create a Curtain Wall Panel

1. Select a panel similar to the one you want to create (e.g., select a solid panel to create a new solid panel type). If it is locked, unlock it by clicking (Prevent or allow change of element position).

2. In Properties, click (Edit Type), or, in the *Modify | Curtain Panels* tab>Properties panel, click (Type Properties).

3. In the Type Properties dialog box, click **Duplicate** to create a copy of the existing family type.

4. Give the panel a new name that describes its purpose (e.g., **Brick** or **Aluminum**). The new name automatically includes the family name, such as **System Panel**.

5. Set the *Thickness*, *Offset*, and *Material* and any other parameters as required. Many materials are available in the Materials dialog box that opens when you click (Browse) in the Materials list.

6. Click **OK** to close the dialog box and finish the panel. It is automatically applied to the panel you selected for modification.

- The *Thickness* of the material is centered on the grid if you did not specify an *Offset*. If you want the panel to be recessed in the wall, use a negative offset. If you want the panel to stand out from the wall, use a positive offset.

- Materials with patterns, such as the glass block shown in Figure 3–17, do not display the pattern when the view is zoomed out far. Zoom in to view the material.

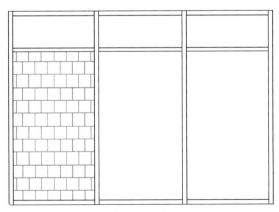

**Figure 3–17**

© 2016, ASCENT - Center for Technical Knowledge®

# Attaching Mullions to Curtain Grids

Mullions are the frameworks for curtain wall panels, as shown in Figure 3–18. They can be many sizes, shapes, and materials. Add them as the final step in your curtain wall design after you have placed the grid lines.

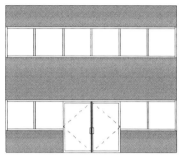

**Figure 3–18**

## How To: Add Mullions

1. In the *Architecture* tab>Build panel, click ⊞ (Mullion).
2. In the Type Selector, select the mullion style. There are no modifiable properties when you insert a mullion.
3. In the *Modify | Place Mullion* tab>Placement panel, select a

   *Create Mullion on* method: ⊞ (Grid Line), ⊞ (Grid Line

   Segment), or ⊞ (All Grid Lines), as shown in Figure 3–19.

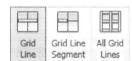

**Figure 3–19**

4. Select the grid line on which you want to place the mullion. If the grid line is inside a grid, the mullion is placed on the grid's center line. If it is on the edge of the wall, the mullion is placed so that its exterior is flush with the outside of the wall.

   - Hold <Shift> to place a mullion only on the selected segment.
   - Hold <Ctrl> to place the mullion on all empty grid segments (i.e., all without mullions).

   - Corner mullion types are designed for the intersection of two curtain walls. They adjust to fit the angle of the intersection.

*Mullions must be placed individually; they cannot be copied or arrayed.*

## Modifying Mullions

To quickly select mullions, right-click on the edge of the curtain wall and select **Select Mullions**. The mullion options include **On Vertical Grid** or **On Horizontal Grid**, **Inner Mullions**, **Border Mullions**, or **Mullions on Host**, as shown in Figure 3–20.

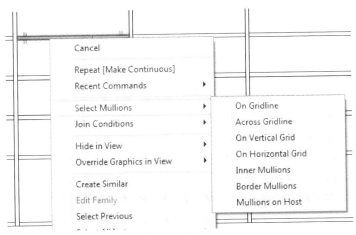

Figure 3–20

- Modify mullion styles by changing their type in the Type Selector.

- If you move a grid line, the mullion moves with it.

- If you delete a grid line, the mullion is also deleted. However, if you delete a mullion, the grid line is not deleted.

- You can change the way mullions intersect. Select the mullion to display the *Modify | Curtain Wall Mullions* tab. In the Mullion panel, click ⊤ (Make Continuous) or ⊥ (Break at Join), You can also do this directly on the mullion, as shown in Figure 3–21.

*Before*                              *After*

Figure 3–21

© 2016, ASCENT - Center for Technical Knowledge®

**Hint: Temporary Hide/Isolate**

You might want to temporarily remove elements from a view, modify the project, and then restore the elements. Instead of completely turning the elements off, you can temporarily hide them.

Select the elements you want to hide (make invisible) or isolate (keep displayed while all other elements are hidden) and click

(Temporary Hide/Isolate). Select the method you want to use, as shown in Figure 3–22.

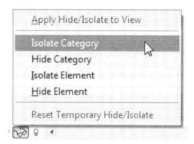

**Figure 3–22**

The elements or category are hidden or isolated. A cyan border displays around the view with a note in the upper left corner, as shown in Figure 3–23. It indicates that the view contains temporarily hidden or isolated elements.

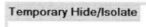

**Figure 3–23**

- Click (Temporary Hide/Isolate) again and select **Reset Temporary Hide/Isolate** to restore the elements to the view.

- If you want to permanently hide the elements in the view, select **Apply Hide/Isolate to View**.

- Elements that are temporarily hidden in a view are not hidden when the view is printed.

# Practice 3a

# Change Elements within a Curtain Wall - Grids

### Practice Objectives

- Modify curtain wall properties.
- Add curtain wall grid lines.

*Estimated time for completion: 10 minutes*

In this practice you will modify a curtain wall using Properties to ensure that the lines match up with other elements. You will also add grid lines that follow the pattern of a nearby wall. The finished elevation is shown in Figure 3–24.

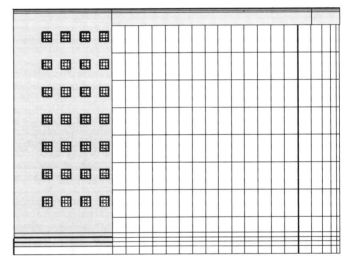

**Figure 3–24**

### Task 1 - Modify the curtain wall.

1. Open the project **Modern-Hotel-Curtain-Walls.rvt**.

2. Open the **Elevations (Building Elevation):South** view.

3. To make the view easier to understand, select one grid line, one column, and one level line. (Hold <Ctrl> to select more than one element.) Then, right-click and select **Hide in View>Category**.

© 2016, ASCENT - Center for Technical Knowledge®

The curtain wall grid does not match up with any of the other features, as shown in Figure 3–25.

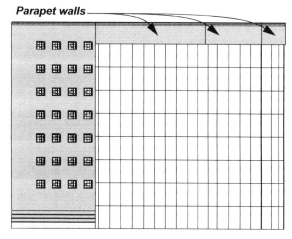

**Figure 3–25**

4. Select the three parapet walls. In Properties, change the *Base Offset* to (negative) **-2' 0"** and click **Apply**. This shortens the parapet.

5. Select the three curtain walls. In Properties, change the *Top Offset* to (negative) **-2' 0"** and click **Apply**. This extends the curtain wall up to the parapet.

6. With the curtain walls still selected, change *the Horizontal Grid Offset* to **4' 0"** (*Offset* field in the *Horizontal Grid* area), as shown in Figure 3–26.

**Figure 3–26**

The grid now fits better, as shown in Figure 3–27.

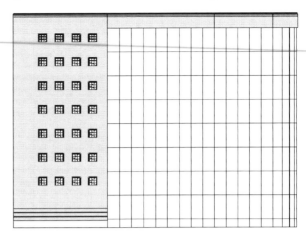

**Figure 3–27**

## Task 2 - Add grid lines.

In this task you will add grid lines to match up with multiple lines at the bottom of the building.

1. Zoom in to the bottom edge of the building and ensure that the brick/CMU and the curtain wall is displayed. Select the grid line and unpin it, as shown in Figure 3–28.

**Figure 3–28**

2. Use  (Align) to move the curtain grid line so it matches with the top of the CMU sill, as shown in Figure 3–29.

**Figure 3–29**

© 2016, ASCENT - Center for Technical Knowledge®

3. In the *Architecture* tab>Build panel, click (Curtain Grid).
4. Add three grid lines aligned with the top of the reveals in the brick, as shown in Figure 3–30.

*Zoom in until the heavier lines of the brick reveals are displayed.*

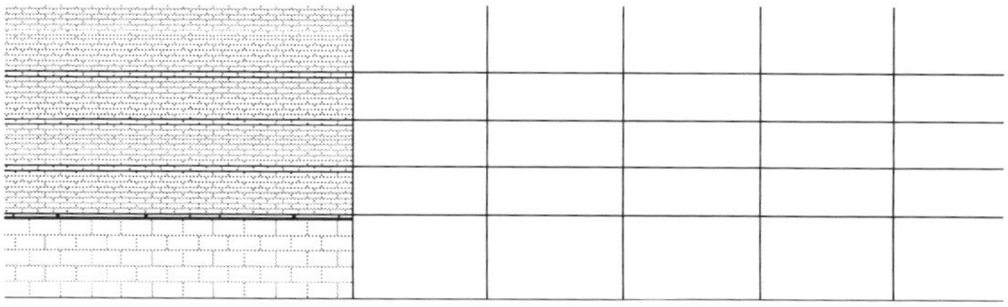

**Figure 3–30**

5. Select these four curtain grid lines (hold <Ctrl> and select each line individually) and move them down **1 1/4"**. Ensure you drag the cursor down before entering the move value. This places them correctly for the mullions, that are added later.
6. Pan over and align and add curtain grid lines to the other two parts of the curtain wall, as shown in Figure 3–31. Ensure you unpin the existing horizontal curtain grid lines before aligning them.

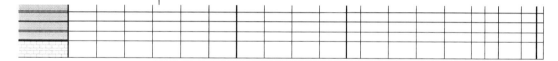

**Figure 3–31**

7. Zoom out until the entire front of the building is displayed.
8. Save the project.

© 2016, ASCENT - Center for Technical Knowledge®

# Practice 3b

# Change Elements within a Curtain Wall - Panels and Mullions

### Practice Objectives

*Estimated time for completion: 15 minutes*

- Add and modify mullions.
- Add a storefront entrance and door panel.

In this practice you will add and modify mullions along the curtain walls. You will also create a storefront that includes a door panel as the front entrance of the building. The finished elevation is shown in Figure 3–32.

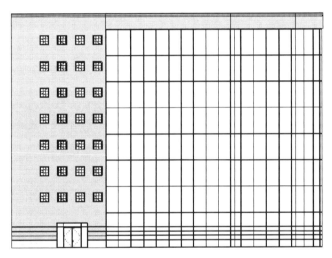

**Figure 3–32**

### Task 1 - Add and modify mullions.

1. Open the project **Modern-Hotel-Mullions.rvt**.

2. Open the **Elevations (Building Elevations): South** view, or work in the 3D view.

3. In the *Architecture* tab>Build panel, click ⊞ (Mullion).

4. In the *Modify | Place Mullion* tab>Placement panel, click ⊞ (All Grid Lines).

5. Select each of the curtain walls. Mullions are place on all of the grid lines.

© 2016, ASCENT - Center for Technical Knowledge®

6. Click 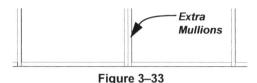 (Modify).

7. At the two lines where the curtain walls meet, extra mullions are added, as shown in Figure 3–33. These are not needed and should be removed.

**Figure 3–33**

8. Select one of the mullions.

9. In the View Control Bar, click ✎ (Temporary Hide/Isolate) and select **Isolate Category**. This makes selecting the mullions you want to delete easier.

10. Delete the extra mullions. Select one mullion, right-click and select **Select Mullions>On Gridline**.

11. Zoom out until all of the curtain walls are displayed.

12. Select the entire bottom row of mullions. You can use the Window selection box to select the entire row.

13. In the *Modify | Curtain Wall Mullions* tab>Mullion panel, click

    (Make Continuous). This changes the mullion direction, as shown in Figure 3–34.

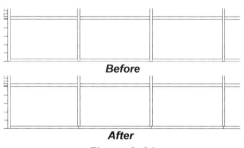

*Before*

*After*
**Figure 3–34**

14. Repeat with the top row of mullions.

15. In the View Control Bar, click ✎ (Temporary Hide/Isolate) and select **Reset Temporary Hide/Isolate**.

16. Save the project.

## Task 2 - Add the storefront entrance.

1. Open the **Floor Plans: Floor 1** view.

2. In the *Architecture* tab>Build panel, click ⬚ (Wall).

3. In the Type Selector, select **Curtain Wall:Storefront**.

4. In Properties, enter the following values:

   - *Base Constraint:* **Floor 1**
   - *Base Offset:* **0' 0"**.
   - *Top Constraint:* **Up to level: Floor 2**
   - *Top Offset:* (negative) **-6' 0"**.

5. Draw the storefront within the existing wall **1'-3"** off of the right gridline, as shown in Figure 3–35.

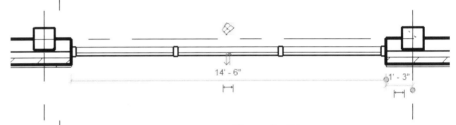

**Figure 3–35**

   - If you draw from right to left, the exterior of the storefront is placed correctly. If you draw from left to right, you need to flip the storefront.

6. Open the **Elevations (Building Elevation): South** view and zoom in on the storefront.

*Type **UP** to unpin the elements.*

7. Window around to select the storefront. Because it was created with a preset type, all of the grids and panels are pinned, as shown on the left in Figure 3–36.

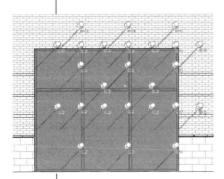 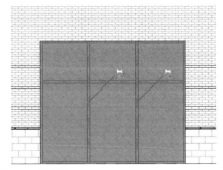

**Figure 3–36**

© 2016, ASCENT - Center for Technical Knowledge®

8. Modify the storefront, as shown in Figure 3–37. Align the horizontal line with the curtain grid line in the main curtain wall and use temporary dimensions to locate the vertical grid lines.

*Ensure you are selecting curtain grid lines as you work and not the mullions. Use <Tab> to cycle through the elements.*

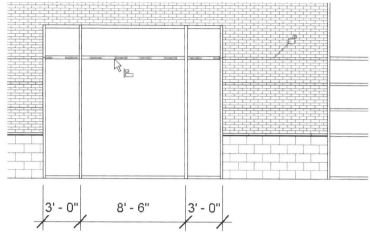

**Figure 3–37**

9. Select the mullions at the top of the storefront and toggle the mullion joins to the top bar so that it is straight across, as shown in Figure 3–38.

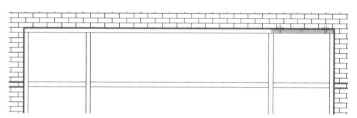

**Figure 3–38**

10. Save the project.

## Task 3 - Add a door in the storefront.

1. In the *Insert* tab>Load from Library panel, click ⬇️ (Load Family). Use this more generic method of loading the curtain wall door family because you cannot use the **Door** command to place doors in curtain walls.

2. In the Load Family dialog box, in the *Doors* folder, select the door **Door-Curtain-Wall-Double-Storefront.rfa**, as shown in Figure 3–39. Click **Open**.

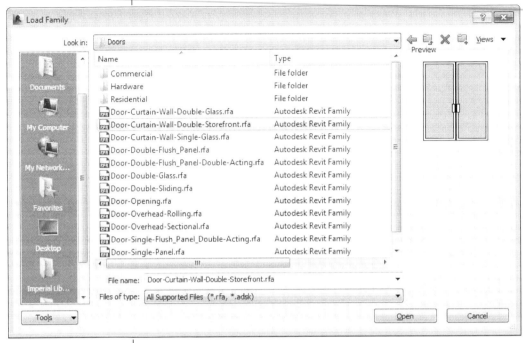

**Figure 3–39**

3. Select the large panel, as shown in Figure 3–40. Use <Tab> to cycle through the selections and then click to select it.

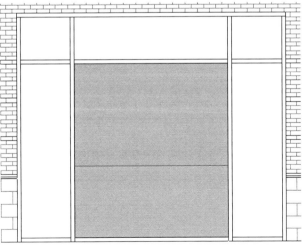

**Figure 3–40**

© 2016, ASCENT - Center for Technical Knowledge®

4. In the Type Selector, select **Door-Curtain-Wall-Double-Storefront.** The panel changes to the door. Delete the mullion at the bottom of the door, as shown in Figure 3–41.

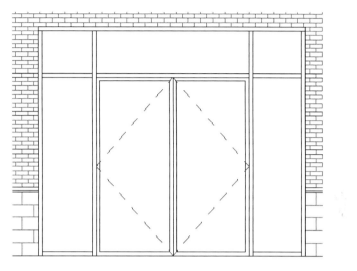

**Figure 3–41**

5. Zoom out until the entire front elevation is displayed.

6. View the project in 3D.

7. Save the project.

# 3.2 Create Compound Walls

System families are created and modified in a project or template file by duplicating an existing element type. Some of these system families (such as walls, roofs, floors, and some ceilings) are compound or layer-based. For example, to modify a compound wall, you edit the type and select the **Structure** parameter. This opens the Edit Assembly dialog box (as shown in Figure 3–42) which enables you to specify each layer of the assembly.

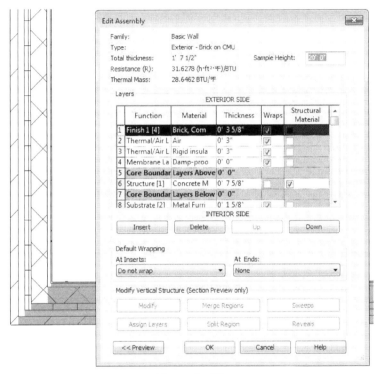

**Figure 3–42**

- Walls are used as the primary example, but floors, roofs, and compound ceilings follow the same pattern.

- Structural Floors often use profiles for metal decking. Creating this type of floor is covered in the profile families topic.

© 2016, ASCENT - Center for Technical Knowledge®

## How To: Create a Compound Wall, Floor, Roof, or Ceiling

1. Start the wall, floor, roof or ceiling command.
2. In Properties, select a type similar to the one you want to create and click 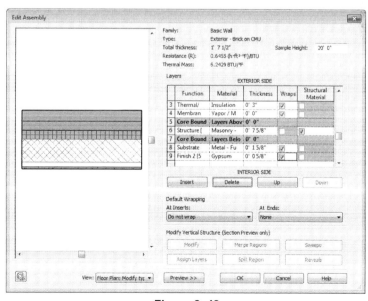 (Edit Type).
3. In the Type Properties dialog box, click **Duplicate...**.
4. In the Name dialog box, enter a name for the new type and click **OK**.
5. Next to the **Structure** parameter, click **Edit...**.
6. In the Edit Assembly dialog box, modify the layers of the assembly as required, and then click **OK**.
7. Modify any Type Parameters in the Type Properties dialog box.
8. Click **OK** to close the dialog box.

---

**Hint: Basic Ceilings**

The basic ceiling system family does not include a structure parameter. Instead, modify the Type by specifying a *Material* for the entire thickness of the ceiling.

---

## Editing Wall, Roof, and Floor Assemblies

In the Edit Assembly dialog box, you can define the layers that make up the compound structure, as shown in Figure 3–43.

*To better visualize the wall, click* **<< Preview** *to open a view of the layers in the structure. You can preview the structure in a plan or section view, and zoom or pan in the preview screen.*

**Figure 3–43**

## Assembly Information

The top of the dialog box lists the *Family* (such as **Basic Wall** or **Floor**), the *Type* that you gave to the new type, and the *Total thickness* (which is the sum of the layers defined in the wall), as shown in Figure 3–44. It also includes *Resistance (R)* and *Thermal Mass* which are automatically calculated from the materials assigned to the layers. You can also set a *Sample Height* for your wall design.

| | | | |
|---|---|---|---|
| Family: | Basic Wall | | |
| Type: | Exterior - Brick on CMU | | |
| Total thickness: | 1' 7 1/2" | Sample Height: | 20' 0" |
| Resistance (R): | 0.6455 (h·ft²·°F)/BTU | | |
| Thermal Mass: | 6.2429 BTU/°F | | |

**Figure 3–44**

## Layers

When you specify the layers for the compound element, you assign them a *Function*, *Material*, and *Thickness*, as shown in Figure 3–45.

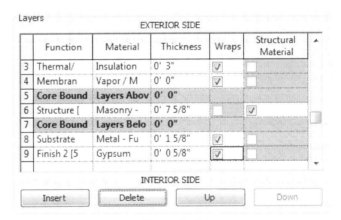

**Figure 3–45**

- Use the buttons to insert additional layers and to rearrange them in the layer list. You can also delete layers from the list.

- The *Core Boundary* function defines the layers above and below the wrapping; a heavier line is displayed when a plan or section view is cut.

© 2016, ASCENT - Center for Technical Knowledge®

- Editing a wall assembly works from the exterior side at the top of the list to the interior side at the bottom. For floors and roofs, you work around the layers above and below the wrap of the *Core Boundary*.

## Options

| Function | Select from a set list of functions in the drop-down list with a priority of highest (1) to lowest (5). High priority layers connect before low priority layers. |
|---|---|
| Structure [1] | The structural support for the wall, floor, or roof. |
| Substrate [2] | A material that acts as a foundation for another material, such as plywood or gypsum board. |
| Thermal/ Air Layer [3] | An open layer for air space. |
| Finish 1 [4] | The exterior finish layer, such as brick for a wall. |
| Finish 2 [5] | The interior finish layer, such as drywall for a wall. |
| Membrane Layer | A vapor barrier. Typically, this is set to a zero thickness. Therefore, it does not have a priority code. |
| Structural Deck (1) | (Floors only) A structural support based on a Deck Profile. You can also specify the Deck Usage with a Bound Layer Above or a Standalone Deck. |
| Material | Select from a list of available materials. Layers clean up if they share the same material. If they do not, a line displays at the join. |
| Thickness | Set the thickness of the particular layer. |

## Wall Only Options

| Sample Height | Displays the height of a wall in section when you are creating it. It does not impact the height of the wall in the project. |
|---|---|
| Default Wrapping | Set up how the heavy line style wraps around openings in walls: *at Inserts* (**Do not wrap**, **Interior**, **Exterior**, or **Both**), and *at Ends* (**None**, **Exterior**, or **Interior**). Wrapping is only visible in plan view. |
| Wraps | Set up individual layers to wrap—select the Wraps option at the end of each layer. |

- Wall wrapping can be set in the assembly or in the Type Properties, as shown in Figure 3–46.

| Wrapping at Inserts | Do not wrap |
|---|---|
| Wrapping at Ends | None |

**Figure 3–46**

- Roofs, floors, and structural slabs have an additional parameter that relates to sloping for drains. When *Variable* is not selected, the slab is set to a constant thickness and the entire element slopes, as shown on the top in Figure 3–47. When *Variable* is selected, only the top layer slopes, as shown on the bottom in Figure 3–47.

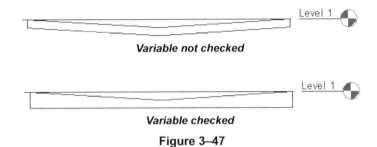

*Variable not checked*

*Variable checked*

**Figure 3–47**

© 2016, ASCENT - Center for Technical Knowledge®

# Practice 3c

# Create Compound Walls

### Practice Objectives

- Create an exterior wall with two different types of layers on the interior and the exterior.
- Create an interior wall that has the same material on either side of the structural core.

*Estimated time for completion: 15 minutes*

In this practice, you will create interior and exterior wall types, and then draw walls using them, as shown in Figure 3–48.

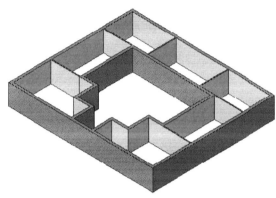

**Figure 3–48**

### Task 1 - Create a Wall type.

1. Start a new project based on the default architectural template and save it as **SW House.rvt**.

*For creating a wall type, it does not matter which command you started with.*

2. In the *Architecture* tab>Build panel or *Structure* tab> Structure panel, click ⬭ (Wall).

3. In Properties, click 🔳 (Edit Type).

4. In the Type Properties dialog box, click **Duplicate...**.

5. In the Name dialog box, type **Exterior – Adobe** and click **OK**.

6. Next to the **Structure** parameter, click **Edit...**.

7. Next to the **Structure [1]** layer, select the *Material* column and click ⌶ (Browse).

8. Expand the Library panel to display it more clearly and select **AEC Materials>Masonry>Brick, Adobe** as shown in Figure 3–49.

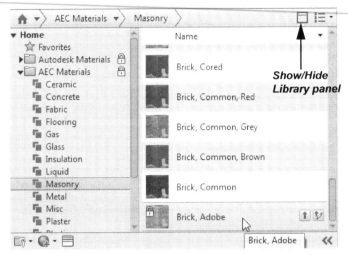

**Figure 3–49**

9. Double-click on **Brick, Adobe** to add it to the list of materials that are available in the project. **Brick, Adobe** is now selected in the Material Browser. Click **OK** to apply the material.

10. In the Edit Assembly dialog box, in the *Thickness* column, type **1'-0"** and verify that **Structural Material** is selected, as shown in Figure 3–50.

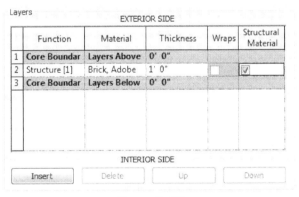

**Figure 3–50**

11. In the *Layers* area, click **Insert**.

© 2016, ASCENT - Center for Technical Knowledge®

In the Material Browser, type **wood** in the search field to narrow the list of materials.

12. Set this layer with *Function* set to **Substrate (2)**, *Material* to **Plywood, Sheathing**, *Thickness* to **1 5/8"**. Click **Down** until the new layer is below the Layers Below Wrap, as shown in Figure 3–51.

13. Add one more layer on the interior side and set *Function* to **Finish 2**, *Material* to **Cherry**, *Thickness* to **5/8"**. Select **Wraps** but not **Structural Material**, as shown in Figure 3–51.

Layers

EXTERIOR SIDE

|   | Function | Material | Thickness | Wraps | Structural Material |
|---|----------|----------|-----------|-------|---------------------|
| 1 | **Core Boundar** | **Layers Above** | **0' 0"** | | |
| 2 | Structure [1] | Brick, Adobe | 1' 0" | ☐ | ☑ |
| 3 | **Core Boundar** | **Layers Below** | **0' 0"** | | |
| 4 | Substrate [2 | Plywood, Sh | 0' 1 5/8" | ☑ | ☐ |
| 5 | Finish 2 [5] | Cherry | 0' 0 5/8" | ☑ | ☐ |

INTERIOR SIDE

**Figure 3–51**

14. Click **OK** to close the Edit Assembly dialog box.

15. Repeat the process to create another new wall type named **Interior – Wood Panel**. In the Type Properties dialog box, change the *Function* to **Interior**.

16. Set up the layer structure as shown in Figure 3–52.

The **Softwood, Lumber** material is found in the AEC Materials list if it is not in the document list.

Layers

EXTERIOR SIDE

|   | Function | Material | Thickness | Wraps | Structural Material |
|---|----------|----------|-----------|-------|---------------------|
| 1 | Finish 2 [5] | Cherry | 0' 0 5/8" | ☑ | ☐ |
| 2 | **Core Boundar** | **Layers Above** | **0' 0"** | | |
| 3 | Structure [1] | Softwood, L | 0' 3 5/8" | ☐ | ☑ |
| 4 | **Core Boundar** | **Layers Below** | **0' 0"** | | |
| 5 | Finish 2 [5] | Cherry | 0' 0 5/8" | ☑ | ☐ |

INTERIOR SIDE

**Figure 3–52**

17. Click **OK** twice to close the dialog boxes.

**Task 2 - Draw walls using the new Wall types.**

1. Set the *Detail Level* to ▨ (Medium).

2. Draw the house shown in Figure 3–53.

   • **Exterior: Exterior – Adobe** and *Height* of **10'-0"**
   • **Interior: Interior – Wood Panel** and *Height* of **10'-0"**

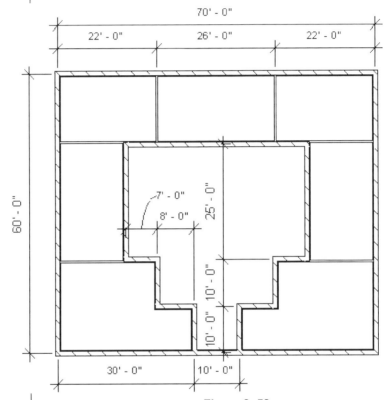

**Figure 3–53**

   • For the Interior walls, set the Location Line to **Finish Face – Interior** or **Finish Face – Exterior** to place the horizontal walls and **Wall Centerline** for the vertical walls.

3. Save the project.

© 2016, ASCENT - Center for Technical Knowledge®

# 3.3 Create a Stacked Wall

A vertically stacked wall is a specific system family that takes two or more existing basic walls and stacks them on top of each other at specific heights, as shown in Figure 3–54. One wall must be variable in height. The basic wall types have to be in place before you create the stacked wall. These walls are created by copying and editing an existing Vertically Stacked Wall type.

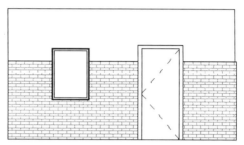

**Figure 3–54**

### How To: Create a Vertically Stacked Wall

1. Start the **Wall** command.
2. In Properties, select an existing stacked wall type and click

   (Edit Type).
3. Duplicate the wall type and give it a new name.
4. In the Type Properties dialog box, next to the **Structure** parameter, click **Edit...**.
5. In the Edit Assembly dialog box, set the *Offset* for how the walls are stacked, and a *Sample Height* for the preview, as shown in Figure 3–55.

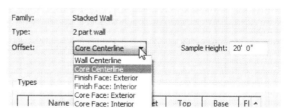

**Figure 3–55**

6. In the *Name* column, select the basic wall types you want to add to the stacked wall, as shown in Figure 3–56.

**Figure 3–56**

7. For each wall type, set the appropriate height and location (Up or Down) in the list. One height must be variable. Set the *Offset* of the wall as required.

8. Click **<< Preview** to see the wall, as shown in Figure 3–57.

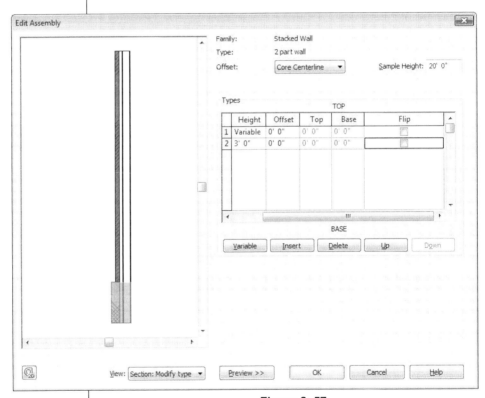

**Figure 3–57**

9. Click **OK** until all of the dialog boxes are closed.

© 2016, ASCENT - Center for Technical Knowledge®

### Hint: Embedding a Wall Inside Another Wall

Another way of creating a compound wall is to embed one wall inside another wall, as shown in Figure 3–58. When you have drawn a host wall, draw another wall on top of, or parallel to it near the host. A warning box opens and recommends that you use **Cut Geometry** to embed the wall in the host wall.

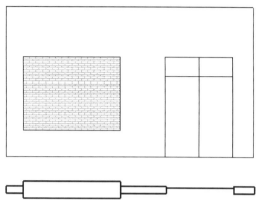

**Figure 3–58**

1. Add the embedded wall to the host wall.
2. Close the warning box.

3. In the *Modify* tab>Geometry panel, click ⌀ (Cut).
4. Select the host wall.
5. Select the wall that cuts the host wall.

- Embedded walls work similar to windows. You can modify the embedded wall with controls.

- Some curtain wall types are created to be automatically embedded in another wall. The type **Curtain Wall: Storefront** is an example. The Type Parameter *Automatically Embed* is available for all curtain wall types.

- You can separate embedded walls. In the *Modify* tab> Geometry panel, expand ⌀ (Cut) and click ⌀ (Uncut Geometry).

# Practice 3d

# Create a Stacked Wall

### Practice Objectives

- Create a vertically stacked wall type.
- Embed a wall into a stacked wall.

*Estimated time for completion: 10 minutes*

In this practice, you will create a vertically stacked wall and use it in a project. You will also embed a curtain wall and another wall type into a host wall, as shown in Figure 3–59.

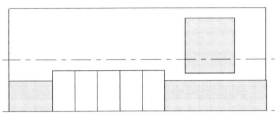

**Figure 3–59**

### Task 1 - Create a stacked wall.

1. Start a new project based on the default architectural or structural template and save it as **Warehouse.rvt**.

2. Start the **Wall** command and select the **Stacked Wall: Exterior – Brick Over CMU w Metal Stud** type.

3. Edit the type and duplicate it to create a new wall type named **Exterior – EIFS over Brick/CMU**.

4. Edit the structure of the new wall.

5. For the top wall, select **Exterior – EIFS on Mtl. Stud**. Leave the *Height* as **Variable** and set the *Offset* to **4”**.

6. For the bottom wall, select **Exterior – Brick on CMU** and set the *Height* to **6’-0”**.

7. Click **OK** to close all of the open dialog boxes.

8. Draw a rectangular building **50’-0” x 30’-0”** using the new wall style.

9. Display the walls in 3D to verify that the Brick/EIFS are displayed on the exterior.

10. Save the project.

© 2016, ASCENT - Center for Technical Knowledge®

## Task 2 - Create an embedded wall.

1. Open the **Floor Plans: Level 1** view.
2. On the south face of the building, add a wall using **Curtain Wall: Storefront** at an *Unconnected Height* of **8'-0"**. Place it directly on the center line of the existing wall along only a portion of the wall. It automatically cuts the existing wall.
3. Open the **Floor Plans: Level 2** view.
4. Add another wall on the same face using **Basic Wall: Exterior – Brick on Mtl. Stud**. This time a warning box opens.
5. Close the warning box.
6. In the *Modify|Place Wall* tab>Geometry panel, click (Cut).
7. Select the host wall.
8. Select the wall that cuts the host wall.
9. In the *Elevations* area, open the **South** view.
10. Flip the orientation of the brick insert as required.
11. Change the size of the embedded wall using the controls, but do not move it down into the lower brick wall.
12. Save the project.

# 3.4 Differentiate System and Component Families

Families are model or annotation elements that have been grouped together and set up with dimensions and other parameters. Families are parametric, meaning that they can be changed without having to recreate the elements. For example, when you change the *Height* and *Depth* of the storage pedestal shown in Figure 3–60, the other parts move with it.

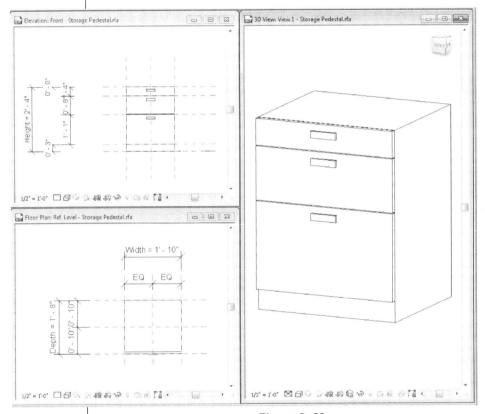

**Figure 3–60**

- *Component Families* (e.g., doors, air handling units, columns, etc.) are defined in the Family Editor and loaded into a project. One family can have many types.

- Many families are complex and time-consuming to create, but creating them all follows the same basic process.

© 2016, ASCENT - Center for Technical Knowledge®

# How To: Create a Component Family (Overview)

1. In the Application Menu, click 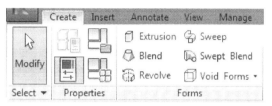 (New) and select **Family**.
2. In the New Family - Select Template File dialog box, select the template you want to use and click **Open**.
3. Set the parametric framework by adding reference planes/lines in plan and elevation views. This is a very important step when working with parametric families.
4. Label and dimension the reference planes/lines to control the movement of the elements and create parameters.
5. Flex the model to ensure the parameters change as expected.
6. Use the Forms tools (shown in Figure 3–61) to draw the elements.

**Figure 3–61**

7. Lock the elements to the reference planes/lines.
8. Flex the elements again by changing the parameters to ensure that they are working.
9. Create family types with different parameters, as required.
10. Save the family.

11. Click (Load into Project) to test the family in a project.

---

**Hint: Other Family Types**

- *System Families* are preset in the templates used to create projects (e.g., walls, roofs, slabs, ducts, pipes, and conduit). You create new types by modifying existing parameters.

- *In-Place Families* are component families created directly in a project and are dependent on the model geometry (e.g., custom gutters, special trim, or built-in columns).

---

*Flexing a model:*
*Changing the dimensions of a model to test its parametric features.*

## Preparing to Create Families

As you create families, you should plan ahead by asking a variety of questions, including:

- Is this family going to be used by one project (in-place) or by many projects (component)?

- Do you need different 2D representations in different views? What about 3D elements?

- Is this going to be a host-based or stand-alone family?

- Do you need various sizes of this family component?

- Are you going to post the family on Autodesk Seek?

> **Hint: Host-based vs. Stand-alone Families**
>
> *Host-based* families are dependent on a host. Examples include downlights (which require a ceiling) and sconces (which require a wall), as shown in Figure 3–62.
>
> *Stand-alone* families do not need a host. Examples include the desk and table lamp shown in Figure 3–62.
>
>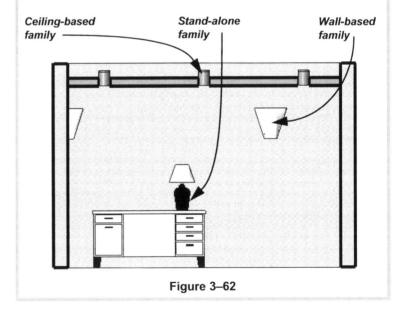
>
> Figure 3–62

© 2016, ASCENT - Center for Technical Knowledge®

# Saving Custom Family Files

When you create custom family files, you should save them to a location shared by the entire company, similar to the Autodesk Revit library. For easy access, set the custom library as the primary or secondary library available when you load a family.

## How To: Specify the File Location for Custom Libraries

1. In the Application Menu, click **Options**.
2. In the Options dialog box, select the *File Locations* tab.
3. Click **Places...**.
4. In the Places dialog box, click ✚ (Add Value). A new *Library Name* is added to the list. Specify the name and path for the library, as shown in Figure 3–63.

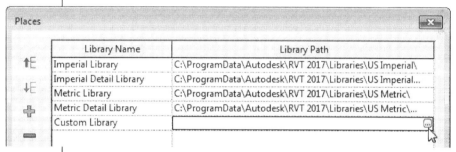

**Figure 3–63**

5. Click ↑E (Move Rows Up) and ↓E (Move Rows Down) to reorder the list of library names.
6. Click **OK** to close the dialog boxes.

- The library at the top of the list will be the default location when loading families.

# 3.5 Work with Family Parameters

Autodesk Revit families can be parametric (i.e., controlled by parameters). These parameters are the framework for creating family elements. They are based on reference planes that are dimensioned and labeled, as shown in Figure 3–64.

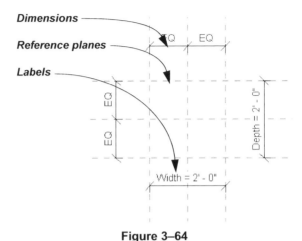

**Figure 3–64**

Before you draw any elements in a family, set up the parametric framework:

1. Place reference planes at critical locations.
2. Dimension the reference planes and label some of them so they can be manipulated.
3. Flex the dimensioned and labeled reference planes to ensure that they function as expected.

## How To: Draw Reference Planes

1. In the Family Editor, in the *Create* tab>Datum panel, click

    (Reference Plane).
2. In the *Modify | Place Reference Plane* tab>Draw panel, click

    (Line) or    (Pick Lines).
3. Draw or select the lines that define the location of the plane.
4. Draw or select other lines as required.

• The number of reference planes you need depends on what you are drawing.

• Reference planes display in plan and elevation views, but not in 3D views.

© 2016, ASCENT - Center for Technical Knowledge®

## Reference Plane Options

- By default, the origin of a family is the center of the space where you create the family. In most templates, this is located at the intersection of the existing reference planes. You can also specify your own origin by modifying the properties of two intersecting reference planes to specify that they define the origin, as shown in Figure 3–65.

**Figure 3–65**

- Reference planes do not display in the project when you insert the family type, but might impact snap and alignment behavior.

  - In Properties, under *Other*, set the **Is Reference** parameter to the plane you want to use, as shown in Figure 3–66.

  - If you do not want a reference plane to be a snap or an alignment, set the **Is Reference** parameter to **Not a Reference**.

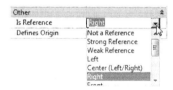

**Figure 3–66**

**Enhanced** in 2017

- After placing a reference plane, you can name it by clicking on **<Click to name>** and typing in the text box, as shown in Figure 3–67, or in Properties.

**Figure 3–67**

- Naming a reference plane enables you to use it to set the work plane when you are ready to add geometry to the family.

### Reference Lines

Reference Lines, as shown in Figure 3–68, are similar to reference planes, but have distinct start and end points. They can be drawn using a wide variety of geometry, such as rectangles, circles, or arcs. Typically, they are used for angled elements.

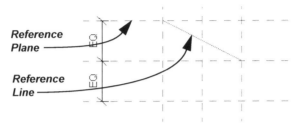

**Figure 3–68**

- In the Family Editor, in the *Create* tab>Datum panel, click
  (Reference Line).

- Reference lines cannot be named.

## Adding Dimensions and Labels

Add dimensions and labels to reference planes to start the constraining process, as shown in Figure 3–69. For example, you might want to run a string of dimensions and then set the distances to be equal by clicking on the associated **EQ** symbol. This moves the reference planes into place. Labeling a dimension creates a parameter that can be modified in the Family Types dialog box.

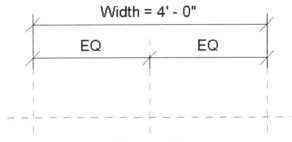

**Figure 3–69**

© 2016, ASCENT - Center for Technical Knowledge®

## How To: Label a Dimension

1. Select the dimension you want to label.
2. In the *Modify | Dimensions* tab>Label Dimension panel, select an existing label from the drop-down list, as show in Figure 3–70. You can also right-click on the dimension text, select **Label**, and choose from the list as shown in Figure 3–71.

**Enhanced**
in 2017

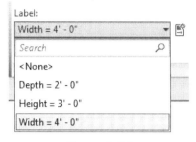

**Figure 3–70**

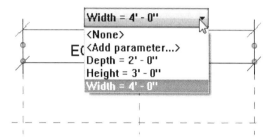

**Figure 3–71**

## How To: Add a Label

1. Select the dimension you want to label.
2. In the *Modify | Dimensions* tab>Label Dimension panel, click

   (Create Parameter).
3. In the Parameter Properties dialog box, in the *Parameter Type* area, select **Family**, as shown in Figure 3–72.

*To use this option, shared parameters must be created in your system.*

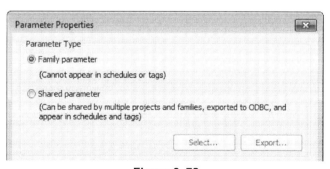

**Figure 3–72**

4. In the *Parameter Data* area, specify the *Name*, as shown in Figure 3–73. The *Type of Parameter* is automatically set to **Length** and the *Group parameter under* is set to **Dimensions**, because the parameter is a dimension.

*When naming a parameter, it is good practice to use title casing and a short name without abbreviations. Parameters are case sensitive.*

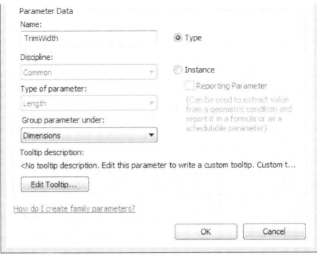

Figure 3–73

5. Select **Type** or **Instance**.
   - **Type** applies it to all instances of a family when it is inserted into a project. To modify it, you need to change the Type Properties.
   - **Instance** applies it to individual instance when inserted into a project. It can be modified directly in Properties.
6. Add a tooltip description, if required.
7. Click **OK**. The dimension is labeled and ready to be flexed.

- If you add too many labeled dimensions, the software warns that you have over-constrained the sketch. You cannot ignore this warning. The label is not created in this case.

**New**
in 2017

- You can change the *Type* or *Instance* setting of a label parameter. Select the related dimension and in the *Modify Dimension* tab>Label Dimension panel, select (or clear) **Instance Parameter**, as shown in Figure 3–74.

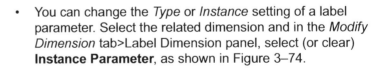
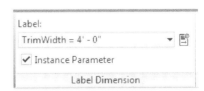

Figure 3–74

© 2016, ASCENT - Center for Technical Knowledge®

## Flexing Geometry

Once you have established dimensions and labeled them, you need to verify that the parameters work correctly with each other. To do this, flex the geometry by changing the value of a label (as shown in Figure 3–75), or using the Family Types dialog box.

**Figure 3–75**

- Select the labeled dimension and then the dimension text to change the value.

- To see all of the values you can flex at one time and to add formulas and non-dimension parameters, you need to work in the Family Types dialog box.

### How To: Flex the Geometry in the Family Types Dialog box

**Enhanced**
in **2017**

*You might have to move the dialog box to display the elements you are adjusting.*

1. In the *Create* or *Modify* tab>Properties panel, click

   (Family Types). The Family Types dialog box displays as shown in Figure 3–76.

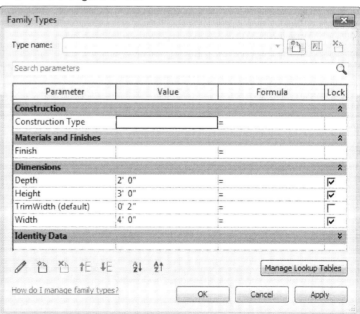

**Figure 3–76**

2. Change the labeled parameters and click **Apply**.
3. Do the elements move correctly? Try several modifications.
4. Set the parameters as required and click **OK** to finish the command.

## Creating and Modifying Parameters

In addition to creating labels (parameters specifically for dimensions), you can add parameters that store other information (such as the material of the element, as shown in Figure 3–77, the wattage of a light fixture, or the reinforcement cover setting in concrete). You can also add formulas to parameters so that they change when a related parameter changes.

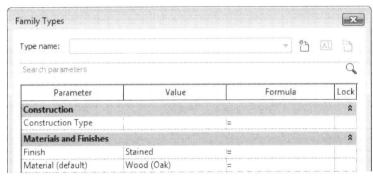

Figure 3–77

- Instance parameters include (default) after the name, as shown in Figure 3–77. The assigned value is then used when the component is inserted into a project. It can be changed in Properties when the component is selected.

*Other options are covered in later topics.*

- The Family Types dialog box contains options for editing, creating, and organizing parameters, as shown in Figure 3–78.

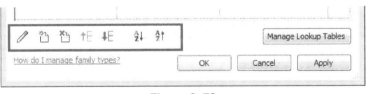

Figure 3–78

| | **Edit Parameter** | Displays the Parameter Properties dialog box, where you can change the name, group, or tooltip, or switch between **Type** and **Instance**. You can also change the parameter to reference a shared parameter. |
|---|---|---|

© 2016, ASCENT - Center for Technical Knowledge®

| | | |
|---|---|---|
| | **New Parameter** | Opens the Parameter Properties dialog box, where you can setup a new parameter. |
| ↑E , ↓E | **Move parameter up/down** | Enables you to organize the parameters in each group. |
| | **Delete parameter** | Removes the selected parameter. |
| ↓²ᵃ , ↑²ᵃ | **Sort parameters in ascending/ descending order** | Sets the order of the parameters to alphabetical order and removes any changes you might have made. |

## How To: Create Parameters

1. In the Family Editor, in the *Create or Modify* tab>Properties panel, click  (Family Types).

2. In the Family Types dialog box click  (New Parameter).
3. In the Parameter Properties dialog box, set up the Parameter Data, as shown in Figure 3–79.

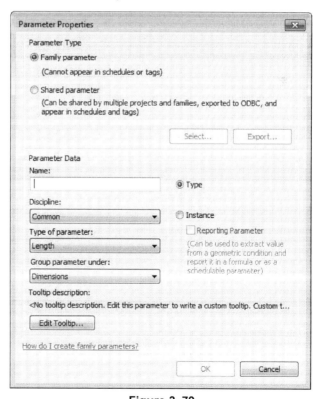

**Figure 3–79**

- The *Discipline* can be set to **Common**, **Structural**, **HVAC**, **Electrical**, **Piping**, or **Energy**. The *Type of Parameter* list changes according to the discipline.

4. Click **OK**.
5. Create or modify additional parameters. When you are finished, click **OK**.

## Common Parameter Types

| | |
|---|---|
| **Text** | A text parameter can host any type of information that consists of both numbers and letters. Examples could be the fabric color or part number of the element. |
| **Integer** | Any value that is always represented by a whole number. Examples could be the number of chairs that fit around a conference table or the number of shelves in a bookcase. |
| **Number** | Any numeric value: whole, decimal, or fraction. You can use formulas with **Number** parameters. |
| **Length** | When you label dimensions, you create **Length** parameters. You can use formulas with **Length** parameters. |
| **Area** | Establishes the area of an element. It is numeric and can have formulas applied to it. |
| **Volume** | Establishes the volume of an element. It is numeric and can have formulas applied to it. |
| **Angle** | Establishes the angle of an element. It is numeric and can have formulas applied to it. |
| **Slope** | Displays a slope, as set in the Field Format. |
| **Currency** | Displays the amount in dollars or other currencies, as set up in the Field Format. |
| **Mass Density** | Displays the mass per unit volume of material. |
| **URL** | Specifies a link to a web site. |
| **Material** | Provides a place to assign a material from the list of materials that are set up in the project. |
| **Image** | Creates a parameter at which you can add a raster image connected to the family. |
| **Yes/No** | Used with instance parameters where you need a **Yes** or **No** answer to a question listed in the name. The default is **Yes**. |
| **<Family Type>** | Opens a dialog box where you can select from the list of family types, such as doors, furniture, or tags. |

© 2016, ASCENT - Center for Technical Knowledge®

## How To: Add Formulas to Parameters

1. In the *Create* or *Modify* tab>Properties panel, click
   (Family Types).
2. In the Family Types dialog box, in the *Formula* column, add
   formulas to the parameters. In the example shown in
   Figure 3–80, the *Shelf Height* is defined as the **Height**
   divided by **4**. When you change the *Shelf Height* or *Height*,
   the other value updates according to the formula.

| Dimensions | | | |
|---|---|---|---|
| Depth | 2' 0" | = | ☑ |
| Height | 6' 0" | = | ☑ |
| ShelfHeight | 1' 6" | = Height / 4 | ☑ |
| TrimWidth | 0' 2" | = | ☐ |
| Width | 4' 0" | = | ☑ |

**Figure 3–80**

You can use several types of formulas with families:

| | |
|---|---|
| **Arithmetic** | Basic arithmetic operations in formulas include addition (+), subtraction (-), multiplication (*), division (/), exponentiation, logarithms, and square roots. |
| **Trigonometric** | Trigonometric functions include sine, cosine, tangent, arcsine, arccosine, and arctangent. |
| **Conditional** | Conditional functions include comparisons in a condition (e.g., <, >, =, etc.) and Boolean operators with a conditional statement (e.g., AND, OR, NOT, etc.). See the Autodesk Revit Help files for more information about creating conditional statements. |

- You can enter numbers as integers, decimals, or fractions. Conditional statements can include numeric values, numeric parameter names, or **Yes/No** parameters.

- Formulas are case-sensitive. Therefore, if you have created a dimension label named **Height**, ensure that the formula that uses this label also has the H capitalized (e.g., **Height * 2**).

### Hint: Formulas in Projects

You can use a formula to specify the length of a wall by typing it in the temporary dimension. Start with an equal sign (e.g., =12 / 3 + 4). The example shown in Figure 3–81 returns the number 8 (interpreted as 8'-0") in the dimension. Formulas also work with numerical values in Properties.

**Figure 3–81**

© 2016, ASCENT - Center for Technical Knowledge®

# Practice 3e

# Work with Family Parameters

### Practice Objectives

- Add reference planes.
- Dimension and label reference planes.
- Add a formula to a parameter.
- Flex the framework.

*Estimated time for completion: 20 minutes*

In this practice, you will create a family file based on a template and view the existing reference planes. You will also create reference planes, dimension them, and label the dimensions, as shown in Figure 3–82. You will add a formula to control a parameter and then test the framework by changing parameter values.

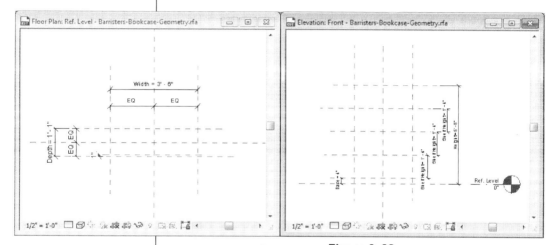

**Figure 3–82**

### Task 1 - Open a family template.

1. Close all open projects.

2. On the Start page, under the *Families* area, select **New**.

3. In the New Family - Select Template File dialog box, select the template **Furniture.rft** from the Revit Library and click **Open**.

4. In the *View* tab>Windows panel, click ⊟ (Tile) (or type **WT**).

---

5. The four open views display so you can see each of them. Type **ZA** (the shortcut for **Zoom All to Fit**) to fit the view in all of the windows.

6. Two existing reference planes are included in the file, as well as **Ref.Level**.

7. Save the family in the practice files folder as **Barrister Bookcase.rfa**.

## Task 2 - Create plan view reference planes.

1. Maximize the **Ref. Level** view.

2. Create four new reference planes, one on each side of the existing planes, as shown in Figure 3–83. Do not worry about the exact location yet.

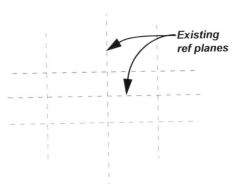

Figure 3–83

3. Add dimensions between each reference plane and across the top and side, as shown in Figure 3–84. Set the interior dimensions to **Equal**.

*Your dimensions might vary depending on where you originally placed the reference planes.*

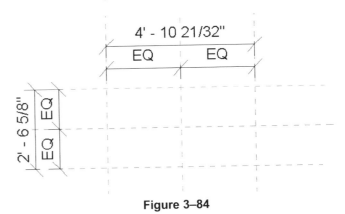

Figure 3–84

© 2016, ASCENT - Center for Technical Knowledge®

4. Select the overall horizontal dimension. In the *Modify |*

   *Dimensions* tab>Label Dimension panel, click 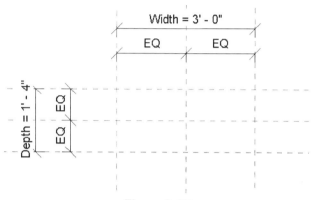 (Create Parameter).

5. In the Parameter Properties dialog box, in the *Parameter Data* area, ensure that **Type** is selected and then type the name **Width**. Click **OK**.

6. Repeat the process for the overall vertical dimension and name the parameter **Depth**.

7. Select the *Width* dimension and click on the text. Change it to **3'-0"**. Repeat the process and set the *Depth* to **1-'4"**, as shown in Figure 3–85.

**Figure 3–85**

8. Create one more horizontal reference plane **1"** inside the front reference plane and name it **Door Face**. Dimension and lock it in place, as shown in Figure 3–86.

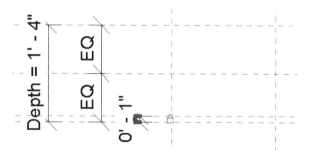

**Figure 3–86**

9. Flex the framework by changing the *Width* dimension to **3'-6"** and the *Depth* dimension to **1'-1"**.

10. Verify that the other reference planes have remained in place.

11. Save the family file.

## Task 3 - Create front view reference planes.

1. Open the **Elevations: Front** view.

2. Create the reference planes and dimensions and label them, as shown in Figure 3–87.

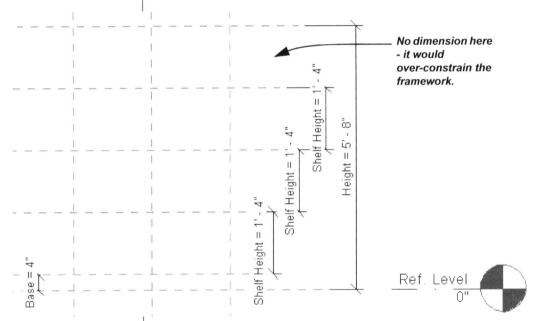

**Figure 3–87**

- Each of the shelf height dimensions must be separate. Once you have created one shelf height parameter, you can apply the same label to the other dimensions.

3. In the *Modify* (or *Create*) tab>Properties panel, click (Family Types).

© 2016, ASCENT - Center for Technical Knowledge®

*The parameters
automatically display in
alphabetical order. You
can reorganize them as
required.*

4.  In the Family Types dialog box, set up a formula for the *Shelf Height*, as shown in Figure 3–88. Lock the **Height** parameter and the **Shelf Height** parameter also locks.

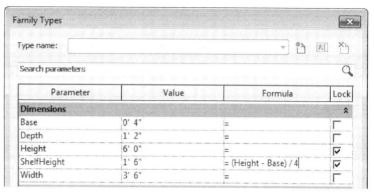

**Figure 3–88**

5.  Move the dialog box to one side and try several different values. Click **Apply** to apply the changes to the family. Verify that all of the reference planes move together. Click **OK**.

6.  Save the family.

# 3.6 Create a New Family Type

An important aspect of Family Types is that it helps you *flex* or test the parametric dimensions you set up, as well as helps you create formulas for parameters. A further use for Family Types is the ability to create preset sizes for insertion into a project. When you select the related command, the types display in the Type Selector, as shown in Figure 3–89 for a desk component.

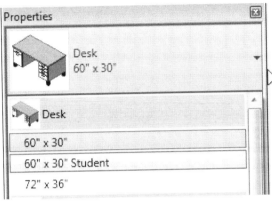

Figure 3–89

## How To: Create Family Types

1. In the Family Editor, in the *Create* or *Modify* tab>Properties panel, click ⊞ (Family Types).

2. At the top of the Family Types dialog box, click ⬑ (New Type), as shown Figure 3–90.

Enhanced  in 2017

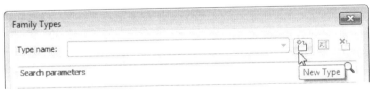

Figure 3–90

- You can type a part or all of a parameter's name to limit the number of parameters that display. This enables you to modify the values more quickly.

© 2016, ASCENT - Center for Technical Knowledge®

3. In the Name dialog box, type a name for the Family Type (as shown in Figure 3–91) and click **OK**.

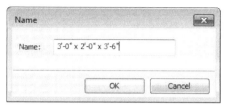

**Figure 3–91**

- Select a name that is useful for the entire set of types, typically a size.
- The name of the family always precedes the name of the type. Therefore, you do not need to re-enter that information.

4. In the Family Types dialog box, set the *Value(s)* for that size (as shown in Figure 3–92) and click **Apply**.

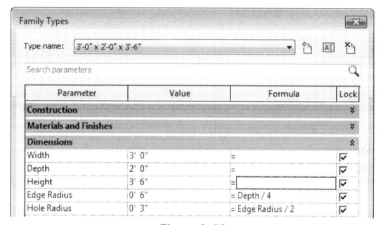

**Figure 3–92**

5. Repeat the process. You can create as many different types as you need.
6. Verify that all of the types are functioning correctly.
7. Click **OK** to finish the command.
8. Save the family.
9. Load the family into a project and test the new types you have created.

- In the *Family Types* area, click ▣ (Rename Type) and ▣ (Delete Type) as required, to modify the list.

- To edit a type, select the type name, change the value(s), and click **Apply**.

### Hint: Exporting and Importing Family Types

Family Types can be exported to a text file and then imported into a related family. This can save you time when creating different versions of the same basic category.

- In the Application Menu, expand 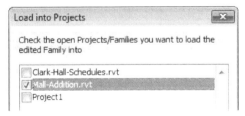 (Export), scroll down and click (Family Types). In the Export As dialog box, select a location and name. Click **Save**.

- In the *Insert* tab>Import panel, click (Import Family Types). In the Import Family Types dialog box, select the required text file, and click **Open**.

## Working with Families in Projects

To continue testing your family it helps to see how it works in a project. You can load a family into one or more projects while in the Family Editor. You must have a project open before doing this.

### How To: Load a Family into a Project

1. In the Family Editor panel, click (Load into Project). The panel is displayed in all of the Family Editor tabs.
2. If only one project is open, the family is automatically loaded into it. If you have more than one project open, the Load into Projects dialog box opens. Select the project(s) to load into, as shown in Figure 3–93.

**Load into Projects**

Check the open Projects/Families you want to load the edited Family into

- ☐ Clark-Hall-Schedules.rvt
- ☑ Mall-Addition.rvt
- ☐ Project1

**Figure 3–93**

3. The project opens with the family loaded. Often, the related command is started with the new family selected in the Type Selector.

- If you have finished working on the family you can click (Load into Project and Close).

© 2016, ASCENT - Center for Technical Knowledge®

# Practice 3f

*Estimated time for completion: 10 minutes*

# Create a New Family Type

### Practice Objectives

- Create family types of different sizes.
- Test the family in a project.

In this practice, you will create Family Types for different sizes of the bookcase. Your will then test the bookcase family in a project by placing each of the different types, as shown in Figure 3–94.

**Figure 3–94**

### Task 1 - Create Family Types.

1. In the practice files folder, open **Barristers-Bookcase-Types.rvt**.

2. In the *Create* or *Modify* tab>Properties panel, click 🗔 (Family Types).

3. In the Family Types dialog box, click 🗋 (New Type).

4. In the Name dialog box, type **3'-0" x 5'-0"** and click **OK**.

5. In the *Dimensions* area, verify or set the following values for the parameters as shown in Figure 3–95:

  • *Width:* **3'-0"**

  • *Height:* **5'-0"**

  • *Depth:* **1'-1"**

  • *Base:* **4"**

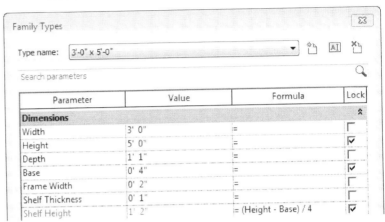

**Figure 3–95**

6. Click **Apply**.

7. Repeat these steps for the following sizes:

  • **3'-0" x 6'-0"**

  • **3'-6" x 5'-0"**

  • **3'-6" x 6'-0"**

8. In the Family Types dialog box, test each of the new named types.

9. Click **OK**.

10. Save the family.

© 2016, ASCENT - Center for Technical Knowledge®

## Task 2 - Use the family in a project.

1. In the practice files folder, open
   **Barristers-Bookcase-Project.rvt**.

2. In the *View* tab>Windows panel, expand (Switch
   Windows). Select a Barrister-Bookcase family view.

3. In the Family Editor panel, click (Load into Project).
   - If there is only one project open, the family file is
     automatically loaded into that project.
   - If more than one project is open, the Load into Projects
     dialog box opens. Select the project you want to load and
     click **OK**.

4. The **Component** command is automatically started with the
   Barristers Bookcase family selected.

5. Place one of each type in the project.

6. Create a 3D view to see the differences.

7. Save the project.

# 3.7 Use Family Creation Procedures

Once parametric framework has been created, it is recommended to add actual geometry to the family file, as shown in Figure 3–96. The components in a family can include 3D solids and voids as well as 2D symbolic lines. You can also include model lines, model text, and annotation text.

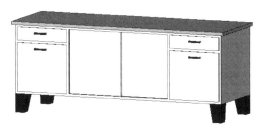

**Figure 3–96**

## Creating 3D Elements

There are five methods of creating solid forms, as shown in Figure 3–97. Each method uses a sketched 2D profile as the basis of the 3D shape.

**Figure 3–97**

*Void forms use the same creation methods.*

- **Extrusion** pushes the profile out in one direction.
- **Blend** links two profiles together.
- **Revolve** rotates the profile around an axis.
- **Sweep** extends a profile along a path.
- **Swept Blend** connects two different profiles along a path.

© 2016, ASCENT - Center for Technical Knowledge®

New
in 2017

**Hint: Selecting Void Forms**

Solids and voids are considered separate categories. You can use the **Filter** command to select them separately, as shown in Figure 3–98.

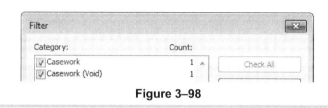

**Figure 3–98**

## Extrusions

Extrusions are the simplest elements to create. All you need to do is draw a closed profile using Autodesk Revit sketch tools and assign a depth for the extrusion, as shown in Figure 3–99.

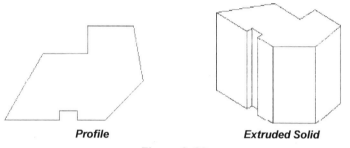

*Profile*                     *Extruded Solid*

**Figure 3–99**

### How To: Create Solid Extrusions

1. In the *Create* tab>Forms panel, click ⬚ (Extrusion).
2. In the Options Bar, set the *Depth* for the extrusion, as shown in Figure 3–100.

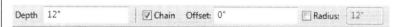

**Figure 3–100**

- A positive value for the depth extrudes up or toward you depending on the work plane. A negative value extrudes down or away from you.

3. In the *Modify | Create Extrusion* tab>Draw panel, use the sketch tools to create the profile for the extrusion. You can add dimensions and reference planes as required, to create the profile. They will not display when the extrusion is finished.

4. In the Mode panel, click ✓ (Finish Edit Mode) to create the extrusion.
5. In the *Modify | Extrusion* tab, make changes to the extrusion as required.

*By default, **Start** is at the work plane and **End** is at the depth.*

6. In Properties, you can adjust the *Extrusion Start* and *Extrusion End*, the *Visible* and *Visibility/Graphics Overrides*, and *Material*. You can also change it from a **Solid** to a **Void** or vice versa, and place it in the *Subcategory* of **Hidden Lines** or **Overhead Lines**.

• In the *Create* tab>Work Plane panel, click ▣ (Set) to select the plane on which you want to draw a profile (e.g., on top of another extrusion).

# Blends

Blends are defined by two profiles: one for the base (bottom) and one for the top. The two profiles are connected by the solid element. If the base and top do not have the same number of corners, adjust the vertex connection, as shown in Figure 3–101.

*If the entire blended element is not displayed in plan view, select the View name in the Project Browser, and then in Properties, modify the View Range Cut Plane.*

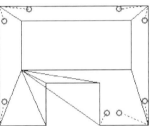 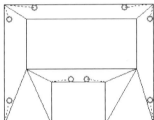

**Figure 3–101**

## How To: Create Solid Blends

1. In the *Create* tab>Forms panel, click ⬙ (Blend).
2. In the *Modify | Create Blend Base Boundary* tab>Draw panel, use the sketch tools to draw the base profile.

3. In the Mode panel, click ⬙ (Edit Top).
4. In the Options Bar, set the *Depth* for the top.
5. Draw the top profile using the sketch tools.

6. If the intersections are complex, click ⬙ (Edit Vertices) and ensure that all of the connections work correctly.

7. Click ✓ (Finish Edit Mode) to create the blend.

© 2016, ASCENT - Center for Technical Knowledge®

8. The *Modify | Blend* tab displays, where you can edit the base or the top. You also have access to the Properties of the blend.

- When you click 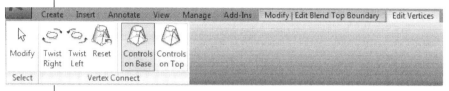 (Edit Vertices), open blue dots are displayed on the dotted lines. These lines are suggested connections. Select the dot to toggle the connection on or off, and repeat with other corners to obtain the required connections. Use the tools in the *Edit Vertices* tab>Vertex Connect panel, as shown in Figure 3–102, to modify the vertices.

**Figure 3–102**

## Revolves

A revolved solid form requires a profile and an axis around which it is revolved, as shown in Figure 3–103. The profile often needs to be sketched in a work plane perpendicular to the *ground*. Before sketching the profile, create a reference plane that you can use for the work plane. For example, if you are creating a dome, create two intersecting reference planes at the center of the dome and name them. Then, when you start the revolution, you can select one reference plane for your work plane and the other for your axis.

*You can name a reference plane in Properties.*

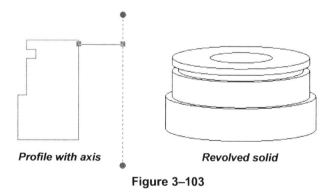

**Profile with axis**          **Revolved solid**

**Figure 3–103**

## How To: Create Solid Revolves

1. In the *Create* tab>Forms panel, click ⬚ (Revolve).
2. In the *Modify | Create Revolve* tab>Work Plane panel, click

   ⬚ (Set). In the Work Plane dialog box, select the plane on which you want to draw the profile. A prompt warns you if you need to change views to draw in that work plane.

3. In the Draw panel, click ⬚ (Boundary Line) and draw the profile.

4. In the Draw panel, click ⬚ (Axis Line) and draw or select the axis about which the profile will rotate.

5. Click ⬚ (Finish Edit Mode) to create the solid.
6. The *Modify | Revolve* tab displays, where you can edit the revolve. You can also change the Properties (such as the *End Angle* and *Start Angle*).

*The axis can be an edge of the profile or some distance away if there is an opening.*

## Sweeps

A sweep is similar to an extrusion. However, instead of only extruding in one direction, it follows a path that can have multiple segments, as shown in Figure 3–104. You define the path first and then create the profile on the path.

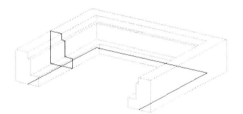

**Figure 3–104**

## How To: Create Solid Sweeps

1. In the *Create* tab>Forms panel, click ⬚ (Sweep).

2. In the *Modify | Sweep* tab>Sweep panel, click ⬚ (Sketch Path) or ⬚ (Pick Path). Draw or select the path you want the sweep to follow.

3. Click ⬚ (Finish Edit Mode).

© 2016, ASCENT - Center for Technical Knowledge®

*Click  (Load Profile) to load additional profiles into the family file for use with the sweep.*

*The profile plane is automatically drawn on the first line of the path. It is the red dot with the green line through it, as shown in a 3D view in Figure 3–105. The red dot is the place where the profile and path intersect.*

4. In the Sweep panel, select a profile from the list or click (Select Profile), and then click (Edit Profile) to sketch a profile.
   - The Go To View dialog box opens if you need to change views to draw the profile. Select the view in which you want to draw the profile and click **Open View**.
5. Draw the profile for the sweep on the profile plane, as shown in Figure 3–105.

*Figure 3–105*

6. Click (Finish Edit Mode) twice to complete the process.
7. The *Modify | Sweep* tab displays, where you can edit the sweep. In Properties, you can change several options of the profile along with the other standard options.

# Swept Blends

Swept blends consist of a path and two profiles, as shown in Figure 3–106. The profiles can have different shapes. The path must be one segment, which can be a line, an arc, or a spline.

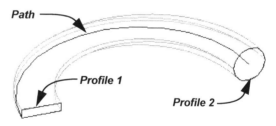

*Figure 3–106*

## How To: Create Solid Swept Blends

1. In the *Create* tab>Forms panel, click (Swept Blend).
2. In the *Modify | Swept Blend* tab>Swept Blend panel, click (Sketch Path) or (Pick Path). Draw or select the path you want the swept blend to follow. You can only have one segment in the path.

3. Click ✔ (Finish Edit Mode).

4. In the Swept Blend panel, click ▷ (Select Profile 1).

5. Select a profile from the list or create a new profile using ▱ (Edit Profile).

6. Click ▷ (Select Profile 2) and repeat the process. It does not need to be the same size or shape as the first profile.

7. In the Swept Blend panel, click ▱ (Edit Vertices) and align the vertices. This controls the twist of the swept blend.

8. Click ✔ (Finish Edit Mode).

9. In the *Modify | Swept Blend* tab, make any changes as required.

10. In Properties, set any options as required.

## Aligning and Locking

It is important to lock and align sketches to reference planes (rather than other family elements) so that they can be flexed parametrically. The padlock symbol displays when you snap to reference planes while drawing. Select the padlock to lock the element to the reference plane, as shown in Figure 3–107.

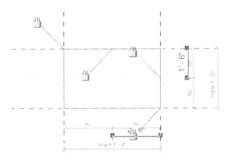

**Figure 3–107**

- When using the ⟋ (Pick Line) option, in the Options Bar, you can select **Lock** to automatically lock the sketch line to the selected reference plane.

- You can also use the **Align** command to align and lock elements to reference planes.

- You can temporarily hide other elements before sketching to ensure that you only work with the reference planes.

© 2016, ASCENT - Center for Technical Knowledge®

**New**
in 2017

- Tangency Locks display when you add arcs that are tangent to other lines, as shown in Figure 3–108. Close the padlock to keep the tangency as the element is flexed.

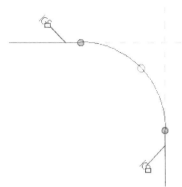

Figure 3–108

## Setting Room Calculation Points

Some families (e.g., lighting fixtures, specialty equipment, casework, furniture, etc.) can be placed so that the default center of the element is not in the room where it needs to be counted, as shown in Figure 3–109. You can adjust this by modifying the Room Calculation Point, making the family a room-aware family.

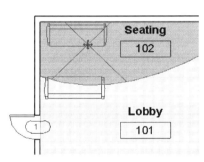

Seating
102

Lobby
101

*Before room calculation point*

| <Furniture Schedule> | | | |
|---|---|---|---|
| A | B | C | D |
| Family and Type | Room: Number | Room: Name | Count |
| Sofa-Pensi | 101 | Lobby | 1 |
| Sofa-Pensi | 102 | Seating | 1 |
| Grand total: 2 | | | |

*After room calculation point*

| <Furniture Schedule> | | | |
|---|---|---|---|
| A | B | C | D |
| Family and Type | Room: Number | Room: Name | Count |
| Sofa-Pensi | 102 | Seating | 2 |
| Grand total: 2 | | | |

Figure 3–109

- Room Calculation Points must be set in the family.

## How To: Set a Room Calculation Point

1. Open the Family file.
2. In Properties, select Room Calculation Point, as shown on the left in Figure 3–110.
3. Move the room calculation point to the required location, as shown on the right in Figure 3–111.

**Figure 3–110**

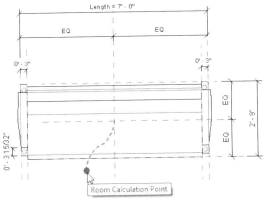

**Figure 3–111**

4. Save and load (or reload) the family file into the project.

© 2016, ASCENT - Center for Technical Knowledge®

# Practice 3g

# Use Family Creation Procedures

### Practice Objectives

- Create solid extrusion elements.
- Align and lock the elements to reference planes.
- Join the geometry of elements.

*Estimated time for completion: 20 minutes*

In this practice, you will create extruded solids for the base, frame, shelves, and back of a bookcase, and lock them in place with dimensions. You will also join the solid elements together to form one unit, as shown in Figure 3–112.

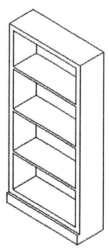

**Figure 3–112**

### Task 1 - Create a base for the bookcase.

1. In the practice files folder, open **Barrister-Bookcase-Geometry.rfa**.

2. Open the **Floor Plans: Ref. Level** view.

3. In the *Create* tab>Forms panel, click (Extrusion). In the Options Bar, set the *Depth* to **4"**.

4.  In the *Modify | Create Extrusion* tab>Draw panel, use the sketch tools to draw a rectangle across the outside intersections of the reference planes. Lock all four lines to the reference planes, as shown in Figure 3–113.

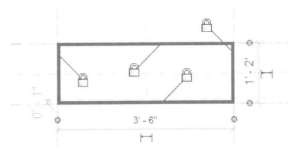

**Figure 3–113**

5.  Click (Finish Edit Mode).

6.  Open the **Elevations: Front** view.

7.  In the *Modify* tab>Modify panel, click (Align). Align the top of the extrusion to the *Base* reference plane and lock it.

8.  Save the family.

## Task 2 - Create the frame and shelves for the bookcase.

1.  In the *Create* tab>Work Plane panel, click (Set).

2.  In the Work Plane dialog box, set the *Name* to **Reference Plane : Door Face** and click **OK**.

3.  Start the **Extrusion** command.

© 2016, ASCENT - Center for Technical Knowledge®

4. Draw four reference planes inside the existing reference planes. Dimension and label them as shown in Figure 3–114.

*Drawing the reference planes inside the extrusion helps to keep the primary views from getting cluttered.*

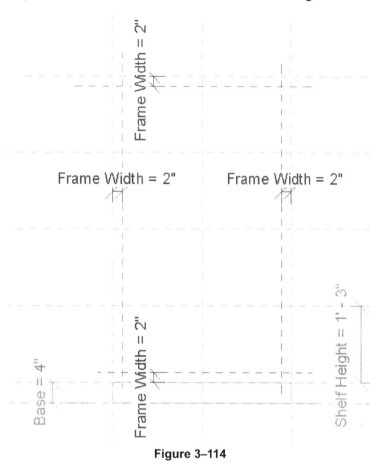

**Figure 3–114**

5. In the Family Types dialog box, flex the *Height* and *Width* of the overall bookcase to verify that the new **Frame Width** parameters move as expected.

6. Return to the *Modify | Create Extrusion* tab and select **Rectangle**.

7. In the Options Bar, set the *Depth* to **1'-0"**.

8. Draw and lock two rectangular sketches to the reference planes, as shown in Figure 3–115.

*Hint: type **SI** to force the snap to the intersection of the reference planes.*

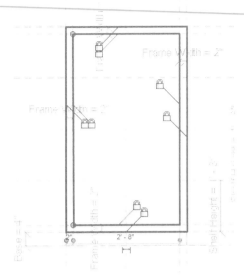

**Figure 3–115**

9. Click ✔ (Finish Edit Mode).

10. Start the **Extrusion** command again.

11. Draw two reference planes on either side of the shelf height reference plane. Dimension and label them as shown in Figure 3–116. Repeat with the other two shelf height locations.

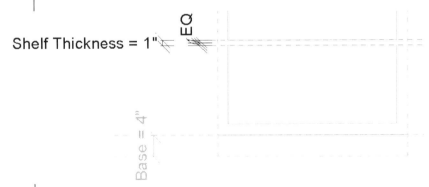

**Figure 3–116**

© 2016, ASCENT - Center for Technical Knowledge®

- To make the labels more readable, change the scale to **1"=1'-0"**. You can also create an additional dimension type with the *Read Convention* set to **Horizontal** and use it for the **Shelf** parameters, as shown in Figure 3–116.

12. In the *Modify | Create Extrusion* tab>Draw panel, select **Rectangle**.

13. In the Options Bar, ensure that the *Depth* is set to **1'-0"**.

14. Draw the sketch around each shelf, as shown in Figure 3–117. Lock the sketches to the reference planes.

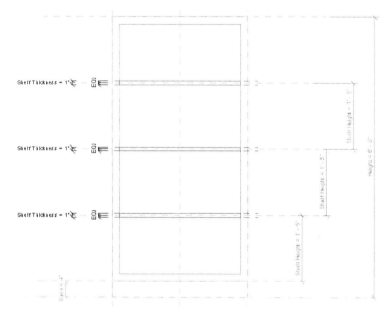

**Figure 3–117**

15. Click ✔ (Finish Edit Mode).

16. Open the Family Types dialog box and move the *Height*, *Width*, and *Depth* to the top of the parameters list.

17. Flex the *Height* and *Width* of the overall bookcase to verify the new **Shelf Thickness** parameters move as expected. Finish the flexing with the *Height* set to **5'-0"** and the *Width* to **3'-0"**.

18. Save the family.

## Task 3 - Create the back of the bookcase.

1. Open the **Elevations: Left** view.

2. Align and lock the back of the frame and shelf extrusions to the back reference plane (on the left).

3. Open the **Floor Plans: Ref. Level** view.

4. Start the **Extrusion** command again.

5. Add a reference plane **1/4"** from the back of the bookcase. Dimension and lock it in place, as shown in Figure 3–118.

*Create a label if you want to change the size of the back.*

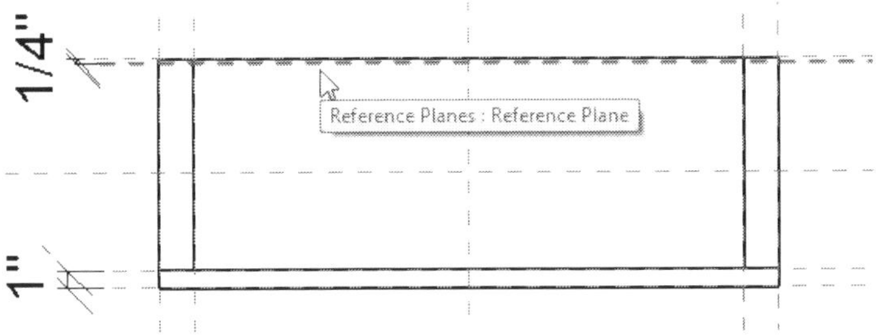

**Figure 3–118**

6. Return to the *Modify | Create Extrusion* tab and select **Rectangle**.

7. In the Options Bar, set the *Depth* to **2'-6"**. (This is less than the bookcase height. You will adjust it later.)

8. Draw a rectangular sketch across the back and lock it to the reference planes.

9. Click   (Finish Edit Mode).

© 2016, ASCENT - Center for Technical Knowledge®

10. Open the **Elevations: Left** view. Switch the **Visual Style** to 🗇 (Hidden Line). The back extrusion is shown in Figure 3–119.

11. Align and lock the top of the back panel with the top reference plane, as shown in Figure 3–120.

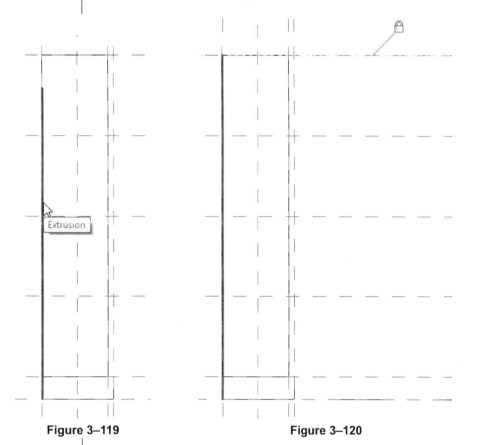

**Figure 3–119**　　　　　　　**Figure 3–120**

12. Switch to a 3D view. The base, frame, shelves, and back are all separate elements, as shown in Figure 3–121.

13. In the *Modify* tab>Geometry panel, click (Join) and join the four elements. The bookcase should display as shown in Figure 3–122.

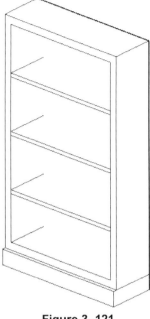

| **Figure 3–121** | **Figure 3–122** |

14. Save the family.

© 2016, ASCENT - Center for Technical Knowledge®

# Modeling

This chapter includes instructional content to assist in your preparation for the following topic and objectives for the Autodesk® Revit® Architecture Certified Professional exam.

## Autodesk Certification Exam Objectives in this Chapter

| Exam Topic | Exam Objective | Section |
|---|---|---|
| Modeling | • Create a building pad | • 4.1 |
| | • Define floors for a mass | • 4.2 |
| | • Create a stair with a landing | • 4.3 |
| | • Create elements such as a floors, ceilings, or roofs | • 4.4 to 4.6 |
| | • Generate a toposurface | • 4.7 |
| | • Model railings | • 4.8 |
| | • Edit a model element's material (door, window, furniture) | • 4.9 |
| | • Change a generic floor/ceiling/roof to a specific type | • 4.10 |
| | • Attach walls to a roof or ceiling | • 4.11 |
| | • Edit room-aware families | • 4.12 |

# 4.1 Create a Building Pad

A building pad on a toposurface cuts or fills the surface around the area of the pad. You can create the pad from existing walls or sketch it with lines. The example in Figure 4–1 shows the site with a building pad in section.

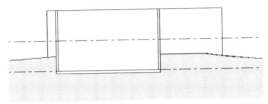

**Figure 4–1**

- A pad is an element in the project that might be in the same plane as a floor.

- A pad affects the surrounding surface and a floor element does not.

- Pads can be turned off in the Visibility/Graphic Overrides dialog box.

## How To: Create a Building Pad

1. Open the site plan view with an existing toposurface. Building pads must be drawn on a toposurface.
2. In the *Massing & Site* tab>Model Site panel, click

   ▣ (Building Pad).
3. In the *Modify | Create Pad Boundary* tab>Draw panel, click

   ⌐ (Boundary Line). You can use any of the Draw tools or

   click ▧ (Pick Walls) to establish the outline of the building pad.
4. In Properties, specify a *Level* and a *Height Offset from Level* for the depth of the pad and set any phasing as needed.

5. Click ✔ (Finish Edit Mode).

- The sketch of a pad must form a closed loop, but can contain additional loops inside to display openings (such as a courtyard). If you have several buildings, create a pad for each one.

- You can slope pads in one direction for drainage using

   ◿ (Slope Arrow).

© 2016, ASCENT - Center for Technical Knowledge®

# Practice 4a

# Create a Building Pad

*Estimated time for completion: 10 minutes*

## Practice Objectives

- Create a property line by sketching.
- Add a building pad.

In this practice you will add a property line and a building pad to a toposurface, as shown in Figure 4–2.

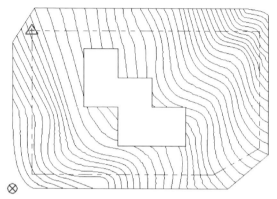

**Figure 4–2**

### Task 1 - Create a property lines.

1. In the practice files folder, open **New-Site-Pad.rvt**.

2. Open the **Site** plan view if it is not already open.

3. In the *Massing & Site* tab>Modify Site panel, click

   (Property Line).

4. In the Create Property Line dialog box, select **Create by sketching** as shown in Figure 4–3.

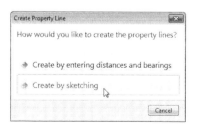

**Figure 4–3**

5. Sketch the property line, as shown in Figure 4–4.

*Use the Survey Point as the start point of the property line.*

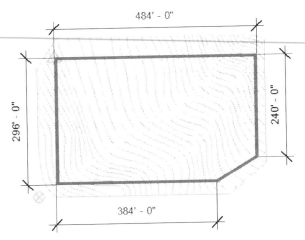

**Figure 4–4**

6. Click ✔ (Finish Edit Mode).

## Task 2 - Create a building pad.

1. In the *Massing & Site* tab>Model Site panel, click
   ▣ (Building Pad).

2. In the *Modify | Create Pad Boundary* tab>Draw panel, click
   ⌐L (Boundary Line). Use the Draw tools to establish the outline of the building pad, as shown in Figure 4–5.

*Use the Survey Point to identify the start point of the pad.*

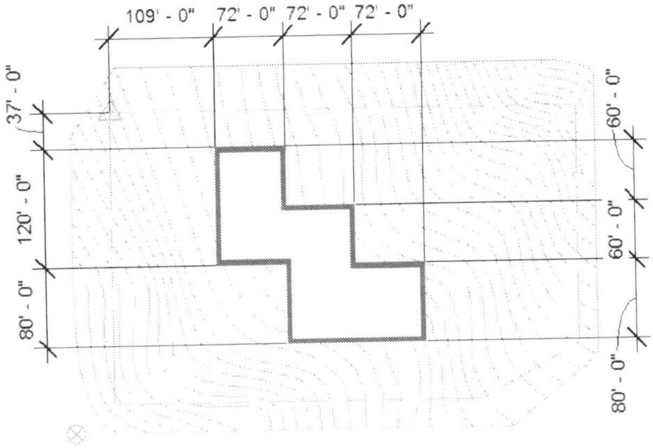

**Figure 4–5**

© 2016, ASCENT - Center for Technical Knowledge®

3. In Properties, verify that the *Level* is **Level 1** and the *Height Offset from Level* is set to **0**.

4. Click 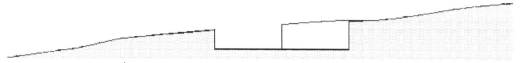 (Finish Edit Mode).

5. Open the **Site Section** view and see how the pad cuts the site, as shown in Figure 4–6.

**Figure 4–6**

6. Save the project.

# 4.2 Define Floors for a Mass

To create floors in a massing study, you must first create Mass Floors. These are the basis for creating floors and also help track the floor area of the building. Once you have the mass floors in a project, you can click ⬢ (Floor by Face) to add the floor elements on the faces.

### How To: Create Mass Floors

1. Select a mass.
2. In the *Modify | Mass* tab>Model panel, click ⬢ (Mass Floors).
3. In the Mass Floors dialog box, select the levels where you want floor area faces to be located, as shown in Figure 4–7, and click **OK**.

*If you have a lot of levels to select hold the <Ctrl> or <Shift> key to select multiple.*

Figure 4–7

The mass floors display in the massing study, as shown in Figure 4–8.

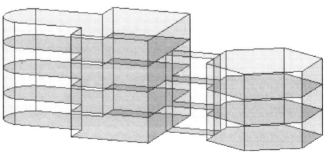

Figure 4–8

Mass floors keep track of the area, exterior surface area, volume, and perimeter of each floor. This information can be used in schedules and tags.

© 2016, ASCENT - Center for Technical Knowledge®

# Practice 4b

## Define Floors for a Mass

*Estimated time for completion: 10 minutes*

*Some levels are higher than the current height of the masses, By selecting them now, they will automatically be applied when the height of the masses is changed.*

### Practice Objectives

- Add mass floors.
- Use existing schedules to track the coverage of the site and the gross area of the mass, while making changes to one of the towers
- Add walls, floors, roofs, and curtain systems to the finished mass towers.

In this practice, you will add mass floors to specified levels, as shown in Figure 4–9.

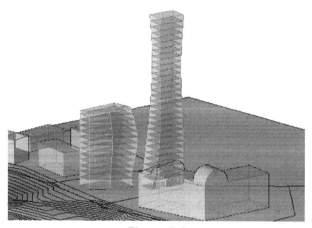

**Figure 4–9**

### Task 1 - Add Massing Floors.

1. In the practice files folder, open **Edmon-Towers-Building.rvt**.

2. Select the two curved masses included in the project.

3. In the *Modify | Mass* tab>Model panel, click 🗇 (Mass Floors).

4. Select all of the levels in the Mass Floors dialog box and click **OK**. The new mass floors display as shown in Figure 4–9.

# 4.3 Create a Stair with a Landing

As with other Autodesk Revit elements, stairs are *smart* parametric elements. With just a few clicks, you can create stairs of varying heights and designs, complete with railings. Stairs can be created by assembling stair components (as shown in Figure 4–10), or by sketching a custom layout.

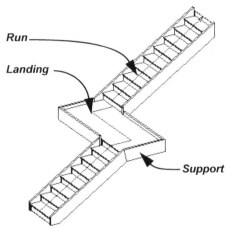

**Figure 4–10**

When creating component-based stairs, there are three parts of a stair that can be assembled, as shown in Figure 4–10:

- **Runs:** The actual stair tread and riser elements. These include straight runs which can be combined for multi-landing stairs, spiral stairs and L-shaped and U-shaped Winders.

- **Landings:** The platform between runs. These are typically created automatically and then modified if required.

- **Supports:** The stringer or carriage that structurally holds the stair elements. These can be created automatically or you can pick the edges where you want the different types to go. These can be placed on either side of the stairs or in the center of the stairs.

- Railings are typically added within the **Stair** command. They display after you complete the stair.

- You can select and edit each of the components while you are in edit mode, or after the stair has been created.

© 2016, ASCENT - Center for Technical Knowledge®

- Each component of the stair is independent but also has a relationship to the other components. For example, if steps are removed from one run they are added to connected runs to maintain the overall height, as shown in Figure 4–11.

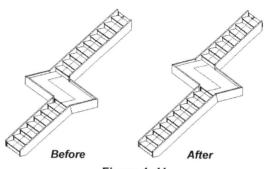

**Before**          **After**

**Figure 4–11**

---

**Hint: Stairs and Views**

When creating stairs you can work in either plan or 3D views. It can help to have the plan view and a 3D view open and tiled side by side. Only open the views in which you want to work and type **WT** to tile the views.

---

**Creating Runs**

To create a component stair, you must first place the run elements. There are six different options available in the Components panel, as shown in Figure 4–12, and described as follows:

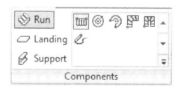

**Figure 4–12**

| | | |
|---|---|---|
| 〽 | **Straight** | Draws a straight run by selecting the start and end points of the run. |
| ◎ | **Full-Step Spiral** | Draws a spiral run based on a start point and radius. |
| ⟲ | **Center-Ends Spiral** | Draws a spiral run based on a center point, start point, and end point. |
| ⌐ | **L-Shape Winder** | Draws an L-shaped winder based on the lower end. |

| | | |
|---|---|---|
| ⊞ | **U-Shape Winder** | Draws a U-shaped winder based on the lower end. |
| ✎ | **Create Sketch** | Opens additional tools where you can sketch stair boundary and risers individually. |

- Component stairs can include a mix of the different types of runs.

## How To: Create a Component-based Stair with Straight Runs

1. In the *Architecture* tab>Circulation panel, click 🖎 (Stair by Component).
2. In the Type Selector, select the stair type, as shown in Figure 4–13.

*The stair type can impact all of the other settings. Therefore, it is important to select it first.*

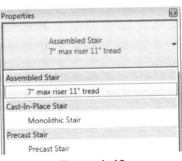

**Figure 4–13**

3. In Properties (shown in Figure 4–14), set the parameters for the *Base Level* and *Top Level*, and any other information that is needed.

*Multistory Top Level enables you to create multiple runs of stairs based on Levels. The levels need to be the same height for this to work.*

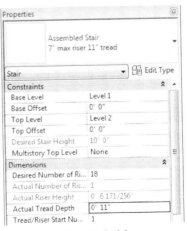

**Figure 4–14**

© 2016, ASCENT - Center for Technical Knowledge®

4. In the *Modify | Create Stairs* tab>Tools panel, click

   (Railing), select a railing type in the Railings dialog box as shown in Figure 4–15, and specify whether the *Position* is on the **Treads** or **Stringer**. Click **OK**.

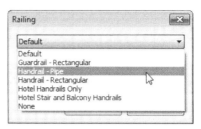

*Railings can also be added and modified after the stair has been placed.*

**Figure 4–15**

5. In the *Modify | Create Stair* tab>Components panel, click

   (Run) and then click (Straight).

6. In the Options Bar (shown in Figure 4–16), specify the following options:

   • **Location Line:** Select **Exterior Support: Left**, **Run: Left**, **Run: Center**, **Run: Right**, or **Exterior Support: Right**.

   • **Offset:** Specify a distance from the Location Line. This is typically used if you are following an existing wall but do not need to have the stairs directly against them.

   • **Actual Run Width:** Specify the width of the stair run (not including the supports).

   • **Automatic Landing:** Creates landings between stair runs (recommended).

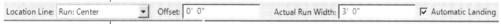

**Figure 4–16**

7. Click on the screen to select a start point for the run. A box displays, indicating the stair orientation and the number of risers created and remaining, as shown in Figure 4–17.

*If you are creating a complex stair pattern, sketch reference planes in the **Stairs** command to help you select the start and end points of each run.*

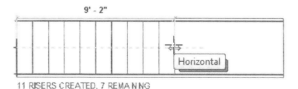

9' - 2"

Horizontal

11 RISERS CREATED, 7 REMANING

**Figure 4–17**

*If the stair is going in the wrong direction, click*

*(Flip) in the Modify | Create Stair tab>Tools panel.*

- For straight stairs of a single run, select a second point anywhere outside the box to create the run.
- For multi-landing or u-shaped stairs, select a second point inside the box for the length of the first run. Then select a start point and an end point for the next run.

8. Click (Finish Edit Mode) to create the stairs, complete with railings.

# Creating Other Types of Runs

While most stairs are created using straight runs there are times when you need to create specialty runs, such as spirals and winders.

### How To: Create a Full-Step Spiral Run

1. Start the **Stair** command and set up the Properties as required.
2. In the Components panel, click (Full-Step Spiral).
3. Select the center point of the spiral.
4. Select (or type) the radius of the spiral. The run is created as shown in Figure 4–18.

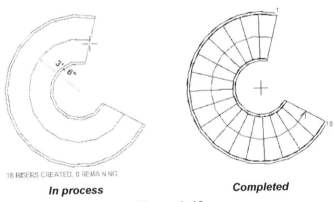

18 RISERS CREATED, 0 REMAINING

*In process*                    *Completed*

**Figure 4–18**

### How To: Create a Center-Ends Spiral Run

1. Start the **Stair** command and set up the Properties as required.
2. In the Components panel, click (Center-Ends Spiral).
3. Select the center of the spiral.
4. Select (or type) the radius of the spiral, as shown on the left in Figure 4–19.

© 2016, ASCENT - Center for Technical Knowledge®

*You can create spiral stairs with landings with this option.*

5. Drag the cursor to display the number of risers as shown on the right in Figure 4–19.

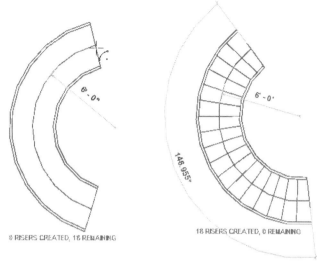

Select the radius          Select the end of the run

**Figure 4–19**

## How To: Create Winder-based stairs.

1. Start the **Stair** command and set up the Properties as required.

2. In the Components panel, click (L-Shape Winder) or (U-Shape Winder).

3. Click a start point to place the overall stair.

4. Select the stair and use the arrow controls to modify the length as shown in Figure 4–20.

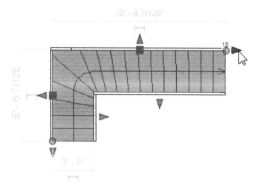

**Figure 4–20**

---

## Creating Landings

Landings are typically created automatically between any breaks in runs. Once finishing the stair, you can easily modify the landings to create custom designs. There are two additional options to create landings, as shown in Figure 4–21:

- **Pick Two Runs:** Places the landing at the correct height between the runs.

- **Create Sketch:** Enables you to draw the shape of the landing, but you must place it at the correct height.

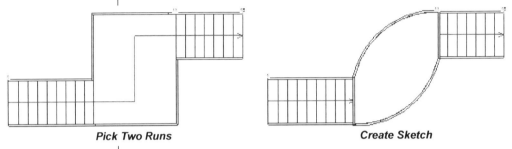

*Pick Two Runs*                                        *Create Sketch*

**Figure 4–21**

- You can connect runs with a landing as long as the start level and end level of the runs are at the same height.

## Adding Supports

Stair supports are included in the stair type if required. However, you might want to delete them and add them later. (This only works if the stair type has supports that are specified in the Type properties.)

### How To: Add Stair Support Components

1. If there are no supports, in the *Modify | Create Stair* tab> Components panel, click ✏ (Support) and then click ⚞ (Pick Edges).
2. Select the edge on which you want to place the support. Hover over the first support and press <Tab> if you have more than one connected edge on which you want to place the supports.
3. Finish the stair assembly as required.

                          © 2016, ASCENT - Center for Technical Knowledge®

# Practice 4c

# Create a Stair with a Landing

*Estimated time for completion: 25 minutes*

### Practice Objectives

- Create a component stairs.
- Cut out floors where stairs penetrate them.

In this practice you will create u-shaped stairs, including multi-story stairs in the stairwell, as shown in Figure 4–22. You will also modify the floors for stair openings and (if you have time) add a shaft to create an opening for the upper floors.

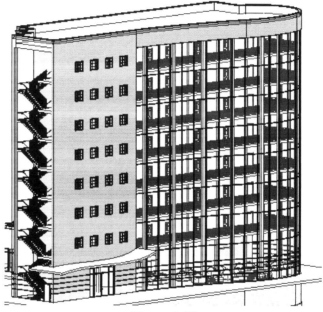

**Figure 4–22**

### Task 1 - Create the stairs on the first floor.

1. Open the project **Modern-Hotel-Stairs.rvt**.

2. Open the **Floor Plans**: **Floor 1 - Stair 1** view. This is a callout from the main floor plan.

3. Hide the grid lines, sections, and crop region.

4. In the *Architecture* tab>Circulation panel, click 🖑 (Stair).

5. In Properties, set or verify the following parameters:

- Stair Type: **Assembled Stair: Hotel Stairs**
- Base Level: **Floor 1**
- Top Level: **Floor 2**
- Base Offset: **0' 0"**
- Top Offset: **0' 0"**

6. In the *Modify | Create Stair* tab>Tools panel, click

    (Railing). In the Railings dialog box, select **Hotel Stair Guardrail-Floor 1**, as shown in Figure 4–23. Verify that the *Position* is set to **Treads** and click **OK**.

*The Guardrails are different for the upper floors. Therefore, there are two different stair guardrail styles.*

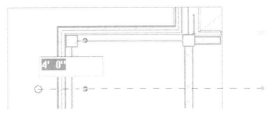

Railing

Default

Default
Glass Panel - Bottom Fill
Guardrail - Rectangular
Handrail - Rectangular
Hotel Balcony Guardrail
Hotel Stair Guardrail-Floor 1
Hotel Stair Guardrail-Floor X
Hotel Stair Handrail-Wall-Floor 1
Hotel Stair Handrail-Wall-Floor X
None

Figure 4–23

7. In the *Modify | Create Stair* tab>Work Plane panel, click

    (Ref Plane). Draw a horizontal reference plane **4' 0"** from the inner edge of the top wall of the stairwell, as shown in Figure 4–24. Click   (Modify).

4' 0"

Figure 4–24

8. In the *Modify | Create Stair* tab>Components panel, click

    (Run).

9. In the Options Bar, set the *Location Line* to **Run: Left**, set *Offset* to **0' 0"**, the *Actual Run Width* to **3' 8"**, and select **Automatic Landing**.

© 2016, ASCENT - Center for Technical Knowledge®

10. Pick the start point of the first run on the wall close to the door, as shown in Figure 4–25. The exact location is not important at this point. Pick a second point near the reference plane.

11. Pick the start point for the second run at the intersection of the wall and reference plane as shown in Figure 4–25. Pick the second point past the ghost image of the completed number of stairs.

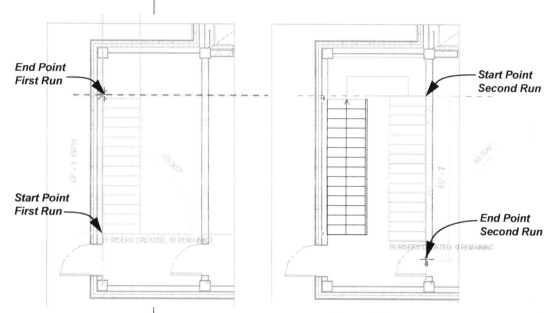

**Figure 4–25**

12. The run on the left wall might not be in the right place. Select the run and click ✛ (Move). Select a point on the top riser and then on the reference plane, as shown in Figure 4–26.

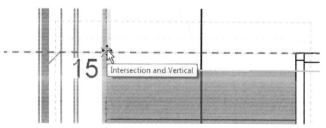

**Figure 4–26**

13. Depending on how you drew the runs you might also need to modify the run lengths. The left should have 1 to 16 steps and the right should have Steps 17 to 31. Select the stairs on the left and use the arrow shape handle at the base of the stairs, to change the number of stairs as required.

14. Click 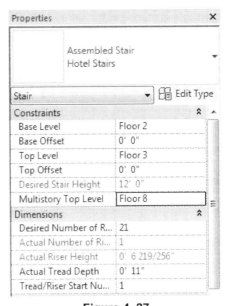 (Finish Edit Mode).

15. Save the project.

## Task 2 - Create the Upper Floor stairs.

1. Open the **Floor Plans: Floor 2** view and zoom in on the left stairwell. You should see the **DN** annotation and part of the stairs from the level below.

2. Use **Temporary/Hide** to clean up the view to have it display more clearly.

3. Click (Stair).

*All of the floor heights are the same between the 2nd and 8th floors, so you can create a multistory stair.*

4. In Properties, verify that the *Base Level* is set to **Floor 2** and the *Top Level* is set to **Floor 3** and set the *Multistory Top Level* to **Floor 8**. Note the *Desired Number of Risers*, as shown in Figure 4–27. This number is much smaller because the height between Floor 2 and Floor 3 is only 12' 0".

Properties

Assembled Stair
Hotel Stairs

Stair — Edit Type

| Constraints | |
|---|---|
| Base Level | Floor 2 |
| Base Offset | 0' 0" |
| Top Level | Floor 3 |
| Top Offset | 0' 0" |
| Desired Stair Height | 12' 0" |
| Multistory Top Level | Floor 8 |
| Dimensions | |
| Desired Number of R... | 21 |
| Actual Number of Ri... | 1 |
| Actual Riser Height | 0' 6 219/256" |
| Actual Tread Depth | 0' 11" |
| Tread/Riser Start Nu... | 1 |

Figure 4–27

© 2016, ASCENT - Center for Technical Knowledge®

5. In the *Modify | Create Stair* tab> Tools panel, click
   (Railing). In the Railing dialog box, set the *Railing Type* to **Hotel Stair Guardrail-Floor X**. Click **OK**.

6. In the Work Plane panel, click (Reference Plane) and add a horizontal reference plane **4' 0"** from the inner side of back wall. Click (Modify).

7. Add the stair runs as in Task 1, modifying the runs as required to display stairs 1 to 11 on the left and 12 to 21 on the right as shown in Figure 4–28.

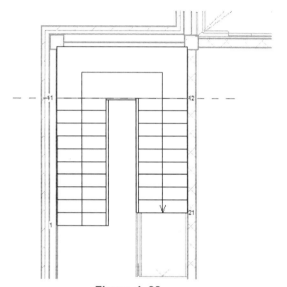

**Figure 4–28**

8. Click (Finish Edit Mode).

9. To see the stairs on all of the floors, open the **Sections (Building Section): East-West Section** and set the Visual Style to 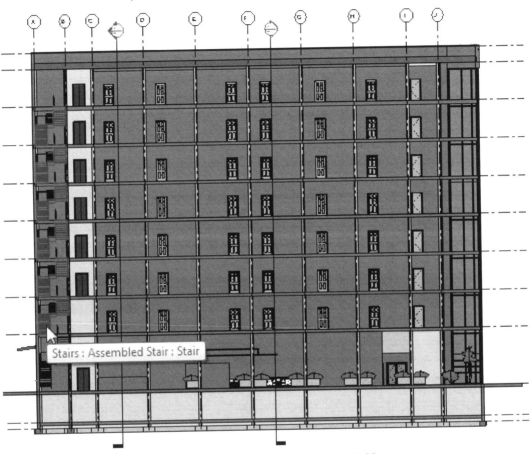 (Consistent Colors), as shown in Figure 4–29.

**Figure 4–29**

10. If you have time at the end of the practice, create stairs from the Basement to Floor 1 and save the project.

---

**Task 3 - Modify the second floor stair openings.**

---

1. Open the **Floor Plans: Floor 2** view.

2. Select the floor. (It is easiest to select one of the balconies.)

3. In the *Modify | Floors* tab>Mode panel, click (Edit Boundary).

© 2016, ASCENT - Center for Technical Knowledge®

4. Modify the boundary line so that it creates an opening for the stairs, as shown in Figure 4–30.

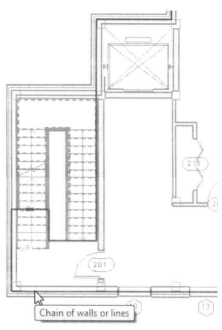

**Figure 4–30**

5. Click (Finish Edit Mode). Do not attach the walls to the floor.

6. Zoom out to display the entire second floor.

7. Save the project.

8. If you have time at the end of the practice, modify the floor for the Floor 1 stair opening to the Basement. Place a shaft for the Floor 3 through Floor 8. You can use a shaft here because the openings are the same on all of the floors.

9. Save the project.

# 4.4 Create Elements Such as Floors, Ceilings, or Roofs - Floors

The **Floor** command can generate any flat or sloped surface, such as floors, balconies, decks, and patios, as shown in Figure 4–31. Typically created in a plan view, the floor can be based either on bounding walls or on a sketch that you draw to define the outline.

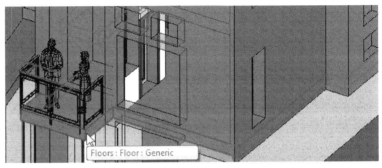

Floors : Floor : Generic

**Figure 4–31**

- The floor type controls the thickness of a floor.

## How To: Add a Floor

1. In the *Architecture* tab>Build panel, expand (Floor) and click (Floor: Architectural) or (Floor: Structural). You are placed in sketch mode where other elements in the drawing are grayed out.
2. In the Type Selector, set the type of floor you want to use. In Properties, set any other options you might need.
3. In the *Modify | Create Floor Boundary* tab>Draw panel, click (Boundary Line).

   - Click (Pick Walls) and select the walls, setting either the inside or outside edge. If you have selected a wall, you can click (Flip) to switch the inside/outside status of the boundary location, as shown in Figure 4–32.

*The lines in the sketch must form a closed loop. You can use tools in the Modify panel to adjust intersections.*

© 2016, ASCENT - Center for Technical Knowledge®

- Click ✏ (Line) or one of the other Draw tools and draw the boundary edges.

4. Click 🗔 (Slope Arrow) to define a slope for the entire floor.

5. Click 🗔 (Span Direction) to modify the direction for floor spans. It comes in automatically when you place the first boundary line, as shown in Figure 4–32.

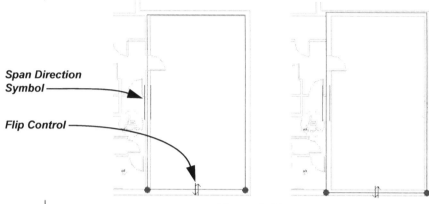

**Span Direction Symbol**

**Flip Control**

**Figure 4–32**

6. Click ✔ (Finish Edit Mode) to create the floor.

- If you are using 🗔 (Pick Walls), select the **Extend into wall (to core)** option in the Options Bar if you want the floor to cut into the wall. For example, the floor would cut through the gypsum wall board and the air space but stop at a core layer such as CMU.

- If you select one of the boundary sketches, you can also set *Cantilevers* for *Concrete* or *Steel*, as shown in Figure 4–33.

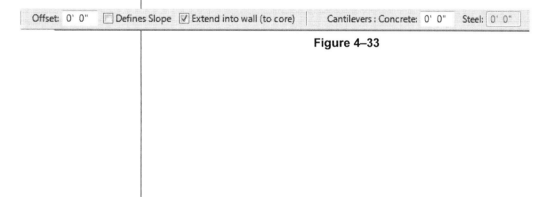

**Figure 4–33**

- To create an opening inside the sketch, create a separate closed loop inside the first one, as shown in Figure 4–34.

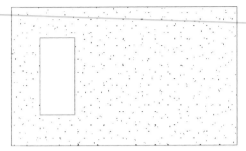

**Figure 4–34**

- If you create a floor on an upper level, an alert box displays prompting if you want the walls below to be attached to the underside of the floor and its level. If you have a variety of wall heights, it is better to click **No** and attach the walls separately.

- Another alert box might open as shown in Figure 4–35. You can automatically join the geometry or can do so at a later time.

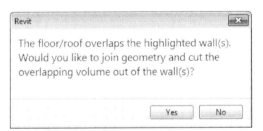

**Figure 4–35**

© 2016, ASCENT - Center for Technical Knowledge®

- Floors can be placed on top of floors. For example, a structural floor can have a finish floor of tile or carpet placed on top of it, as shown in Figure 4–36. These floors can then be scheduled separately.

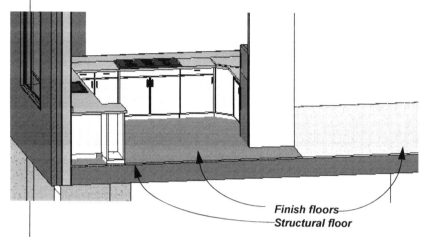

*Finish floors*
*Structural floor*

**Figure 4–36**

## Modifying Floors

You can change a floor to a different type in the Type Selector. In Properties, you can modify parameters including the *Height Offset From Level*, as shown in Figure 4–37. When you have a floor selected, you can also edit the boundaries.

**Enhanced**
in **2017**

*Many of the parameters in Properties are used in schedules, including Elevation at Top (Bottom) and Elevation at Top (Bottom) Core for multi-layered floors.*

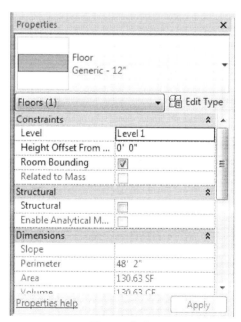

**Figure 4–37**

## How To: Modify the Floor Sketch

1. Select a floor. You might need to highlight an element near the floor and press <Tab> until the floor type displays in the Status Bar or in a tooltip, as shown in Figure 4–38.

**Figure 4–38**

2. In the *Modify | Floors* tab>Mode panel, click  (Edit Boundary). You are placed in sketch mode.
3. Modify the sketch lines using the draw tools, controls, and the various modify tools.

4. Click  (Finish Edit Mode).

- Double-click on a floor to move directly to editing the boundary.

- Floor sketches can be edited in plan and 3D views, but not in elevations. If you try to edit in an elevation view, you are prompted to select another view in which to edit.

---

**Hint: Selecting Floor Faces**

If it is difficult to select the floor edges, toggle on the Selection Option  (Select Elements by Face). Then can select the floor face, and not only the edges.

---

© 2016, ASCENT - Center for Technical Knowledge®

# Joining Geometry

*Cutting a section through the objects you want to join helps to display them more clearly.*

**Join Geometry** is a versatile command used to clean up intersections. The elements remain separate, but the intersections are cleaned up. It can be used with many types of elements including floors, walls, and roofs. In Figure 4–39, the wall on the left and the floor have been joined, but the wall on the right has not been joined with the floor and therefore does not display the lines that define the intersection edges.

**Geometry joined**          **Geometry not joined**

**Figure 4–39**

## How To: Join Geometry

1. In the *Modify* tab>Geometry panel, expand (Join) and click (Join Geometry).
2. Select the elements to join.

- If you toggle on the **Multiple Join** option in the Options Bar, you can select several elements to join to the first selection.

- To remove the join, expand (Join), click (Unjoin Geometry), and select the elements to unjoin.

# Practice 4d

# Create Elements Such as Floors, Ceilings, or Roofs - Floors

### Practice Objectives

- Add floors.
- Copy a floor to multiple levels.

*Estimated time for completion: 30 minutes*

In this practice you will create or modify floors in the Basement, first floor, and second floor of a project. You then copy the floor on the second floor to other related levels and clean up connections between the floors and wall. The second floor with balconies is shown in Figure 4–40.

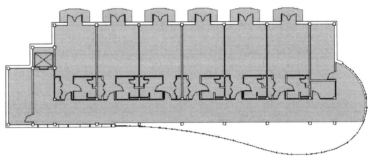

**Figure 4–40**

### Task 1 - Add the basement floor.

1. Open the project **Modern-Hotel-Floors.rvt**.

2. Open the **Floor Plans: Basement** view.

3. In the *Architecture* tab>Build panel, click  (Floor).

4. In the Type Selector, select **Floor: Concrete-1-'0"**.

5. In the *Modify | Create Floor Boundary* tab>Draw panel, click  (Pick Walls) and select the inside face of the exterior foundation walls.

6. Click  (Finish Edit Mode).

© 2016, ASCENT - Center for Technical Knowledge®

7.  If an error dialog box opens, click **Continue**. Use the modify tools to ensure that the boundary is a closed loop. (Hint: On the right side of the building, move the wall end of the stairwell up until it connects with the curved wall.)

8.  Click ✓ (Finish Edit Mode) again.

9.  When the alert box opens, click **Yes**. The floor pattern displays as shown in Figure 4–41.

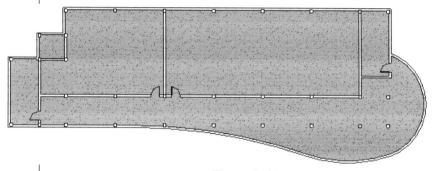

Figure 4–41

10. Click in empty space to release the floor selection.

*Press <Enter> to repeat the last command.*

11. Start the **Floor** command again.

12. In the Type Selector, select **Floor: Tile**. In Properties, set the *Height Offset from Level* to **1/4"** to match the thickness of the tile.

13. Draw the boundary around the stair wells and hall as shown in Figure 4–42.

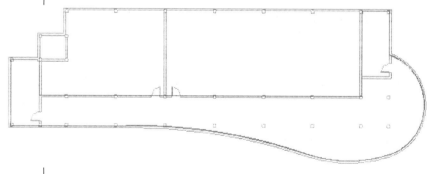

Figure 4–42

14. Click ✓ (Finish Edit Mode).

15. When prompted to join overlapping geometry, click **Yes**.

16. Click in empty space to release the selection and zoom in to display the different floor coverings, as shown in Figure 4–43.

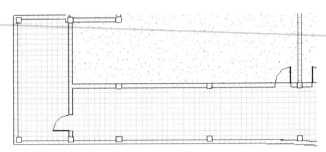

**Figure 4–43**

17. Save the project.

## Task 2 - Modify a floor as a platform for the building.

1. Open the **Floor Plans**: **Floor 1 with Pool** view.

2. Hide the grid lines, tags, and elevation markers.

3. Select the existing floor around the pool building. In the *Modify | Floors* tab>Mode panel, click (Edit Boundary).

4. Modify the boundary as shown in Figure 4–44.

*Modifying the boundary of this floor creates a platform for the building.*

**Select this outline to modify**

**Change the outline to look like this**

**Remove this line**

**Figure 4–44**

5. Click (Finish Edit Mode).

© 2016, ASCENT - Center for Technical Knowledge®

6. When prompted to attach walls to the floor, click **No**. Some of the walls need to be attached, but not all of them.

7. Click in empty space to release the selection.

8. View the building in 3D. It now has a base to rest on.

9. Save the project.

## Task 3 - Add the second floor with balconies.

1. Open the **Floor Plans: Floor 2** view.

2. In the View Control Bar, click ♀ (Reveal Hidden Elements).

3. Select one of the text notes in the imported CAD file. Right-click and select **Unhide in View>Elements**.

4. Click ▣ (Close Reveal Hidden Elements).

*The linked CAD file has been imported to prevent problems with the software finding the correct information for the practice.*

5. Select any element that makes it difficult to display the outline of the floor and balcony. In the View Control Bar, click

*Using Temporary Hide/Isolate cleans up the view temporarily as you create the floor.*

    (Temporary Hide/Isolate) and select **Hide Category**.

6. In the *Architecture* tab>Build panel, click   (Floor).

7. In the Type Selector, select **Floor: Generic - 12"**.

8. In the *Modify | Create Floor Boundary* tab>Draw panel, click

  (Boundary Line) and   (Pick Walls).

9. In the Options Bar, set the *Offset* to **0' 0"** and select **Extend into wall (to core)**.

10. Select the main outside walls. The sketch line displays at the core of the wall, as shown in Figure 4–45. Do not select the three curved walls.

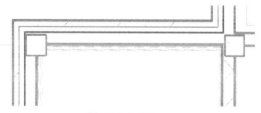

**Figure 4–45**

11. Change to 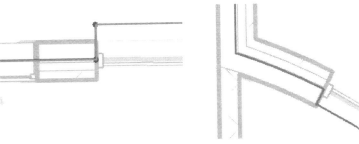 (Pick Lines) and select the lines of walkways in the linked CAD file. (The text notes displays as **LINE OF WALKWAYS** and points to it).

12. Use draw and modify tools to fix the connections at the wall and walkway, as shown in Figure 4–46.

**Figure 4–46**

13. Pan over to one of the balconies.

14. Use (Pick Lines) to draw the outline of the balcony.

15. Use drag controls to have the balcony lines meet the floor line.

16. Use (Split Element) with **Delete Inner Segment** selected on the Options Bar, and cut the line as shown in Figure 4–47.

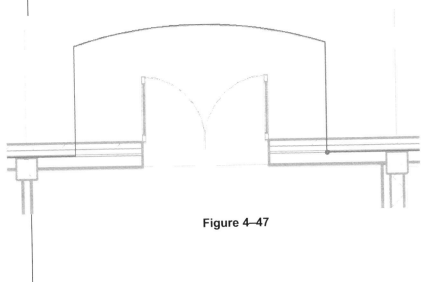

**Figure 4–47**

© 2016, ASCENT - Center for Technical Knowledge®

17. Click ⬚ (Modify) and select the balcony elements.

18. Copy the elements to the other balconies and split the lines to create one continuous sketch.

19. Click ✔ (Finish Edit Sketch).

20. When the alert box shown in Figure 4–48 displays, click **Yes** to cut overlapping geometry out of the walls.

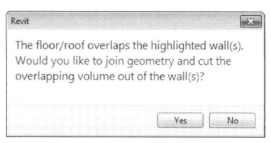

**Figure 4–48**

21. Click in empty space to release the floor selection.

22. Hide the imported CAD file in the view.

23. In the View Control Bar, click ⬚ (Temporary/Hide Isolate) and select **Reset Temporary/Hide Isolate**. The elements you hid earlier display.

24. Save the project.

---

### Task 4 - Copy the second floor to other floors and clean up floor connections with the walls.

---

1. In the **Floor Plans: Floor 2** view, select the new floor.

2. In the *Modify | Floors* tab>Clipboard panel, click ⬚ (Copy to the Clipboard).

3. In the Clipboard panel, expand ⬚ (Paste) and click ⬚ (Aligned to Selected Levels).

4. In the Select Levels dialog box, select **Floor 3** through **Floor 8**, as shown in Figure 4–49. Click **OK**.

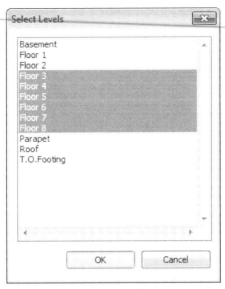

**Figure 4–49**

5. Open a 3D view and rotate it to display the new floors placed in the building, as shown in Figure 4–50.

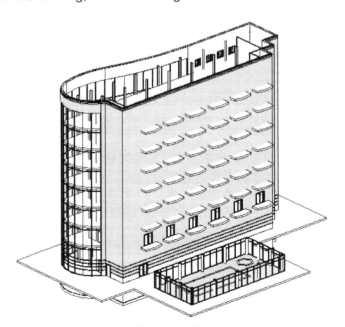

**Figure 4–50**

6. Return to the **Floor Plans: Floor 2** view again.

© 2016, ASCENT - Center for Technical Knowledge®

7.  Select all of the interior walls and interior doors of the guest rooms as well as the exterior doors to the balcony. (Hint: You can open the floor plan of any of the floors between Floor 3 and Floor 8 to display the elements that need to be copied.)

    *   Hold down <Shift> to clear the selection of anything you did not want, such as the exterior walls and the interior stairwell and elevator walls.

    *   Use ⛛ (Filter) to filter out items you do not want to copy, such as the columns, door tags, elevations, and views.

8.  Copy the selected elements to the clipboard and paste them to the same levels as the floors.

9.  Open several of the floor plan views to verify the placement of the guest room walls and doors.

10. Return to the 3D view to display the building with all of the doors and guest rooms, as shown in Figure 4–51.

**Figure 4–51**

11. Zoom in on the back of the building. The floor slabs that extend to the balconies are not joined with the walls and therefore do not display a line across the connection between the wall and balcony, as shown in Figure 4–52. Zoom out to display all of the floors.

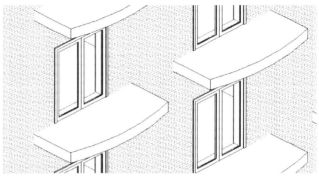

**Figure 4–52**

12. In the *Modify* tab>Geometry panel, expand ⬡ (Join) and click ⬡ (Join Geometry). In the Options Bar, select **Multiple Join**.

13. Select the back exterior wall and then select each floor with a balcony to join the wall and floors, as shown in Figure 4–53. Floor 2 is already joined and does not need to be selected.

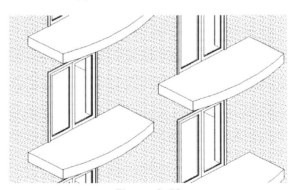

**Figure 4–53**

14. Zoom out to see the entire building.

15. Save the project.

© 2016, ASCENT - Center for Technical Knowledge®

# 4.5 Create Elements Such as Floors, Ceilings, or Roofs - Ceilings

Adding ceilings to Autodesk Revit models is a straightforward process. To place a ceiling, click inside areas that are bounded by walls, and the ceiling is created, as shown in the large room on the right in Figure 4–54. You can also sketch custom ceilings when required. Any fixtures you attach to a ceiling displays in reflected ceiling plans, as well as in sections and 3D views.

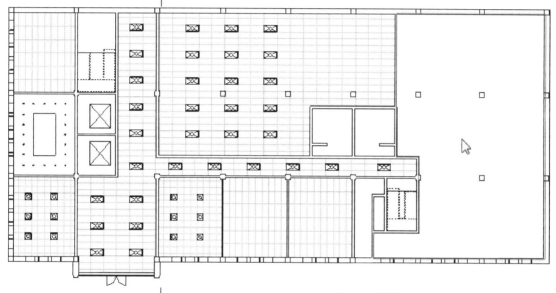

**Figure 4–54**

- Ceiling plans are typically created by default when you add a level with a view, as shown in Figure 4–55.

*If you do not want a level to have a ceiling plan, you can right-click on its name in the Project Browser and select **Delete**.*

**Figure 4–55**

## How To: Create an Automatic Boundary Ceiling

1. Switch to the appropriate Ceiling Plan view.

2. In the *Architecture* tab>Build panel, click 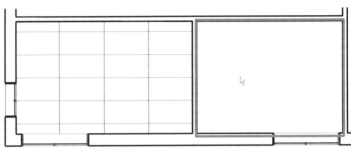 (Ceiling).

3. In the Type Selector, select the ceiling type. In Properties, set the *Height Offset from Level*.

4. In the *Modify | Place Ceiling* tab>Ceiling panel, verify that

   (Automatic Ceiling) is selected. Click inside a room to create a ceiling, as shown in Figure 4–56.

**Figure 4–56**

5. Continue adding ceilings to other rooms, as required.

---

**Hint: Room Bounding Status**

Elements (such as walls, floors, ceilings, and roofs) have a *Room Bounding* parameter set in Properties. In most cases, this is turned on by default as these elements typically define areas and volumes.

The **Automatic Ceiling** tool uses this parameter to identify walls that set the outline of a ceiling. If you turn off this parameter for a wall (such as a partial height wall), the **Automatic Ceiling** tool ignores the wall.

Ceilings can also be used as a Room Bounding for volume calculations.

---

• To modify a ceiling boundary, select a ceiling and either:

   • In the *Modify |Ceilings* tab>Mode panel, click (Edit Boundary), or

   • Double-click on the ceiling.

© 2016, ASCENT - Center for Technical Knowledge®

# Sketching Ceilings

To add a ceiling to part of a room (as shown in Figure 4–57) or to have two different ceiling types at separate levels, you need to sketch a ceiling.

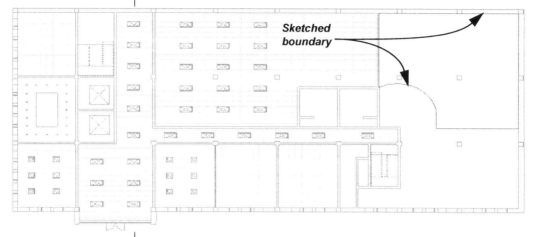

*Sketched boundary*

**Figure 4–57**

## How To: Sketch a Ceiling

1. In the *Architecture* tab>Build panel, click  (Ceiling).
2. In the *Modify | Place Ceiling* tab>Ceiling panel, click

    (Sketch Ceiling).

3. In the Draw panel, click  (Line) or  (Pick Walls) and define a closed loop for the ceiling boundary, similar to sketching a floor boundary.

4. Click  (Finish Edit Mode) to create the ceiling.

• To include a hole in a ceiling, draw the hole as part of the sketch. The hole must be a closed loop completely inside the ceiling boundary.

• In the *Architecture* tab>Opening panel, you can also use

    (Opening By Face),  (Shaft Opening) or  (Vertical Opening) to cut a hole in a ceiling that is separate from the sketch.

---

**Hint: Selecting Ceiling Faces**

If it is difficult to select the ceiling without the grids, you can toggle on the Selection Option ⬚ (Select elements by face). Then you can select the ceiling face, and not only the edges. If you double-click on the ceiling face (or a grid line) the Edit Boundary options are displayed.

---

## Modifying Ceiling Grids

*To change a rectangular ceiling tile pattern from horizontal to vertical, select a grid line and rotate it 90 degrees.*

When using acoustical tile ceiling types, you can reposition the grid locations by moving or rotating the gridlines, as shown in Figure 4–58.

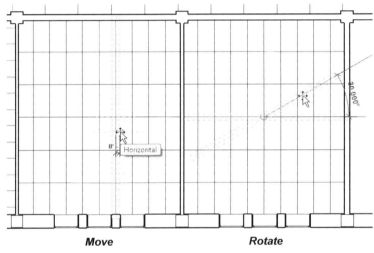

**Move**                    **Rotate**

**Figure 4–58**

### How To: Move a Ceiling Grid

1. Select a grid line in the ceiling that you want to modify.

2. In the *Modify | Ceilings* tab>Modify panel, click ✛ (Move).

3. Move the cursor to one side and type a distance, such as **1'-0"** or **6"**.

### How To: Rotate a Ceiling Grid

1. Select a grid line in the ceiling that you want to modify.

2. In the *Modify | Ceilings* tab>Modify panel, click ↻ (Rotate).

3. In the Options Bar, type an *Angle* or use ↻ (Rotate) to visually select the angle.

---

   © 2016, ASCENT - Center for Technical Knowledge®

# Practice 4e

# Create Elements Such as Floors, Ceilings, or Roofs - Ceilings

## Practice Objectives

*Estimated time for completion: 15 minutes*

- Create automatic ceilings with grids.
- Add ceiling components.

In this practice, while working in a reflected ceiling plan, you will add acoustical tile ceilings to several support spaces. You will then add light fixtures and air terminals, as shown in Figure 4–59.

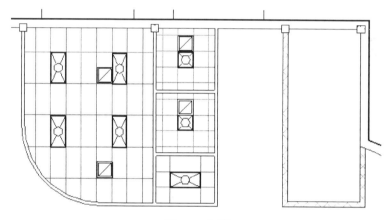

**Figure 4–59**

## Task 1 - Create ceilings with ceiling grids.

1. Open the drawing **Modern-Hotel-Ceilings.rvt**.

2. Open the **Ceiling Plans: Floor 1** view.

   - To clarify the drawing, you might want to hide the grids, elevations, and sections categories. A quick way to do this is to select one of each element and then use the **Visibility Hide** shortcut by pressing <V> and then pressing <H>.

3. In the *Architecture* tab>Build panel, click  (Ceiling).

4. In the Type Selector, verify that **Compound Ceiling: 2' x 4' ACT System** is selected.

5. Click inside the four support rooms, as shown in Figure 4–60.

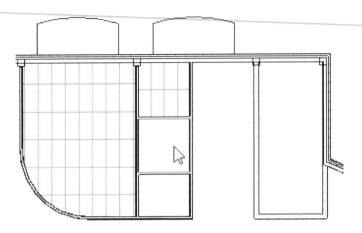

**Figure 4–60**

6. Start the **Modify** command and select one grid line in each restroom. In the Type Selector, select **Compound Ceiling: 2' x 2' ACT System**. In Properties, set the *Height Offset from Level* to **9' 0"**.

---
**Task 2 - Add ceiling components.**

---

1. In the *Architecture* tab>Build panel, click  (Component).

2. In the Mode panel, click (Load Family) and load the following components from the associated folders:

   - Lighting>Architectural>Internal: **Downlight Recessed Can.rfa, Troffer Light 2x2 Parabolic.rfa**, and **Troffer Light 2x4 Parabolic.rfa**
   - Mechanical>MEP>Air-Side Components>Air Terminals: **Return Register.rfa** and **Supply Diffuser.rfa**

*Hold <Ctrl> to select more than one element.*

*The air terminals found in the Architectural folder are only 2D. If you don't have access to the MEP folder, you can use these instead.*

3. Add the ceiling fixtures, as shown in Figure 4–61.

- Select a ceiling grid line and use **Move** to modify the grid to suit the location of the fixtures.
- Select a light fixture and place it on the grid. Press <Esc> and select the light fixture. Press <Spacebar> to rotate the light 90 degrees.
- Use snaps or **Align** to place it exactly on the grid.
- Copy it to the other locations.
- Place return registers in each room. Set the *Offset* from the Level to the height of the ceiling before placing them.

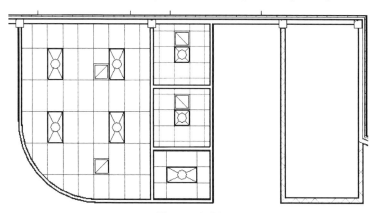

**Figure 4–61**

4. Save the project.

# 4.6 Create Elements Such as Floors, Ceilings, or Roofs - Roofs

The Autodesk Revit software provides two main ways of creating roofs:

- **Footprint:** Created in a floor plan view by defining the area to be covered.

- **Extrusion:** Created in an elevation or section by defining a profile sketch.

The footprint method can generate most common roof types, including flat, shed, gable, and hip roofs. The extrusion method is needed for an odd-shaped roof or a roof with two slopes on the same face, as shown in Figure 4–62.

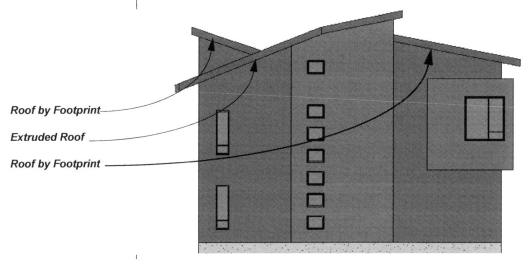

Roof by Footprint

Extruded Roof

Roof by Footprint

**Figure 4–62**

- Other roof options, found in the Roof drop-down list, include **Roof by Face**, which is used with Massing elements, **Roof Soffit**, which connects the edge of the roof to the wall, **Fascia**, which places a flat board on the outside edge of the roof and **Gutter**, which adds a gutter on the edge of the roof.

© 2016, ASCENT - Center for Technical Knowledge®

## Creating Roofs by Footprint

To create a flat roof, or any basic single-sloped roofs (hip, shed, or gable), start with a plan view and define a sketch or "footprint" around the area that you want the roof to cover, as shown in Figure 4–63.

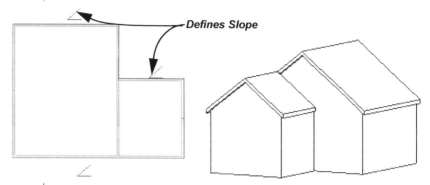

*Defines Slope*

**Figure 4–63**

You control the type of roof by specifying which edge(s) define the slope:

- No edges sloped = flat roof
- One edge sloped = shed roof
- Two opposing edges sloped = gable roof
- All edges sloped = hip roof

### How To: Add a Roof by Footprint

1. Open a plan view at the roof level of the building.

2. In the *Architecture* tab> Build panel, expand ⬜ (Roof) and click ⬜ (Roof by Footprint).

3. In the *Modify | Create Roof Footprint* tab>Draw panel, click ⬚ (Pick Walls) or ╱ (Line) or any other Draw tool to create the roof footprint. You can include arcs in the sketch.

    - The lines must form a closed boundary with no overlapping lines.

    - Use commands such as ⬆ (Trim), to modify the lines as required.

© 2016, ASCENT - Center for Technical Knowledge®

4. Select and modify each segment of the sketch as required using the Options Bar, Properties, or controls, as shown in Figure 4–64.

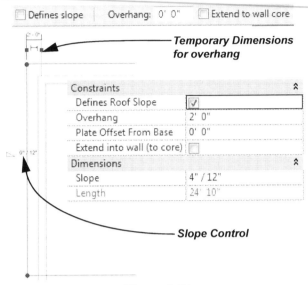

**Figure 4–64**

5. Click ✓ (Finish Edit Mode).
6. An alert box might open, as shown in Figure 4–65. You can attach the highlighted walls to the roof now or later.

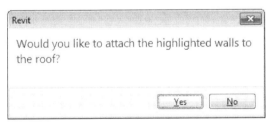

**Figure 4–65**

7. The roof is still selected and you can set the options for the entire roof in Properties. These include the roof type, *Base Offset from Level*, *Rafter Cut*, and *Cutoff Level* options.

© 2016, ASCENT - Center for Technical Knowledge®

# Attaching Walls to Roofs

Attaching walls to the roof extends the walls up to the roof, as shown in Figure 4–66. You attach walls while you are still in the roof command, or you can use the **Attach Top/Base** options later in the design process.

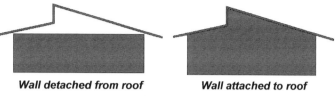

**Wall detached from roof**          **Wall attached to roof**

**Figure 4–66**

- **Attach Top/Base** can also be used with walls that are against sloping floors or topographic site features.

## How To: Attach Walls to Roofs

1. Select the wall or walls that you want to attach to the roof.

2. In the *Modify | Walls* tab>Modify Wall panel, click ▣ (Attach Top/Base). Verify that *Attach Wall* is set to **Top**, as shown in Figure 4–67.

**Figure 4–67**

3. Select the roof. The walls are trimmed or extended to the roofline.

- To edit a roof, either:

  - Double-click on the edge of the roof

  - With the roof selected, click ▱ (Edit Footprint).

  You can then modify the sketch and all of the options for each segment.

## Hint: Setting Up a Roof Plan

When creating a roof, add a level with a floor plan view where the bottom of the roof should be located. If there are roofs at different heights, create a level for each location.

Most plan views are typically cut at 3'-0" to 4'-0" above the bottom of the level, as shown in Figure 4–68. However, this does not work with pitched roofs, whose structures can reach 20'-0" high or more. To change the height of the area shown in the roof plan, change the *View Range* in View Properties.

  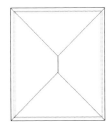

*View Range Cut Plane @ 4'-0"*   *View Range Cut Plane @ 30'-0"*

**Figure 4–68**

# Creating Roofs by Extrusion

Extruded roofs enable you to create complex roof forms, such as the curved roof shown in Figure 4–69. Extruded roofs are based on a sketch of the roof profile in an elevation or section view. The profile is extruded between a start and end point.

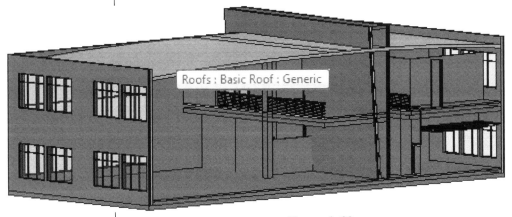

**Figure 4–69**

© 2016, ASCENT - Center for Technical Knowledge®

## How To: Create an Extruded Roof

1. Open an elevation or a section view.

2. In the *Architecture* tab>Build panel, expand 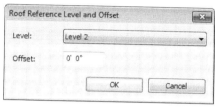 (Roof) and click  (Roof by Extrusion).

3. In the Work Plane dialog box, select the Work Plane on which you want to sketch the roof profile, and click **OK.**

4. In the Roof Reference Level and Offset dialog box, as shown in Figure 4–70, specify the base *Level* and *Offset* (if any).

*By default, this level is set to the highest one in the project. The offset creates a reference plane at that distance.*

**Figure 4–70**

5. Draw reference planes to help you create the roof profile. Reference planes created within sketch mode do not display once the roof is finished.

6. Use the Draw tools to create the profile, as shown in Figure 4–71.

*Sketch only the shape of the roof in profile, not the thickness.*

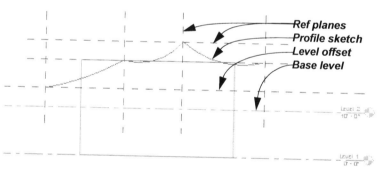

**Figure 4–71**

7. In Properties, set the *Extrusion Start* and *End*.

8. Click  (Finish Edit Mode).

9.  In the Type Selector, select the roof type.

    - The thickness, which is determined by the roof type, is added below the profile sketch line.

10. View the roof in 3D and make any other required modifications. For example, you can use the controls on the ends of the roof to extend the overhang (as shown in Figure 4–72), as well as modify the roof using temporary dimensions and the parameters in Properties.

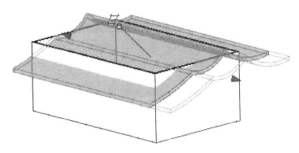

**Figure 4–72**

11. Attach the walls to the roof.

- You can make changes to the roof's profile in one of the following ways:

    - Double-click on the edge of the roof.
    - Select the roof. In the *Modify | Roofs* tab>Mode panel, click  (Edit Profile).

## How To: Modify the Plan View of an Extruded Roof

1.  Open a plan view where the entire roof displays.
2.  Select the roof.
3.  In the *Modify | Roofs* tab>Opening panel, click  (Vertical).
4.  In the *Modify | Create Extrusion Roof Profile* tab>Draw panel, use the tools to create a closed boundary.The boundary can be entirely inside the roof or touching the roof boundaries.

© 2016, ASCENT - Center for Technical Knowledge®

5. Click 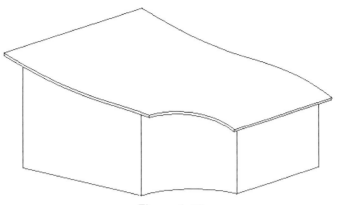 (Finish Edit Mode). The extruded view now has a cutout, as shown in Figure 4–73.

**Figure 4–73**

# Practice 4f

# Create Elements Such as Floors, Ceilings, or Roofs - Roofs by Footprint

### Practice Objectives

- Create flat and sloped roofs using Roof by Footprint.
- Create a roof plan view.

*Estimated time for completion: 25 minutes*

In this practice you will create a flat roof on the main part of the hotel, and flat and sloped roofs over the poolhouse, as shown in Figure 4–74.

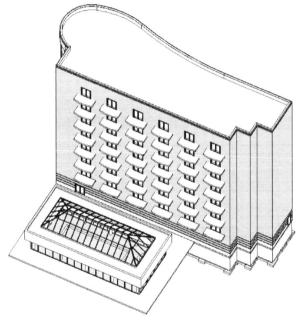

Figure 4–74

### Task 1 - Create a flat roof.

1. Open **Modern-Hotel-Roof-Footprint.rvt**.

2. Open the **Floor Plans: Roof** view and set the *Underlay* to **None**.

3. Hide the grid lines and section and elevation markers.

© 2016, ASCENT - Center for Technical Knowledge®

4. In the *Architecture* tab>Build panel, expand 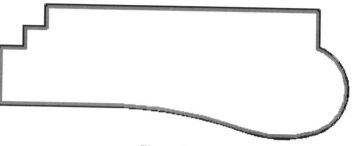 (Roof) and click (Roof by Footprint).

5. In the Options Bar, clear the **Defines slope** option.

6. In the *Modify | Create Roof Footprint* tab>Draw panel, click (Pick Walls) and select the inside of the walls around the building, as shown in Figure 4–75.

**Figure 4–75**

7. Click (Finish Edit Mode).

8. In the Type Selector, select **Basic Roof: Steel Truss - Insulation on Metal Deck - EPDM**.

9. View the building in 3D to display the roof applied below the parapet wall, as shown in Figure 4–76.

**Figure 4–76**

10. Save the project.

## Task 2 - Create a roof plan.

*Hold down <Shift> and the mouse wheel to rotate in 3D view.*

1. Rotate the 3D view until the poolhouse at the back of the building displays. It does not yet have a roof, but several features are in place, including the parapet walls and roof soffit, as shown in Figure 4–77.

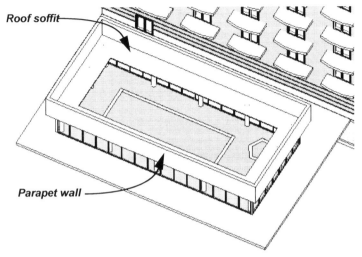

**Figure 4–77**

2. Duplicate (without detailing) a copy of the **Floor Plans: Floor 2** view and rename it as **Roof - Poolhouse**.

3. Verify that this view is open.

4. In Properties, edit the *View Range* and set it up as shown in Figure 4–78. Then click **OK**.

**Figure 4–78**

© 2016, ASCENT - Center for Technical Knowledge®

5. Expand the crop region to display the pool area and then modify it so that only the poolhouse displays, as shown in Figure 4–79. Hide any other elements as required.

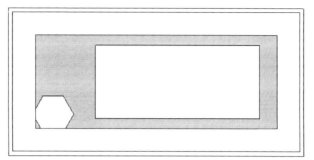

**Figure 4–79**

6. Hide the crop region.

## Task 3 - Create roofs on the poolhouse.

1. In the *Architecture* tab>Build panel, click ⌐ (Roof). The software remembers the most recently used command of **Roof by Footprint**.

2. In the Options Bar, verify that the **Defines slope** option is cleared and there is no overhang.

3. In the *Modify | Create Roof Footprint* tab>Draw panel, click 

   ⌐ (Pick Walls) and select the inside of the parapet walls.

   Use ⌐ (Pick Lines) and select the soffit opening, as shown in Figure 4–80. This creates a flat roof with an opening in it.

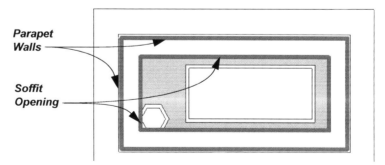

**Figure 4–80**

4. Click ✓ (Finish Edit Mode.)

5. With the roof still selected, set the following:

   - *Type:* Basic Roof: Generic - 12"
   - *Base Level:* **Floor 2**
   - *Base Offset from Level:* (negative) **-2' 0"**

6. Click in the view to release the roof.

7. Click ⬓ (Wall).

8. In Properties, set the following parameters:

   - Wall Type: **Basic Wall: Exterior - EIFS on Mtl.Stud**
   - Location Line: **Finish Face: Interior**
   - Base Constraint: **Floor 2**
   - Base Offset: (negative) **-1' 0"**
   - Top Constraint: **Unconnected**
   - Unconnected Height: **1' 0"**

9. Draw this short wall around the opening, as shown in Figure 4–81.

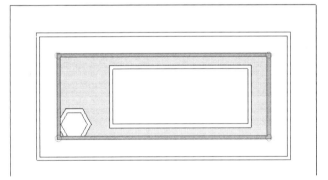

**Figure 4–81**

10. Click ▛ (Roof by Footprint).

11. In the Options Bar, select the **Defines slope** option.

© 2016, ASCENT - Center for Technical Knowledge®

12. Use 🔍 (Pick Walls) and select the outside of the new walls you just created, as shown in Figure 4–82.

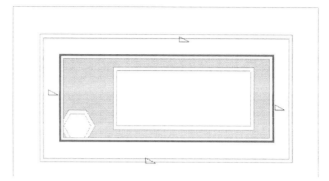

**Figure 4–82**

13. Click ✔ (Finish Edit Mode). In the Message dialog box, click **No** to not attach any walls to the roof.

14. In the Type Selector, select **Sloped Glazing: Pool Roof** and verify that the *Base Level* is **Floor 2**. In the *Grid 1* area, set the *Justification* to **Center**. The new roof displays as shown in Figure 4–83.

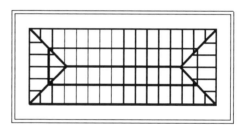

**Figure 4–83**

15. View the entire model in 3D.

16. Save the project.

**Task 4 - Apply slopes to the main flat roof (optional).**

If time permits, select the flat roof on the main hotel and use the Shape Editing tools on the *Modify | Floors* tab to add appropriate drainage slopes.

# Practice 4g

# Create Elements Such as Floors, Ceilings, or Roofs - Roofs by Extrusion

## Practice Objectives

- Create an extruded roof.
- Modify the plan profile of a roof.

*Estimated time for completion: 20 minutes*

In this practice you will create a curved extruded roof to cover the main entrance of the building and modify its plan profile to cover the side entrance, as shown in Figure 4–84.

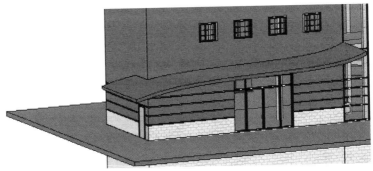

**Figure 4–84**

## Task 1 - Create a roof by extrusion.

1. Open **Modern-Hotel-Roof-Extruded.rvt**.

2. Open the **Elevations (Building Elevation): South** view.

3. Zoom in on the area around the front entrance.

4. In the *Architecture* tab>Build panel, expand 🗔 (Roof) and click ◣ (Roof by Extrusion).

5. In the Work Plane dialog box, verify that **Pick a plane** is selected, and click **OK**.

6. Select the front face of the wall.

7. In the Roof Reference Level and Offset dialog box, set the *Level* to **Floor 2** and click **OK**. A reference plane is set at this level and the drawing is grayed out.

© 2016, ASCENT - Center for Technical Knowledge®

8. Sketch the profile of a roof similar to the one shown in Figure 4–85. It should extend beyond the building to the left but finish at the end of the brick wall on the right.

*The example was created using*

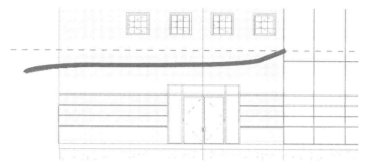

*(Spline).*

**Figure 4–85**

9. In Properties, set the *Extrusion End* to (negative) **-6' 0"**.

10. Click ✔ (Finish Edit Mode).

11. In the Type Selector, select **Basic Roof: Generic - 9"**.

12. View the new roof in 3D. It is mostly inside the building at this point.

### Task 2 - Modify the extruded roof.

1. Open the **Floor Plans: Site** view. This view displays the entire building in plan including all of the roofs.

2. Hide the grid lines and elevation markers by category.

3. Select the Entrance roof and using controls, move the roof outward so that the length is 20' 0", as shown in Figure 4–86.

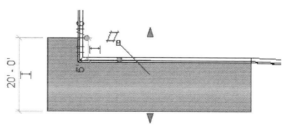

**Figure 4–86**

4. In the *Modify | Roofs* tab>Opening panel, click 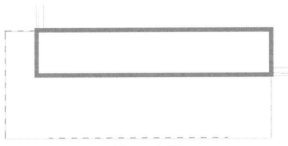 (Vertical).

5. Create a rectangular cutout of the roof for the portion that passes through the building, as shown in Figure 4–87.

**Figure 4–87**

6. Click ✓ (Finish Edit Mode).

7. View the modified roof in 3D. It now wraps around the side of the building to cover the side entrance, as shown in Figure 4–88.

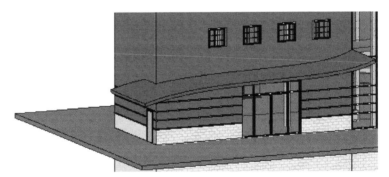

**Figure 4–88**

8. Save the project.

© 2016, ASCENT - Center for Technical Knowledge®

# 4.7 Generate a Toposurface

Once you have the Survey Point and Project Base Point in place, you can create topographical surfaces (toposurfaces), as shown in Figure 4–89.

- You can create a toposurface in three different ways:
  - Specify points directly in the project.
  - Import a CAD file with 3D information.
  - Import a points file (.txt or .cvs) developed by a surveyor.

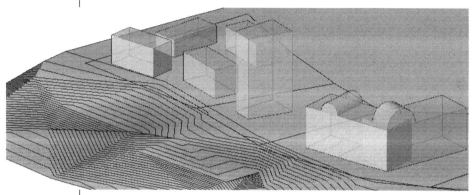

**Figure 4–89**

- You can edit toposurfaces by modifying individual points.

- Site settings that impact the toposurfaces include the contour line display and section graphics.

## How To: Create a Toposurface By Specifying Points

1. Open a site or 3D view.
2. In the *Massing & Site* tab>Model Site panel, click

   ▧ (Toposurface).
3. In the *Modify | Edit Surface* tab>Tools panel, click ⌂ (Place Point).
4. In the Options Bar, set the *Elevation* for the point as shown in Figure 4–90. By default, you are only able to select **Absolute Elevation**. After you create a surface of three points, you can also select **Relative to Surface**.

**Figure 4–90**

5. Click in the drawing area to place the point.
6. Continue placing points. You can vary the elevation as needed. After you have placed three points, a boundary is displayed, connecting them. When you add a point at a different elevation, you see the contour lines forming, as shown in Figure 4–91.

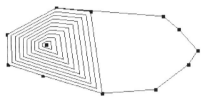

Figure 4–91

7. In the Surface panel, click ✍ (Finish Surface) when you have finished selecting points.

- Points can be added in plan and 3D views.

- To create a neat outer boundary for a toposurface, draw reference planes and then select points at the intersections of the planes.

## How To: Create a Toposurface Using an Imported File

*When importing, do not use the **Current view only** option as you need the 3D information stored in the CAD file.*

1. In a site or 3D view, import a CAD file (DWG, DXF, or DGN) that holds the site information.
2. In the *Massing & Site* tab>Model Site panel, click ⬛ (Toposurface).
3. In the *Modify | Edit Surface* tab>Tools panel, expand ⬛ (Create from Import) and click ⬛ (Select Import Instance).
4. Select the imported file by clicking on the edge of the file.
5. In the Add Points from Selected Layers dialog box, select the layers that hold the points (the layer names vary according to the original drawing file standard), as shown in Figure 4–92.

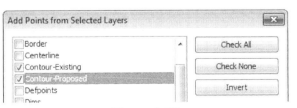

Figure 4–92

© 2016, ASCENT - Center for Technical Knowledge®

6. Click **OK**. The new toposurface is created with points at the same elevations as the imported information.

7. Click ✔ (Finish Surface) to end the command.

8. If you do not need the CAD file for other information, delete it.

- If the CAD file is going to be updated with information (such as the footprint of the building or roads and parking areas), it would be better to link the CAD file. This way, when the up-to-date information is provided, it is included in the project.

## How To: Create a Toposurface from a Points File

1. Open a site or 3D view.

2. In the *Massing & Site* tab>Model Site panel, click 

   ▧ (Toposurface).

3. In the *Modify | Edit Surface* tab>Tools panel, expand 

   🏠 (Create from Import) and click 🏠 (Specify Points File).

4. In the Select File dialog box, select the CSV or comma delimited text file (TXT) that contains the list of points and click **Open**.

5. In the Format dialog box, as shown in Figure 4–93, select the unit format and click **OK**. The options include **Decimal feet**, **Decimal inches**, **Meters**, **Centimeters**, and **Millimeters**.

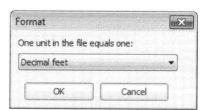

**Figure 4–93**

6. The points create a toposurface in the project. Add additional points as needed and click ✔ (Finish Surface).

- Having many points on a surface slows down system performance. While still in the *Modify | Edit Surface* tab> Tools panel, click 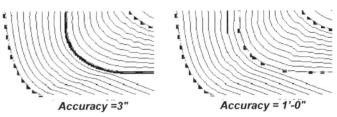 (Simplify Surface) to reduce the number of points. Set the required accuracy, as shown in Figure 4–94, and click **OK**.

*Accuracy =3"*       *Accuracy = 1'-0"*

**Figure 4–94**

## Editing Toposurfaces

You can make changes to a toposurface by adding points or editing existing point locations and elevations, as shown in Figure 4–95. You can also modify the Properties of a toposurface, including material and phasing information.

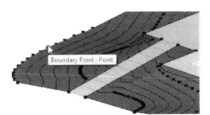

**Figure 4–95**

### How To: Edit a Toposurface

1. Select the toposurface that you want to edit.

2. In the *Modify | Topography* tab>Surface panel, click (Edit Surface).

3. In the *Modify | Edit Surface* tab>Tools panel, click (Place Point) and add more points to the surface.

4. To edit existing points, select one or more points.

5. In the *Interior (or Boundary) Points* tab, you can use various modification tools. You can change the elevation of the points in the Options Bar, as shown in Figure 4–96.

*When adding points, it helps to be in a 3D shaded view so that you can see the effects of your new points.*

© 2016, ASCENT - Center for Technical Knowledge®

**Figure 4–96**

6. Select another point or click in an empty space to finish editing the points.
7. In the *Modify | Edit Surface* tab> Surface panel, click

   (Finish Surface) to end the command.

## Site Settings

In the *Massing & Site* tab>Model Site panel, click ˟ in the panel title. The Site Settings dialog box opens, in which you can set the way contours are displayed in the plan and section views of a toposurface, as shown in Figure 4–97.

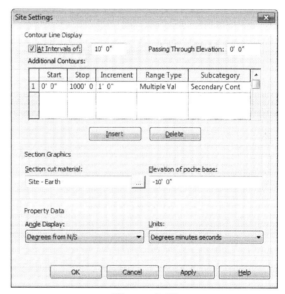

**Figure 4–97**

## Site Setting Options

**Contour Line Display**

| At Intervals of: | Set the distance for the primary contour lines. These display with a heavy line and are not necessarily the places at which you added the points. |
| --- | --- |
| **Passing Through Elevation** | The starting elevation for contour lines. |

**Additional Contours**

| | |
|---|---|
| **Start/Stop** | **Start** is the location for a single additional contour or the first of a series of contours. **Stop** is the end of a series of additional contour lines. |
| **Increment** | The distance between sub-contours when the *Range type* is set to **Multiple Values**. The style is set according to the Subcategory specification. |
| **Range Type** | Set to **Multiple Values** or **Single Value**. When set to multiple, you can specify the start and stop and the increment. When set to **Single Value**, you can specify the location of the single contour in the **Start Value**. Increments are grayed out. |
| **Subcategory** | Select from a list of object styles that define how to display the additional contours. For example, **Secondary Contours** display with a thin line and **Primary Contours** with a wide line. You can create additional options in **Object Styles** under **Topography**. |
| **Insert / Delete** | Insert or delete additional contour descriptions. |

**Section Graphics**

| | |
|---|---|
| **Section cut material** | The default material is set to **Earth**. Click (Browse) to open the Material Browser in which you can select a different material. Additional site related materials can be found in the *AEC Materials: Misc* area at the bottom of the Material Browser. The following shows a section cut using the **Earth** material. |
| **Elevation of poche base** | The height of the poche (or hatching) that displays below the bottom contour line in a section view. It is usually negative. |

**Property Data**

| | |
|---|---|
| **Angle Display** | Select the type of angles to display: **Degrees from N/S** or **Degrees**. |
| **Units** | Select the type of units to display: **Degrees Minutes Seconds** or **Decimal Degrees**. |

© 2016, ASCENT - Center for Technical Knowledge®

# Practice 4h

# Generate a Toposurface

### Practice Objectives

- Import a CAD file with contours.
- Set the Project Base Point and the Survey Point.
- Create a Toposurface from the imported file.
- (Optional) Create a Toposurface using a Points file.

*Estimated time for completion: 10 minutes*

In this practice you will import a CAD file that contains contour information, set the Project Base Point and Survey Point, create a toposurface from the imported file, change the site settings, and add a section as shown in Figure 4–98.

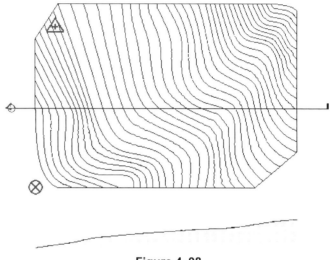

**Figure 4–98**

### Task 1 - Import a CAD file.

1. Start a new project based on the default architectural template.

2. Open the **Floor Plans:Site** view.

3. In the *Insert* tab>Import panel, click  (Import CAD).

*This file was creating using the AutoCAD®️ software.*

4. In the Import CAD Formats dialog box, navigate to the practice files folder and select **Site-DWG.dwg**. Accept the default options and click **Open**.

5. Type **ZE** to zoom out to the extents of the file. The origin of the imported CAD file is placed at the origin of the project, as shown in Figure 4–99.

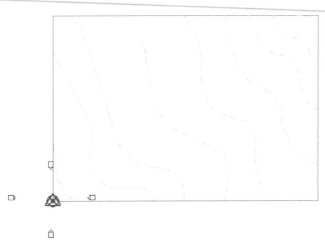

**Figure 4–99**

6. Save the project in the practice files folder as **New-Site.rvt**.

## Task 2 - Set the Project Base Point and the Survey Point.

1. Click on the Project Base Point and set the information as shown in Figure 4–100, and as follows:

   - N/S: **63' 0"**
   - E/W: **75' 0"**
   - Elev: **1856' 0"**
   - Angle to True North: **20 degrees**

*This is information you would receive from surveyors or civil engineers.*

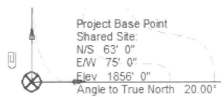

**Figure 4–100**

2. The project elements move with the Project Base Point. Type **ZE** again to display the new location of the site.

3. Select the Survey Point and click ⬚ to unclip it.

© 2016, ASCENT - Center for Technical Knowledge®

4. Set the information as shown in Figure 4–101, and as follows:

- N/S: **354' 0"**
- E/W: **225' 0"**
- Elev: **1864' 0"**

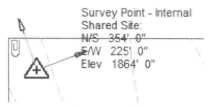

**Figure 4–101**

5. Reclip the Survey Point in its new location.

6. Hide the elevation markers and save the project

## Task 3 - Create a Toposurface from the Imported file.

1. Continue working in the **Floor Plans: Site** view.

2. In the *Massing & Site* tab>Model Site panel, click

   (Toposurface).

3. In the *Modify | Edit Surface* tab>Tools panel, expand

   (Create from Import) and click (Select Import Instance).

4. Select the imported CAD file.

5. In the Add Points from Selected Layers dialog box, click **Check None**. Select the layer **Contour-Existing** (as shown in Figure 4–102) and click **OK**.

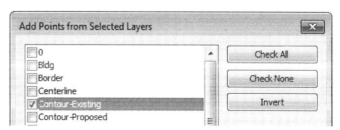

**Figure 4–102**

6. The new toposurface is created with points applied along the contour lines from the CAD file, as shown in Figure 4–103.

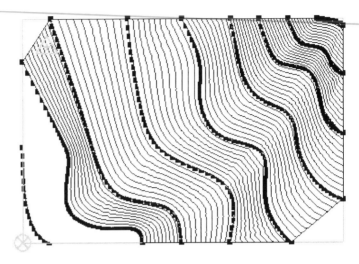

**Figure 4–103**

7. In the *Modify | Edit Surface* tab> Tools panel click

   (Simplify Surface).

8. In the Simplify Surface dialog box, set the *Accuracy* to **1'-0"** (as shown in Figure 4–104) and click **OK**.

**Figure 4–104**

9. Fewer points are placed in the toposurface without

   compromising the actual contour location. Click   (Finish Surface).

10. Hide the linked CAD file.

11. The contour lines are closer together than the ones displayed in the CAD file, as shown in Figure 4–105. This distance is specified in the Site Settings.

© 2016, ASCENT - Center for Technical Knowledge®

12. In the *Massing & Site* tab>Model Site panel title, click ⌐ (Site Settings).

13. In the Site Settings dialog box, in the *Additional Contours* area, set the *Increment* to **2'-0"**, and click **OK**. The distance between the contours changes, as shown in Figure 4–106.

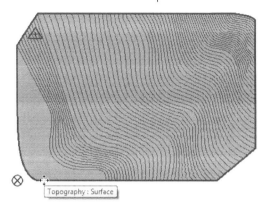

**Figure 4–105**

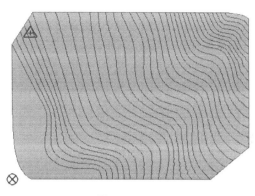

**Figure 4–106**

14. Save the project.

### Task 4 - Create a Site Section.

1. In the *View* tab>Create panel, click ◯ (Section) and draw a horizontal section through the site.

2. In the Project Browser, in the *Section (Building Section)* node, rename the section as **Site Section**.

3. Open the section view. The material displayed in the section is **Earth**, as shown in Figure 4–107, which was specified in the Site Settings.

**Figure 4–107**

4. Save the project.

## Task 5 - (Optional) Create a Toposurface using a Points file.

1. Using Notepad or another text editor, in the practice files folder, open **Topography-Points.txt**. The list of points, shown in part in Figure 4–108, includes three numbers on each line. The format is **Northing (Y), Easting (X), Elevation (ft)**.

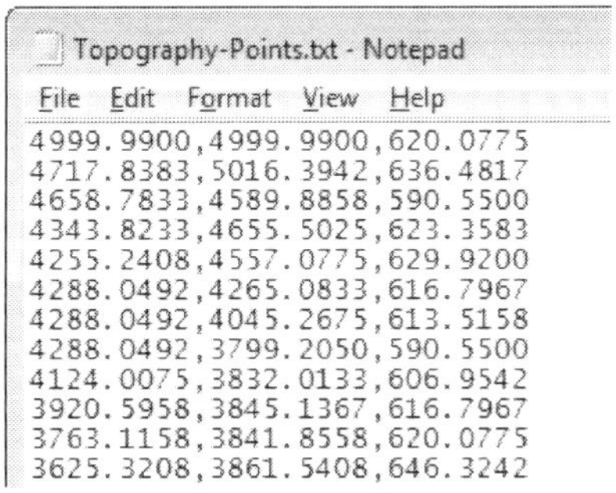

```
Topography-Points.txt - Notepad
File   Edit   Format   View   Help
4999.9900,4999.9900,620.0775
4717.8383,5016.3942,636.4817
4658.7833,4589.8858,590.5500
4343.8233,4655.5025,623.3583
4255.2408,4557.0775,629.9200
4288.0492,4265.0833,616.7967
4288.0492,4045.2675,613.5158
4288.0492,3799.2050,590.5500
4124.0075,3832.0133,606.9542
3920.5958,3845.1367,616.7967
3763.1158,3841.8558,620.0775
3625.3208,3861.5408,646.3242
```

**Figure 4–108**

2. Close the text file.

3. In the practice files folder, open **Topography-Points.rvt**.

4. Open the **Elevations (Building Elevation): South** view.

5. There are two levels. *Level 1* is set to **700'**, which works best with the information provided in the points file for the elevation, which ranges from 590 to 744 feet.

6. Open the default 3D view.

7. In the *Massing & Site* tab>Model Site panel, click

   (Toposurface).

8. In the *Modify | Edit Surface* tab>Tools panel, expand

   (Create from Import) and click (Specify Points File).

9. In the Open dialog box, set the *Files of type* to **Comma delimited Text** and select **Topography-Points.txt.** Click **Open**.

10. In the Format dialog box, select **Decimal feet** and click **OK**.

11. Type **ZE** to zoom to the extents of the file.

© 2016, ASCENT - Center for Technical Knowledge®

12. Click 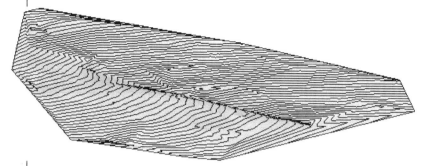 (Finish Surface).

13. Zoom in on the toposurface and investigate it.

14. Modify the Site Settings, Material, and Visual Style as needed to get a better understanding of the site as shown in Figure 4–109.

**Figure 4–109**

15. Save and close the project.

# 4.8 Model Railings

Railings are automatically created with stairs, but you can modify or delete them independently of the stair element. You can also add railings separate from the stairs for other locations, as shown in Figure 4–110.

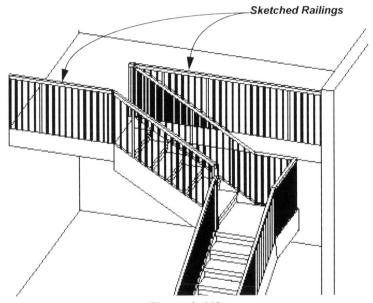

*Sketched Railings*

**Figure 4–110**

*   You can add railings to existing stairs and ramps if they were not included when they were created.

## How To: Add Railings by Sketching

1.  Open a plan or 3D view.
2.  In the *Architecture* tab>Circulation panel, expand

    (Railing) and click  (Sketch Path).
3.  In the Type Selector, specify the railing type.
4.  In the *Modify | Create Railing Path* tab>Tools panel, click

    (Pick New Host) and select the element with which the railing is associated, such as a stair or floor. (This makes the railing take on the slope of the host, and is not required if the host is flat.)

© 2016, ASCENT - Center for Technical Knowledge®

5. Use the Draw tools to draw the lines that define the railings.

6. Click ✓ (Finish Edit Mode) to create the railing.

- The railing must be a single connected sketch. If it is not, you are prompted with a warning, such as that shown in Figure 4–111.

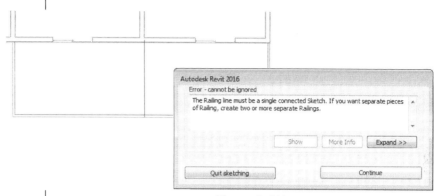

**Figure 4–111**

## How To: Add Railings by Selecting a Host

1. In the *Architecture* tab>Circulation panel, expand

   ▦ (Railing) and click ▦ (Place on Host).

2. In the *Modify | Create Railing Place on Host* tab>Position

   panel, click ▯ (Treads) or ▯ (Stringer).

3. Select the stair or ramp where you want to add the railings.

- **Place on Host** only works if there are no railings on the stair. If you want to add an additional railing (e.g., down the middle of a wide stair) you need to sketch the railing.

## Modifying Railings

Modifying railings can be as simple as changing their type in the Type Selector or as complex as creating custom railing styles. A few of the basic methods include editing the path of a railing, joining railings at different heights, and setting the extensions for the top rails, as shown in Figure 4–112.

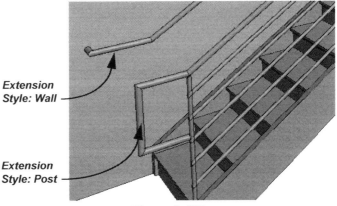

**Figure 4–112**

*   You can delete railings separately from stairs or ramps. However, deleting a stair or ramp automatically deletes related railings.

### Editing the Path of a Railing

To edit the path of a railing, double-click on the railing or select the railing and in the *Modify | Railings* tab>Mode panel, click

 (Edit Path). This places you in edit mode, in which you can modify the individual lines that define the railing, as shown in Figure 4–113. You can create additional lines, but they must be connected to the existing lines.

*Unlike many other elements in edit mode, railings do not have to be in a closed loop.*

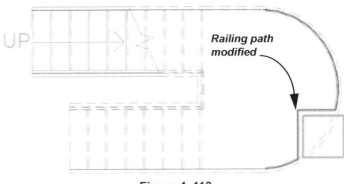

**Figure 4–113**

© 2016, ASCENT - Center for Technical Knowledge®

## Railing Joins

If two railing segments meet in a plan, but are two different heights, you can specify how they interact. While still in edit mode, you can modify each intersection as shown in Figure 4–114.

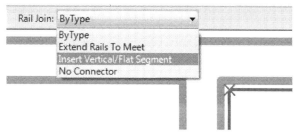

Figure 4–114

## How To: Join Railings at Different Heights

1. Select the railing and in the *Modify | Railings* tab click

   (Edit Path).
2. In the *Modify | Railings>Sketch Path* tab>Tools panel, click

   (Edit Joins).
3. Select the intersection.
4. In the Options Bar, specify the *Rail Join*, as shown in Figure 4–115. The default is **ByType**.
5. If using the default does not produce the required result, select another option in the *Rail Join* drop-down list.

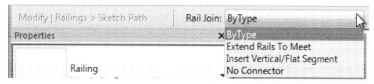

Figure 4–115

- When the *Rail Join* is set to **ByType**, this means that the method of joining the selected intersection is based on parameters in the Type Properties.

## Editing the Top Rail or Handrail

The top rail or handrail of railings can be modified separately from the rest of the railing. This is the first step in customizing the railing system to match many code requirements. For example, you often need to have the handrail extend from the stair as shown in Figure 4–116.

**Figure 4–116**

## How To: Add an Extension to a Top Rail Handrail

1. In a 3D view, hover the cursor over the top rail or handrail. Press <Tab> until it is highlighted and then select it as shown in Figure 4–117.

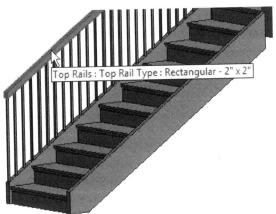

Top Rails : Top Rail Type : Rectangular - 2" x 2"

**Figure 4–117**

© 2016, ASCENT - Center for Technical Knowledge®

2. In the Properties dialog box, click ⊞ (Edit Type). You are editing the type properties of the rail, but not the entire railing system.
3. In the Type Properties dialog box, in the *Extension (Beginning/Bottom)* area, set the *Extension Style*. The options are **None**, **Wall**, **Floor**, and **Post** as shown in Figure 4–118.

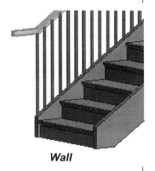

**Wall**

**Floor**

**Post**

Figure 4–118

4. Set the *Length* and select **Plus Tread Depth** if required by the local codes.
5. Click **Apply** to check the addition.
6. Repeat the process for the *Extension (End/Top)*.
7. Make any other changes and click **OK** to finish.

• A Termination can be added if needed. The default rectangular termination works best with the Floor Extension Style but you can also create custom ones.

# Practice 4i

# Model Railings

### Practice Objectives

- Modify railings and handrails.
- Add stand-alone railings.

*Estimated time for completion: 25 minutes*

In this practice you will modify the railings in the stairwells by changing the railings against the wall to a new type. You will also modify the extensions and terminations at the end of the railings. You will then add railings to the interior balconies (as shown in Figure 4–119), and to exterior balconies.

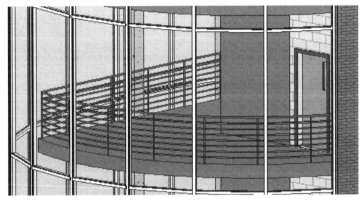

**Figure 4–119**

### Task 1 - Modify the stairwell railings.

1. Open the project **Modern-Hotel-Railings.rvt**.

2. Open the **Floor Plans: Floor 1 - Stair 1** view.

3. Create a camera view looking from the door into the stairwell to display the new stairs and railings.

4. In the Project Browser, in *3D Views*, right-click on the new 3D view and rename it as **Stair 1 - Floor 1.**

*Use <Ctrl>+<Tab> to move between the 3D Camera view and the Floor Plan view.*

5. Modify the controls as required to show the first run of the stair. and set the *Visual Style* to ▦ (Shaded). The top rail and hand rail of the railings display a different material.

© 2016, ASCENT - Center for Technical Knowledge®

6. Select the railing that is against the wall and in the Type Selector, select **Railing: Hotel Stair Handrail-Wall-Floor 1**. The railing type changes as shown in Figure 4–120.

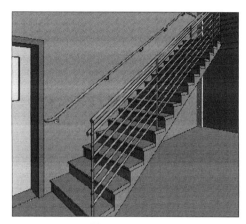

**Figure 4–120**

7. With the handrail still selected, in Properties set the *Tread/String Offset* to **0**. This prevents the handrail from sitting too far off the wall.

8. Open the **Floor Plans: Floor 2** view.

9. Zoom in on the stairwell and select the outside railing. In the Type Selector, change the type to **Railing: Hotel Stair Handrail-Wall-Floor X** and the *Tread/Stringer Offset* to **0**.

10. Create a camera view to display the stairs and railings of the stair going up as shown in Figure 4–121. Select the railing that is partially displayed and hide it. Shade the view to display the components of the railings more clearly.

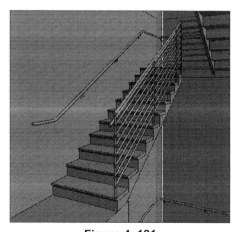

**Figure 4–121**

11. Rename this view as **Stair 1 - Floor 2**.

12. Click inside the camera view. In the inner guardrail, hover the cursor over the separate handrail (not the top rail). Press <Tab> so that only this handrail is highlighted and click to select it.

13. In Properties, click 🔠 (Edit Type).

14. In the Type Properties dialog box, in both the *Extension (Beginning/Bottom)* area and the *Extension (End/Top)* area, set the *Extension Style* to **Floor** and the *Length* to **1' 0"**.

15. In the *Terminations* area, set the *Beginning/Bottom* and *End/Top* to **Termination - Wood - Rectangular**.

16. Click **OK**. The handrail changes as shown in Figure 4–122.

*The railing of the other stair is hidden in this view.*

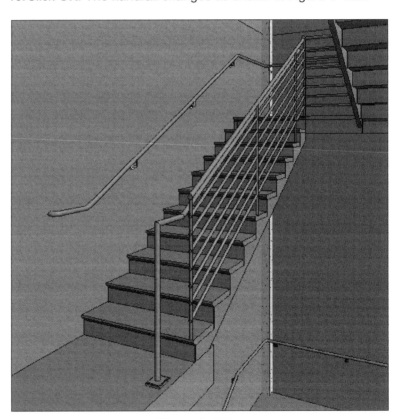

**Figure 4–122**

© 2016, ASCENT - Center for Technical Knowledge®

17. Open one of the other upper floor plans, as shown for Floor 5 in Figure 4–123. The stairs are in place and the guardrail handrail is modified at both ends.

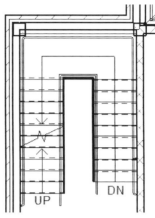

**Figure 4–123**

18. Open a different upper floor view. The changes to the handrails display because it is part of the multi-story stair system.

19. You can also use the **Railing** command to add a guardrail at the floor openings on the stairs.

20. Save the project.

## Task 2 - Add stand-alone railings.

1. Open the **Floor Plans: Floor 2** view and pan and zoom over to the interior balcony (walkway line) as required.

2. In the *Architecture* tab>Circulation panel, expand

   (Railing) and click (Sketch Path).

3. In the Type Selector, select **Railing: Hotel Balcony Guardrail**.

4. Draw a sketch line that is **3"** from the edge of the balcony floor over the lobby of the hotel, as shown in Figure 4–124. Ensure that you include the curved portion at the far end.

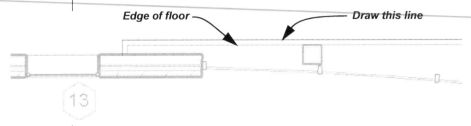

Edge of floor ——— ——— Draw this line

**Figure 4–124**

5. Click ✔ (Finish Edit Mode).

6. Zoom in on one of the outdoor balconies on the back of the building.

7. Add balcony railings, as shown in the sketch in Figure 4–125, using the same parameters as the inside balcony railing.

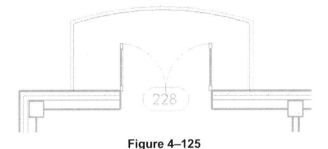

**Figure 4–125**

8. Click ✔ (Finish Edit Mode).

9. Copy the completed railing to the other balconies.

10. Copy all of the railings, inside and out, to the other floors.

11. Open an exterior 3D view and verify the placement of all of the railings.

12. Save the project.

© 2016, ASCENT - Center for Technical Knowledge®

# 4.9 Edit a Model Element's Material (Door, Window, Furniture)

You can easily add additional sizes to existing families of doors or windows that have been loaded into a project. To do this, you create a new type of the required size based on an existing type, as shown in Figure 4–126.

*You can specify materials for door and window sub-elements in the Type Properties.*

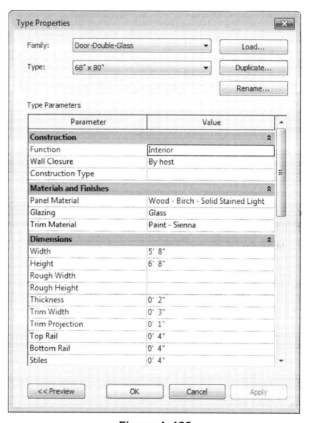

**Figure 4–126**

## How To: Create Additional Door and Window Sizes

1. Start the **Door** or **Window** command.
2. In the Type Selector, select the type you want to modify. In Properties, click ⊞ (Edit Type) or in the *Modify* tab> Properties panel, click ⊞ (Type Properties).

3. In the Type Properties dialog box, click **Duplicate**.
4. Type a new name for the element and click **OK**.
5. In the Type Properties dialog box, change the *Height* and *Width* parameters to match the size.
6. Click **OK** to close the dialog box. The new window or door type is now available for use.

---

**Hint: Measuring Distances**

As you are working in a project, you might need to know some existing distances. Two methods can be used: **Measure Between Two References** and **Measure Along An Element**. Both are available in the Quick Access Toolbar (as shown in Figure 4–127), as well as in the *Modify* tab>Measure panel.

**Figure 4–127**

- To measure between two references, select the references, which can include any snap point, wall lines, or other references (such as door center lines).

- To measure along an element, select the element you want to measure or use <Tab> to select other elements and then click to measure along all of them, as shown in Figure 4–128.

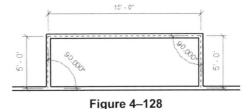

**Figure 4–128**

---

© 2016, ASCENT - Center for Technical Knowledge®

# 4.10 Change a Generic Floor/Ceiling/Roof to a Specific Type

The content that is recommended to review for the Change a Generic Floor/Ceiling/Roof to a Specific Type certification objective is covered in the following section:

- *Section 4.4 Create Elements such as a Floors, Ceilings, or Roofs*
- *Section 4.5 Create Elements Such as Floors, Ceilings, or Roofs - Ceilings*
- *Section 4.6 Create Elements Such as Floors, Ceilings, or Roofs - Roofs*

# 4.11 Attach Walls to a Roof or Ceiling

The content that is recommended to review for the Attach Walls to a Roof or Ceiling certification objective is covered in the following section:

- *Section 4.6 Create elements such as a floors, ceilings, or roofs - Roofs.*

# 4.12 Edit Room-aware Families

The content that is recommended to review for the Edit Room-aware Families certification objective is covered in *Chapter 3: Elements and Families*, in the following section:

- *Section 3.7 Use Family Creation Procedures*

© 2016, ASCENT - Center for Technical Knowledge®

# Chapter 5

# Views

This chapter includes instructional content to assist in your preparation for the following topic and objectives for the Autodesk® Revit® Architecture Certified Professional exam.

## Autodesk Certification Exam Objectives in this Chapter

| Exam Topic | Exam Objective | Section |
| --- | --- | --- |
| Views | • Define element properties in a schedule | • 5.1 |
| | • Control visibility | • 5.2 |
| | • Use levels | • 5.3 |
| | • Create a duplicate view for a plan, section, elevation, drafting view, etc. | • 5.4 |
| | • Create and manage legends | • 5.5 |
| | • Manage view position on sheets | • 5.6 |
| | • Organize and sort items in a schedule | • 5.7 |

# 5.1 Define Element Properties in a Schedule

Schedules extract information from a project and display it in table form. Each schedule is stored as a separate view and can be placed on sheets, as shown in Figure 5–1. Any changes you make to the project elements that affect the schedules are automatically updated in both views and sheets.

*Schedules are typically included in project templates. Ask your BIM Manager for more information about your company's schedules.*

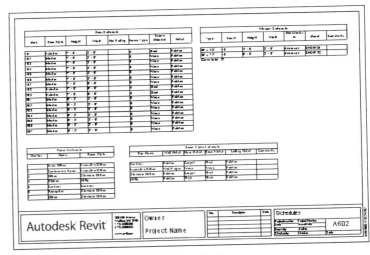

**Figure 5–1**

## How To: Work with Schedules

1. In the Project Browser, expand the *Schedules/Quantities* area, as shown in Figure 5–2, and double-click on the schedule you want to open.

**Figure 5–2**

2. Schedules are automatically filled out with the information stored in the instance and type parameters of related elements that are added to the model.
3. Fill out additional information in either the schedule or Properties.
4. Drag and drop the schedule onto a sheet.

© 2016, ASCENT - Center for Technical Knowledge®

# Modifying Schedules

Information in schedules is bi-directional:

- If you make changes to elements, the schedule automatically updates.

- If you change information in the cells of the schedule, it automatically updates the elements in the project.

## How To: Modify Schedule Cells

1. Open the schedule view.
2. Select the cell you want to change. Some cells have drop-down lists, as shown in Figure 5–3. Others have edit fields.

*If you change a Type Property in the schedule, it applies to all elements of that type. If you change an Instance Property, it only applies to that one element.*

| A | B | C | D |
|---|---|---|---|
| | | | Dimensions |
| Mark | Type | Width | Height |
| | Store Front Double | 8' - 3 1/2" | 9' - 4 1/4" |
| 101 | 36" x 84" | 3' - 0" | 7' - 0" |
| 102 | 24" x 82" | 3' - 0" | 7' - 0" |
| 103 | 30" x 80" | 3' - 0" | 6' - 8" |
| 104 | 30" x 84" | 3' - 0" | 6' - 8" |
| 105 | 32" x 84" | 3' - 0" | 6' - 8" |
| 106 | 36" x 80" | 3' - 0" | 6' - 8" |
| 107 | 36" x 84" | 3' - 0" | 6' - 8" |
| 108 | 36" x 84" | 3' - 0" | 7' - 0" |
| 109 | 36" x 84" | 3' - 0" | 7' - 0" |
| 110 | 72" x 84" | 6' - 0" | 7' - 0" |
| 111 | 72" x 82" | 6' - 0" | 6' - 10" |

**Figure 5–3**

3. Add the new information. The change is reflected in the schedule, on the sheet, and in the elements of the project.

- If you change a Type Property, an alert box opens, as shown in Figure 5–4.

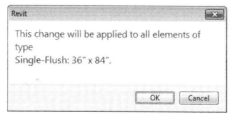

**Figure 5–4**

- When you select an element in a schedule, in the *Modify Schedule/Quantities* tab>Element panel, you can click

  (Highlight in Model). This opens a close-up view of the element with the Show Element(s) in View dialog box, as shown in Figure 5–5. Click **Show** to display more views of the element. Click **Close** to finish the command.

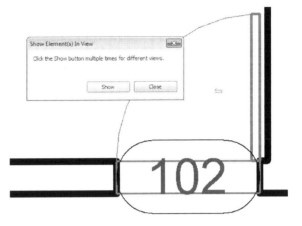

Figure 5–5

## Modifying a Schedule on a Sheet

Once you have placed a schedule on a sheet, you can manipulate it to fit the information into the available space. Select the schedule to display the controls that enable you to modify it, as shown in Figure 5–6.

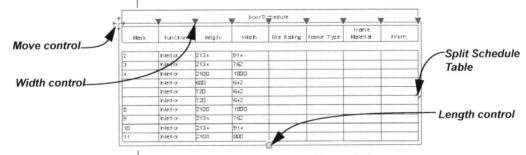

Figure 5–6

- The blue triangles modify the width of each column.

- The break mark splits the schedule into two parts.

- In a split schedule you can use the arrows in the upper left corner to move that portion of the schedule table. The control at the bottom of the first table changes the length of the table and impacts any connected splits, as shown in Figure 5–7.

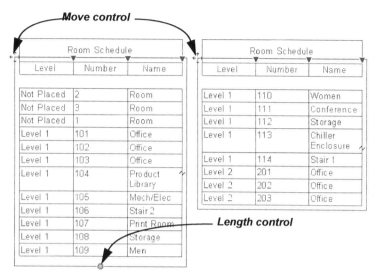

**Figure 5–7**

- To unsplit a schedule, drag the Move control from the side of the schedule that you want to unsplit back to the original column.

# Practice 5a | Define Element Properties in a Schedule

### Practice Objectives

- Update schedule information.
- Add a schedule to a sheet.

*Estimated time for completion: 10 minutes*

In this practice you will add information to a door schedule and to elements that are connected to the schedule. You will then place the schedule on a sheet, as shown in Figure 5–8.

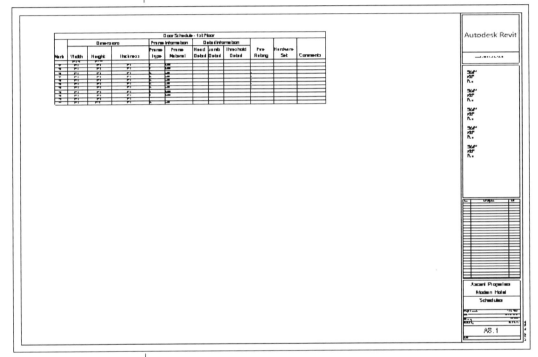

Figure 5–8

### Task 1 - Fill in schedules.

1. Open the project **Modern-Hotel-Schedules.rvt**.

2. In the Project Browser, expand *Schedules/Quantities*. Four schedules have been added to this project.

© 2016, ASCENT - Center for Technical Knowledge®

3. Double-click on **Door Schedule - 1st Floor** to open it. The existing doors in the project are already populated with some of the basic information included with the door, as shown in Figure 5–9.

| Mark | Dimensions | | | Frame Information | | Detail Information | | |
|------|------|------|------|------|------|------|------|------|
| | Width | Height | Thickness | Frame Type | Frame Material | Head Detail | Jamb Detail | Threshold Detail |
| | 8' - 3 1/2" | 9' - 4 1/4" | | | | | | |
| 101 | 3' - 0" | 7' - 0" | 0' - 2" | | | | | |
| 102 | 3' - 0" | 7' - 0" | 0' - 2" | | | | | |
| 103 | 3' - 0" | 6' - 8" | 0' - 2" | | | | | |
| 104 | 3' - 0" | 6' - 8" | 0' - 2" | | | | | |
| 105 | 3' - 0" | 6' - 8" | 0' - 2" | | | | | |
| 106 | 3' - 0" | 6' - 8" | 0' - 2" | | | | | |
| 107 | 3' - 0" | 6' - 8" | 0' - 2" | | | | | |

**Figure 5–9**

4. The first door in the list does not have a mark associated with it. Click in the empty *Mark* cell. In the *Modify Schedules/ Quantities* tab>Element panel, click ⬚ (Highlight in Model). The front door that is part of a curtain wall displays and is highlighted, even though storefront doors are typically not included in Door Schedules. There are no other views to display. Click **Close** in the Show Element(s) in View dialog box.

5. Select one of the single exterior doors other than the front door.

6. In Properties, set a *Frame Type* as **A**, *Frame Material* as **Steel**, and *Finish* as **Coated**.

7. Click ⬚ (Edit Type).

8. In the Type Properties dialog box, in the *Identity Data* area, set the *Fire Rating* to **A**.

9. Click **OK** to finish.

10. Return to the Door Schedule. (Press <Ctrl>+<Tab> to switch between open windows.)

11. Note that the *Frame Type* and *Frame Material* display for one door and the matching exterior doors also have a fire rating. Use the drop-down list and change the options for the matching doors, as shown in Figure 5–10.

### \<Door Schedule - 1st Floor\>

| A | B | C | D | E | F | G | H | I |
|---|---|---|---|---|---|---|---|---|
| | | Dimensions | | Frame Information | | | Detail Information | |
| Mark | Width | Height | Thickness | Frame Type | Frame Material | Head Detail | Jamb Detail | Threshold Detail |
| | 6' - 3 1/2" | 9' - 4 1/4" | | | | | | A |
| 101 | 3' - 0" | 7' - 0" | 0' - 2" | A | Steel | | | A |
| 102 | 3' - 0" | 7' - 0" | 0' - 2" | A | Steel | | | |
| 103 | 3' - 0" | 6' - 8" | 0' - 2" | | | | | |
| 104 | 3' - 0" | 6' - 8" | 0' - 2" | | | | | |

Figure 5–10

12. In the Door Schedule view, specify the *Fire Rating* for some other doors in the schedule. When you change the fire rating, you are prompted to change all elements of that type. Click **OK**.

13. Open the **Floor Plans: Floor 1** view.

14. Select the door to the office, then right-click and select **Select All Instances>In Entire Project**.

15. Look at the Status Bar beside ▽ (Filter) and note that more doors have been selected than are in the current view.

16. In Properties, set the *Frame Type* and *Frame Material* for these doors.

*No visual changes to the door display because these are just text properties.*

17. Press \<Esc\> to clear the selection when you are finished.

18. Switch back to the schedule view to see the additions. Not all of the doors are showing because the schedule has been limited to the 1st floor doors.

19. Save the project.

---

### Task 2 - Add schedules to a sheet.

---

1. In the Project Browser, open the sheet **A8.1 - Schedules**.

2. Drag and drop the **Door Schedule - 1st Floor** view onto the sheet, as shown in Figure 5–11.

© 2016, ASCENT - Center for Technical Knowledge®

*Your schedule may look different then the one shown in* Figure 5–11.

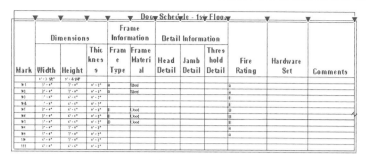

**Figure 5–11**

3. Zoom in and use the arrows at the top to modify the width of the columns so that the titles display correctly.

4. Click in empty space on the sheet to finish placing the schedule.

5. Switch back to the **Floor Plans: Floor 1** view and select the double-swing door at the kitchen.

6. In the Type Selector, change the size to **72" x 82"**. In Properties, add a Frame Type, Frame Material, and Finish.

7. Return to the Door Schedule sheet. The information is automatically populated, as shown in Figure 5–12.

| | Dimensions | | | Frame Information | |
|---|---|---|---|---|---|
| Mark | Width | Height | Thickness | Frame Type | Frame Material |
| | 8' - 3 1/2" | 9' - 4 1/4" | | | |
| 101 | 3' - 0" | 7' - 0" | 0' - 2" | A | Steel |
| 102 | 3' - 0" | 7' - 0" | 0' - 2" | A | Steel |
| 103 | 3' - 0" | 6' - 8" | 0' - 2" | | |
| 104 | 3' - 0" | 6' - 8" | 0' - 2" | | |
| 105 | 3' - 0" | 6' - 8" | 0' - 2" | B | Wood |
| 106 | 3' - 0" | 6' - 8" | 0' - 2" | B | Wood |
| 107 | 3' - 0" | 6' - 8" | 0' - 2" | B | Wood |
| 108 | 3' - 0" | 7' - 0" | 0' - 2" | | |
| 109 | 3' - 0" | 7' - 0" | 0' - 2" | | |
| 110 | 6' - 0" | 7' - 0" | 0' - 2" | | |
| 111 | 6' - 0" | 6' - 10" | 0' - 2" | C | Aluminum |

**Figure 5–12**

8. Return to the 3D view.

9. In the Quick Access Toolbar, click (Close Hidden Windows.

10. Save the project.

# 5.2 Control Visibility

Views are a powerful tool as they enable you to create multiple versions of a model without having to redraw building elements. For example, you can have views that are specifically used for working on the model, while other views are annotated and used for construction documents. Different disciplines can have different views that show only the features they require, as shown in Figure 5–13.

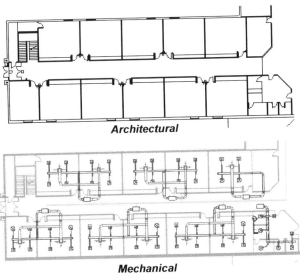

**Architectural**

**Mechanical**

**Figure 5–13**

The view display can be modified in the following locations:

- View Control Bar
- Properties
- Right-click menu
- Visibility/Graphic Overrides dialog box

© 2016, ASCENT - Center for Technical Knowledge®

## Hiding and Overriding Graphics

Two common ways to customize a view are to:

- Hide individual elements or categories

- Modify how graphics display for elements or categories (e.g., altering lineweight, color, or pattern)

An element is an individual item (i.e., one wall in a view), while a category includes all instances of a selected element (i.e., all walls in a view).

In the example shown in Figure 5–14, a Furniture Plan has been created by turning off the structural grids category, and then graying out all of the walls and columns.

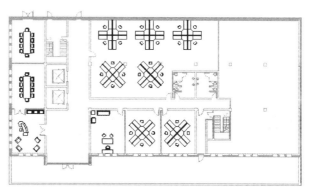

Figure 5–14

### How To: Hide Elements or Categories in a view

1. Select the elements or categories you want to hide.
2. Right-click and select **Hide in View>Elements** or **Hide in View>Category**, as shown in Figure 5–15.
3. The elements or categories are hidden in current view only.

*A quick way to hide entire categories is to select an element(s) and type **VH**.*

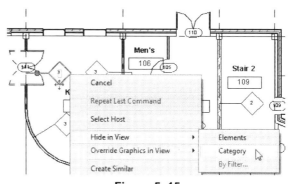

Figure 5–15

# How To: Override Graphics of Elements or Categories in a View

1. Select the element(s) you want to modify.
2. Right-click and select **Override Graphics in View>By Element** or **By Category**. The View-Specific Element (or Category) Graphics dialog box opens, as shown in Figure 5–16.

*The exact options in the dialog box vary depending on the type of elements selected.*

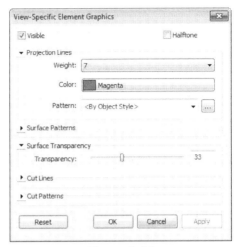

Figure 5–16

3. Select the changes you want to make and click **OK**.

## View-Specific Options

- Clearing the **Visible** option is the same as hiding the elements or categories.

- Selecting the **Halftone** option grays out the elements or categories.

- The options for Projection Lines, Surface Patterns, Cut Lines, and Cut Patterns include **Weight**, **Color**, and **Pattern**, as shown in Figure 5–16.

- **Surface Transparency** can be set by moving the slider bar, as shown in Figure 5–17.

Figure 5–17

© 2016, ASCENT - Center for Technical Knowledge®

- The View-Specific Category dialog box includes the **Open the Visibility Graphics dialog...** button which opens the full dialog box of options.

## The Visibility/Graphic Overrides dialog box

The options in the Visibility/Graphic Overrides dialog box (shown in Figure 5–18) control how every category and sub-category of elements is displayed per view.

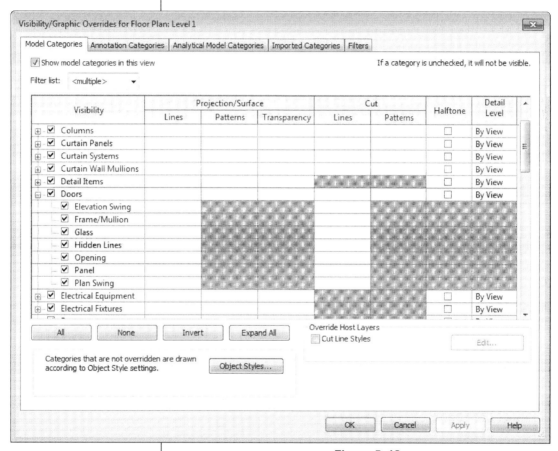

**Figure 5–18**

To open the Visibility/Graphic Overrides dialog box, type **VV** or **VG**. It is also available in Properties: in the *Graphics* area, beside *Visibility/Graphic Overrides*, click **Edit...**.

- The Visibility/Graphic Overrides are divided into *Model, Annotation, Analytical Model, Imported,* and *Filters* categories.

- Other tabs may be available if specific data has been included in the project, including *Design Options*, *Linked Files*, and *Worksets*.

- To limit the number of categories showing in the dialog box select a discipline from the *Filter list,* as shown in Figure 5–19

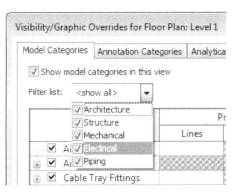

**Figure 5–19**

- To help you select categories, use the **All**, **None**, and **Invert** buttons. The **Expand All** button displays all of the sub-categories.

**Hint: Restoring Hidden Elements or Categories**

If you have hidden categories, you can display them using the Visibility/Graphic Overrides dialog box. To display hidden elements, however, you must reveal the elements first.

1. in the View Control Bar, click ⊡ (Reveal Hidden Elements). The border and all hidden elements are displayed in magenta, while visible elements in the view are grayed out, as shown in Figure 5–20.

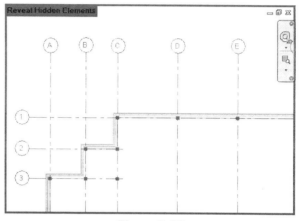

Figure 5–20

2. Select the hidden elements you want to restore, right-click, and select **Unhide in View>Elements** or **Unhide in View>Category**. Alternatively, in the *Modify |* contextual tab> Reveal Hidden Elements panel, click ⌦ (Unhide Element) or ⊞ (Unhide Category).

3. When you are finished, in the View Control Bar, click ⊡ (Close Reveal Hidden Elements) or, in the *Modify |* contextual tab> Reveal Hidden Elements panel click ☒ (Toggle Reveal Hidden Elements Mode).

# View Properties

The most basic properties of a view are accessed using the View Control Bar, shown in Figure 5–21. These include the *Scale*, *Detail Level*, and *Visual Style* options. Additional options include temporary overrides and other advanced settings.

Figure 5–21

Other modifications to views are available in Properties, as shown in Figure 5–22. These options include *Underlays*, *View Range*, and *Crop Regions*.

*The options in Properties vary according to the type of view. A plan view has different parameters than a 3D view.*

**Figure 5–22**

## View Range

The View Range sets the locations of cut planes and view depths in plans, as shown in a section in Figure 5–23.

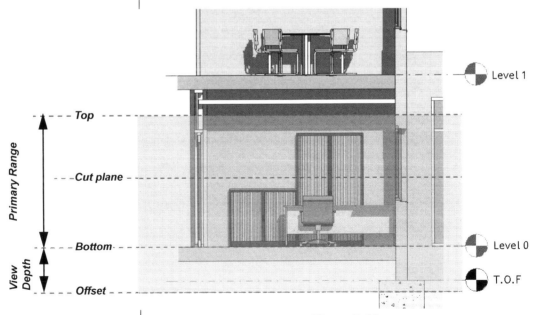

**Figure 5–23**

© 2016, ASCENT - Center for Technical Knowledge®

## How To: Set the View Range

1. In Properties, in the *Extents* area, beside *View Range*, select **Edit…**.
2. In the View Range dialog box, as shown in Figure 5–24, modify the Levels and Offsets for the *Primary Range* and *View Depth.*
3. Click **OK**.

*If the settings used cannot be represented graphically, a warning displays stating the inconsistency.*

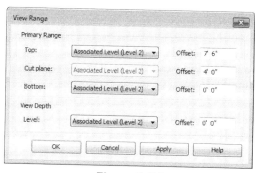

**Figure 5–24**

- A Reflected Ceiling Plan (RCP) is drawn as if the ceiling is reflected by a mirror on the floor so that the ceiling is the same orientation as the floor plan. The cutline is placed just below the ceiling to ensure that any windows and doors below do not display.

## Hint: Depth Clipping and Far Clipping

**Depth Clipping**, shown in Figure 5–25, is a viewing option which sets how sloped walls are displayed if the *View Range* of a plan is set to a limited view.

**Figure 5–25**

**Far Clipping** (shown in Figure 5–26) is available for section and elevation views.

**Figure 5–26**

© 2016, ASCENT - Center for Technical Knowledge®

## Crop Regions

Plans, sections, and elevations can all be modified by changing how much of the model is displayed in a view. One way to do this is to set the Crop Region. If there are dimensions, tags, or text near the desired crop region, you can also use the Annotation Crop Region to include these, as shown in Figure 5–27.

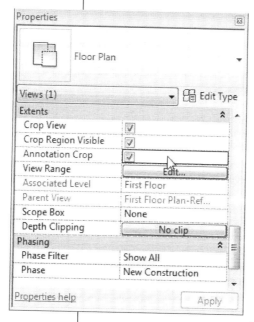

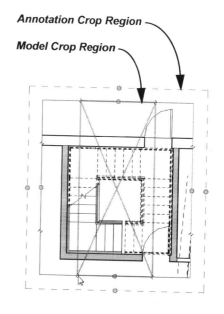

**Figure 5–27**

*Zoom out if you do not see the crop region when you set it to be displayed.*

- The crop region must be displayed to modify the size of the view. In the View Control Bar, click ⛶ (Show Crop Region) Alternatively, in Properties, in the *Extents* area, select **Crop Region Visible**. **Annotation Crop** is also available in this area.

- Resize the crop region using the ◦ control on each side of the region.

*Breaking the crop region is typically used with sections or details.*

- Click ↖ (Break Line) control to split the view into two regions, horizontally or vertically. Each part of the view can then be modified in size to display what is needed and be moved independently.

- It is a best practice to hide a crop region before placing a view on a sheet. In the View Control Bar, click ⛶ (Hide Crop Region).

### Hint: Applying View Templates

A powerful way to use views effectively is to set up a view and then save it as a View Template. To apply a View Template, right-click on a view in the Project Browser and select **Apply View Template Properties....** Then, in the Apply View Template dialog box, select a *Name* in the list (as shown in Figure 5–28) and click **OK**.

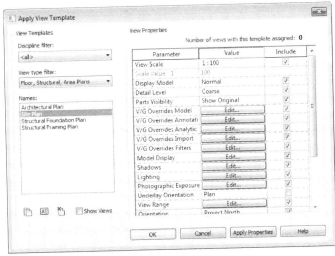

**Figure 5–28**

- View Templates can be preset in Properties so that changes cannot be made to the view.

© 2016, ASCENT - Center for Technical Knowledge®

# 5.3 Use Levels

Levels define stories and other vertical heights (such as a parapet or other reference heights), as shown in Figure 5–29. The default template includes two levels, but you can define as many levels in a project as required. They can go down (for basements) as well as up.

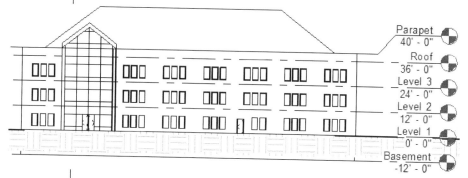

**Figure 5–29**

- You must be in an elevation or section view to define levels.

- Once you constrain an element to a level it moves with the level when the level is changed.

## How To: Create Levels

1. Open an elevation or section view.

2. In the *Architecture* tab>Datum panel, click ⬏ (Level), or type **LL**.

3. In the Type Selector, set the Level Head type if needed.

4. In the Options Bar, select or clear **Make Plan View** as required. You can also click **Plan View Types...** to select the types of views to create when you place the level.

5. In the *Modify | Place Level* tab>Draw panel, click either ⬏ (Pick Lines) to select an element or ⟋ (Line) to draw a level.

6. Continue adding levels as required.

- Level names are automatically incremented as you place them. This automatic numbering is most effective when you use names such as Floor 1, Floor 2, etc. (as opposed to First Floor, Second Floor, etc.). In addition, this makes it easier to find the view in the Project Browser.

- A fast way to create multiple levels is to use the ✎ (Pick Lines) option. In the Options Bar specify an *Offset,* select an existing level, and then pick above or below to place the new level, as shown in Figure 5–30.

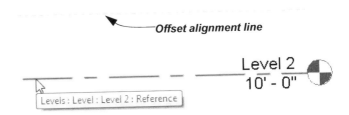

**Figure 5–30**

- When using the ✐ (Line) option, alignments and temporary dimensions help you place the line correctly, as shown in Figure 5–31.

*You can draw the level lines from left to right or right to left depending on where you want the bubble. However, ensure they are all drawn in the same direction.*

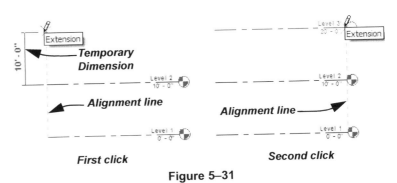

**Figure 5–31**

- You can also use ⟳ (Copy) to duplicate level lines. The level names are incremented but a plan view is not created.

© 2016, ASCENT - Center for Technical Knowledge®

## Modifying Levels

You can change levels using standard controls and temporary dimensions, as shown in Figure 5–32. You can also make changes in the Properties palette.

**Figure 5–32**

- ☑ ☐ (Hide / Show Bubble) displays on either end of the level line and toggles the level head symbol and level information on or off.

- 2D 3D (Switch to 3d / 2d extents) controls whether any movement or adjustment to the level line is reflected in other views (3D) or only affects the current view (2D).

- ↷ (Modify the level by dragging its model end) at each end of the line enables you to drag the level head to a new location.

- 🔒 🔓 (Create or remove a length or alignment constraint) controls whether the level is locked in alignment with the other levels. If it is locked and the level line is stretched, all of the other level lines stretch as well. If it is unlocked, the level line stretches independent of the other levels.

- Click ⌇ (Add Elbow) to add a jog to the level line as shown in Figure 5–33. Drag the shape handles to new locations as required. This is a view-specific change.

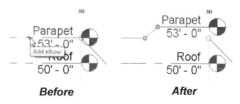

**Before**          **After**

**Figure 5–33**

© 2016, ASCENT - Center for Technical Knowledge®

- To change the level name or elevation, double-click on the information next to the level head, or select the level and modify the *Name* or *Elevation* fields in Properties, as shown in Figure 5–34.

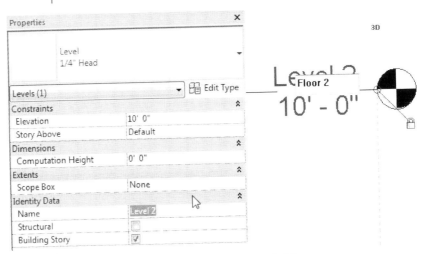

**Figure 5–34**

- When you rename a Level, an alert box opens, prompting you to rename the corresponding views as shown in Figure 5–35.

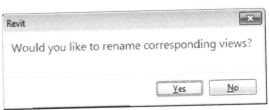

**Figure 5–35**

- The view is also renamed in the Project Browser.

---

**Hint: Copying Levels and Grids from other projects**

Levels and grid lines can be added by drawing over existing levels or grids in an imported or linked CAD file. It can also be copied and monitored from a linked Autodesk® Revit® file. Some projects might require both methods.

---

© 2016, ASCENT - Center for Technical Knowledge®

## Creating Plan Views

By default, when you place a level, plan views for that level are automatically created. If **Make Plan View** was toggled off when adding the level, or if the level was copied, you can create plan views to match the levels.

- Level heads with views are blue and level heads without views are black, as shown in Figure 5–36.

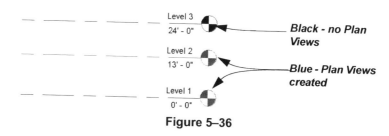

Figure 5–36

*Typically, you do not need to create plan views for levels that specify data, such as the top of a storefront window or the top of a parapet.*

### How To: Create Plan Views

1. In the *View* tab>Create panel, expand 🗐 (Plan Views) and select the type of plan view you want to create, as shown on the left in Figure 5–37.
2. In the New Plan dialog box (shown on the right in Figure 5–37), select the levels for which you want to create plan views.

*Hold down <Ctrl> to select more than one level.*

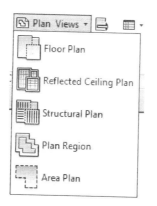
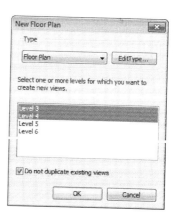

Figure 5–37

3. Click **OK**.

# Practice 5b | # Use Levels

## Practice Objective

- Add and modify levels.

*Estimated time for completion: 10 minutes*

In this practice you will set up the levels needed in the Modern Hotel project, including the floors, the top of the footing, and the parapet, as shown in Figure 5–38.

**Figure 5–38**

## Task 1 - Add and Modify Levels.

1. In the practice files folder, open **Modern-Hotel-Start.rvt**.

2. Open the **Elevations (Building Elevation): North** view.

© 2016, ASCENT - Center for Technical Knowledge®

3. The project has two existing levels named **Level 1** and **Level 2**. These were defined in the template.

4. Zoom in on the level names.

5. Double-click on the name Level 1 and rename it as **Floor 1** as shown in Figure 5–39. Press <Enter>.

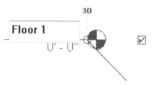

**Figure 5–39**

6. Click **Yes** (press <Enter> or type **Y**) when prompted to rename the corresponding views.

7. Repeat the process and rename *Level 2* as **Floor 2**. Double-click on the height of Floor 2 (10'-0") and change it to **18'- 0"**.

8. In the *Architecture* tab>Datum panel, click (Level).

9. In the *Modify | Place Level* tab>Draw panel, click (Pick Lines). In the Options Bar, set the *Offset* to **12' - 0"**.

10. Hover the cursor over the level line of **Floor 2** and move the cursor slightly upward so that the offset level line is displayed above the **Floor 2** level. Click to create the new level **Floor 3**.

11. Create additional levels until there are a total of eight levels above Floor 1 (up to Floor 9).

12. Rename *Floor 9* as **Roof**. (Rename the corresponding views.)

13. In the Options Bar, clear the **Make Plan View** option and set the *Offset* to **5' 0"**. Create one additional level above the highest level, **Roof**. This level does not need a plan view.

14. Rename the top level as **Parapet**, as shown in Figure 5–40.

**Figure 5–40**

15. Add two levels below **Floor 1**. Name them **Basement** and **T.O. Footing** and set the heights as shown in Figure 5–41. You can modify the levels for clarity using controls such as **Add Elbow**.

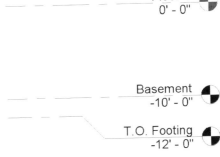

**Figure 5–41**

16. Zoom out to display the entire project.

17. Save the project.

© 2016, ASCENT - Center for Technical Knowledge®

# 5.4 Create a Duplicate View for a Plan, Section, Elevation, Drafting View, etc.

Once you have created a model, you do not have to redraw the elements at different scales or copy them so that they can be used on more than one sheet. Instead, you can duplicate the required views and modify them to suit your needs.

## Duplication Types

**Duplicate** creates a copy of the view that only includes the building elements, as shown in Figure 5–42. Annotation and detailing are not copied into the new view. Building model elements automatically change in all views, but view-specific changes made to the new view are not reflected in the original view.

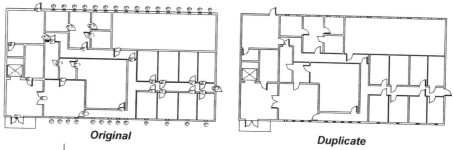

*Original*                                          *Duplicate*

Figure 5–42

**Duplicate with Detailing** creates a copy of the view and includes all annotation and detail elements (such as tags), as shown in Figure 5–43. Any annotation or view-specific elements created in the new view are not reflected in the original view.

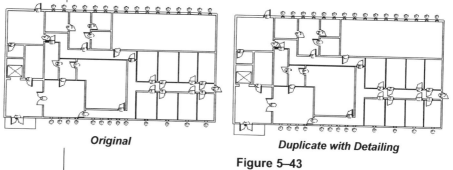

*Original*                          *Duplicate with Detailing*

Figure 5–43

© 2016, ASCENT - Center for Technical Knowledge®

**Duplicate as a Dependent** creates a copy of the view and links it to the original (parent) view, as shown in the Project Browser in Figure 5–44. View-specific changes made to the overall view, such as changing the *Scale*, are also reflected in the dependent (child) views and vice-versa.

**Figure 5–44**

- Use dependent views when the building model is so large that you need to split the building onto separate sheets, while ensuring that the views are all same scale.

- If you want to separate a dependent view from the original view, right-click on the dependent view and select **Convert to independent view**.

## How To: Create Duplicate Views

1. Open the view you want to duplicate.
2. In the *View* tab>Create panel, expand **Duplicate View** and select the type of duplicate view you want to create, as shown in Figure 5–45.

*Most types of views can be duplicated.*

**Figure 5–45**

- Alternatively, you can right-click on a view in the Project Browser and select the type of duplicate that you want to use, as shown in Figure 5–46.

**Figure 5–46**

© 2016, ASCENT - Center for Technical Knowledge®

*You can also press <F2> to start the **Rename** command.*

- To rename a view, right-click on the new view in the Project Browser and select **Rename**. In the Rename View dialog box, type in the new name, as shown in Figure 5–47.

**Figure 5–47**

© 2016, ASCENT - Center for Technical Knowledge®

# Practice 5c

# Control Visibility and Create a Duplicate View

*Estimated time for completion: 10 minutes*

## Practice Objectives

- Duplicate views.
- Modify crop regions.
- Change the visibility and graphic display of elements in views.

In this practice you will duplicate views and then modify them by changing the scale and crop region, hiding some elements, and changing some elements to halftone to prepare them to be used in construction documents. The finished views of the second floor are shown in Figure 5–48, which is a model of the completed building.

**Before**

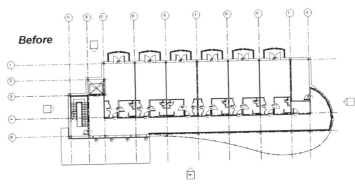

**After**

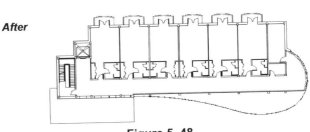

Figure 5–48

## Task 1 - Duplicate and modify the first floor plan view.

1. Open the project **Modern-Hotel-Display.rvt**.

2. Open the **Floor Plans: Floor 1** view. This view includes a variety of tags.

© 2016, ASCENT - Center for Technical Knowledge®

3. In the Project Browser, right-click on the **Floor Plans: Floor 1** view and select **Duplicate View>Duplicate**. This creates a view without all of the tags, but includes the grids and elevation markers.

4. Right-click on the new view and rename it to **Floor 1 Overall**.

5. In the View Control Bar, change the *Scale* to **1/16"=1'-0"**. All of the annotations become larger, as they need to plot correctly at this scale.

6. In the View Control Bar, click 🔲 (Show Crop Region).

7. Select the crop region and drag the control on the top until the pool house displays, as shown in Figure 5–49.

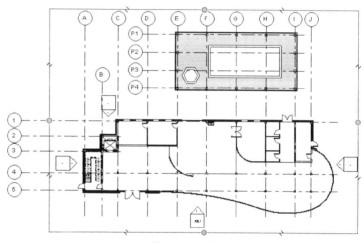

**Figure 5–49**

8. In the View Control Bar, click 🔲 (Hide Crop Region)

9. Select the four horizontal pool grid lines (P1-P4).

10. Right-click and select **Hide in View> Elements**. Only the selected grid lines are hidden.

11. Select one of the elevation markers.

12. Right-click and select **Hide in View>Category**. All of the elevation markers are hidden.

13. In the View Control Bar, click 🔲 (Hide Crop Region).

14. Zoom out to display the entire view. (Hint: Use the shortcuts **ZF** or **ZE**, or double-click the mouse wheel.)

15. Duplicate **Floor 1** again (without Detailing). Rename this view **Floor 1 - Reference**. You will use this later to place callouts and sections.

16. Save the project.

### Task 2 - Duplicate and modify a second floor plan view.

1. Open the **Floor Plans: Floor 2** view.

2. In the Project Browser, right-click on the same view and select **Duplicate View>Duplicate**. This creates a new view without any annotation.

3. Rename this view to **Typical Guest Room Floor Plan**.

4. Select one of the grids and type **VH** (Hide in View Category).

5. Turn on the crop region and bring it in close to the building on all sides. If any of the elevation markers still display, hide them.

6. Turn off the crop region.

7. Select one of the railings along the balconies. Right-click and select **Select All Instances>Visible in View**. The railings are selected as shown in Figure 5–50.

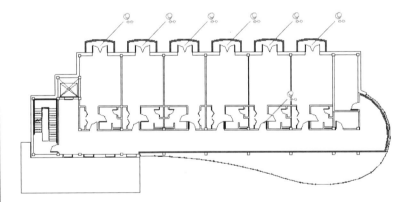

Figure 5–50

© 2016, ASCENT - Center for Technical Knowledge®

8. Right-click again and select **Override Graphics in View > By Element...**

9. In the View-Specific Element Graphics dialog box select **Halftone** and click **OK**.

10. Click in the view to release the selection. The railings are now gray and not as prominent.

11. Close any other projects that may be open.

12. In the Quick Access Toolbar, click ▣ (Close Hidden Windows). Only the Typical Guest Room Floor Plan view should be open.

13. Open the **Floor Plans: Floor 2** view again.

14. Type **WT** to tile the two windows and then type **ZA** so the model displays fully in the view so that you can see the differences in the views.

15. Save the project.

# 5.5 Create and Manage Legends

A legend is a separate view in which you can list the symbols used in your project and provide explanatory notes next to them. They are typically in a table format. Legends can include a list of all annotation symbols you use in your drawings, such as door, window, and wall tags (as shown in Figure 5–51), as well as a list of materials, or elevations of window types used in the project.

| Annotation Legend | |
| --- | --- |
| (grid bubble symbol) | Grid Bubble |
| Name Elevation (level symbol) | Level |
| Room name 101 150SF | Room Tag with Area |
| (section bubble symbol) | Section Bubble |
| (window tag symbol) | Window Tag |
| (wall tag symbol) | Wall Tag |
| (door tag symbol) | Door Tag |
| (callout bubble symbol) | Callout Bubble |
| Room name 150SF | Area Tag |

**Figure 5–51**

• You use ⌐ (Detail Lines) and **A** (Text) to create the table and explanatory notes. Once you have a legend view, you can use commands, such as (Legend Component), (Detail Component), and (Symbol), to place elements in the drawing.

• Unlike other views, legend views can be attached to more than one sheet.

• You can set a legend's scale in the View Status Bar.

• Elements in legends can be dimensioned.

© 2016, ASCENT - Center for Technical Knowledge®

## How To: Create a Legend

1. In the *View* tab>Create panel, expand 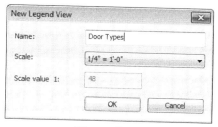 (Legends) and click (Legend) or in the Project Browser, right-click on the *Legends* area title and select **New Legend**.
2. In the New Legend View dialog box, enter a name and select a scale for the legend, as shown in Figure 5–52, and click **OK**.

**Figure 5–52**

3. Place the components in the view first, and then sketch the outline of the table when you know the sizes. Use **Ref Planes** to line up the components.

## How To: Use Legend Components

1. In the *Annotate* tab>Detail panel, expand (Component) and click (Legend Component).
2. In the Options Bar, select the *Family* type that you want to use, as shown in Figure 5–53.

   - This list contains all of the elements in a drawing that can be used in a legend. For example, you might want to display the elevation of all door types used in the project.

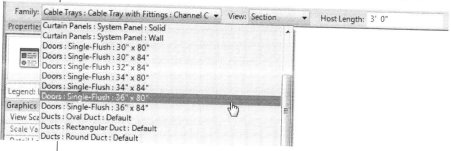

**Figure 5–53**

3. Select the *View* of the element that you want to use. For example, you might want to display the section of the floors or roofs, and the front elevation of the doors (as shown in Figure 5–54) and windows.

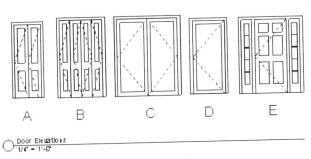

**Figure 5–54**

4. For section elements (such as walls, floors, and roofs), type a distance for the *Host Length*.

• Elements that are full size, such as planting components or doors, come in at their full size.

© 2016, ASCENT - Center for Technical Knowledge®

# Practice 5d

# Create and Manage Legends

*Estimated time for completion: 10 minutes*

### Practice Objective

- Create legends using legend components and text.

In this practice you will create door and window legends (as shown in Figure 5–55), by creating legend views, adding legend components, and labeling the door and window types with text.

13

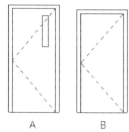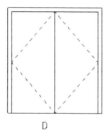

A       B       C       D       E       F

**Figure 5–55**

### Task 1 - Add window and door legends.

1. Open the project **Modern-Hotel-Legends.rvt**.

2. In the *View* tab>Create panel, expand ▦ (Legends) and click ▦ (Legend) to create a new Legend view.

3. Name it **Window Elevations** and set the *Scale* to **1/4"=1'-0"**.

4. In the *Annotate* tab>Detail panel, expand ▱ (Component) and click ⊐⊧ (Legend Component).

© 2016, ASCENT - Center for Technical Knowledge®

5. In the Options Bar, set *Family* to **Windows : Casement 3 x 3 with Trim: 48" x 48"** and *View* to **Elevation: Front**. Place the component in the view. The window displays, as shown in Figure 5–56.

6. In the *Annotate* tab>Text panel, click **A** (Text).

7. In the Type Selector, select **Text: 1/8" Arial Narrow** and add the window number 13 under the window, as shown in Figure 5–56.

13

**Figure 5–56**

8. Create another Legend view. Name it **Door Elevations** and set the *Scale* to **1/4"=1'-0"**.

9. In the Legend view, click (Legend Component) and add the elevations of the doors used in the project.

10. Label the doors as shown in Figure 5–57.

   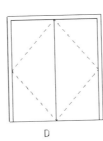  

A      B      C      D      E      F

**Figure 5–57**

11. Save the project.

© 2016, ASCENT - Center for Technical Knowledge®

# 5.6 Manage View Position on Sheets

The process of adding views to a sheet is simple. Drag and drop a view from the Project Browser onto the sheet. The new view on the sheet is displayed at the scale specified in the original view. The view title displays the name, number, and scale of the view, as shown in Figure 5–58.

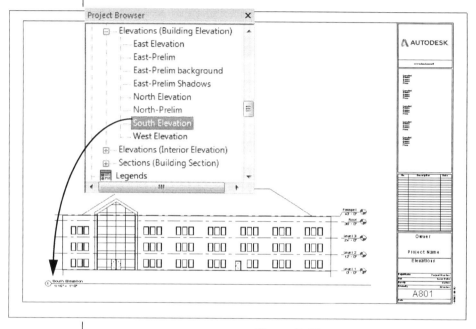

Figure 5–58

## How To: Place Views on Sheets

*Alignment lines from existing views display to help you place additional views.*

1. Set up the view as you want it to display on the sheet, including the scale and visibility of elements.
2. Create or open the sheet where you want to place the view.
3. Select the view in the Project Browser, and drag and drop it onto the sheet.
4. The center of the view is attached to the cursor. Click to place it on the sheet.

## Placing Views on Sheets

- Views can only be placed on a sheet once. However, you can duplicate the view and place that copy on a sheet.

- Views on a sheet are associative. They automatically update to reflect changes to the project.

- Each view on a sheet is listed under the sheet name in the Project Browser, as shown in Figure 5–59.

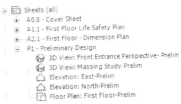

**Figure 5–59**

- You can also use two other methods to place views on sheets:

  - In the Project Browser, right-click on the sheet name and select **Add View...**

  - In the *View* tab>Sheet Composition panel click 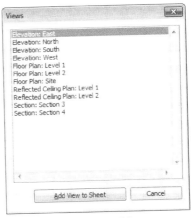 (Place View).

  Then, in the Views dialog box (shown in Figure 5–60), select the view you want to use and click **Add View to Sheet.**

*This method lists only those views which have not yet been placed on a sheet.*

**Figure 5–60**

© 2016, ASCENT - Center for Technical Knowledge®

- To remove a view from a sheet, select it and press <Delete>. Alternatively, in the Project Browser, expand the individual sheet information to show the views, right-click on the view name and select **Remove From Sheet**.

## Moving Views and View Titles

*You can also use the **Move** command or the arrow keys to move a view.*

- To move a view on a sheet, select the edge of the view and drag it to a new location. The view title moves with the view.

- To move only the view title, select the title and drag it to the new location.

- To modify the length of the line under the title name, select the edge of the view and drag the controls, as shown in Figure 5–61.

Figure 5–61

- To change the title of a view on a sheet without changing its name in the Project Browser, in Properties, in the *Identity Data* area, type a new title for the *Title on Sheet* parameter, as shown in Figure 5–62.

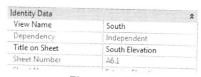

Figure 5–62

## Rotating Views

- When creating a vertical sheet, you can rotate the view on the sheet by 90 degrees. Select the view and set the direction of rotation in the *Rotation on Sheet* drop-down list in the Options Bar, as shown in Figure 5–63.

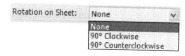

Figure 5–63

- To rotate a view to an angle other than 90 degrees, open the view, turn on and select the crop region and use the **Rotate** command to change the angle.

## Working Inside Views

To make small changes to a view while working on a sheet:

- Double-click *inside* the view to activate it.
- Double-click *outside* the view to deactivate it.

Only elements within the viewport are available for modification. The rest of the sheet is grayed out, as shown in Figure 5–64.

*Only use this method for small changes. Significant changes should be made directly in the view.*

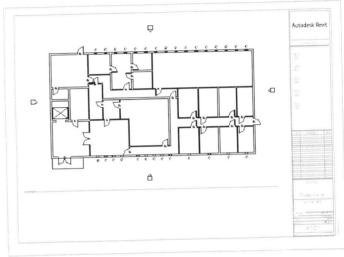

**Figure 5–64**

- You can activate and deactivate views by right-clicking on the view or by using the tools found on the *Modify | Viewports* and *Views* tab>Sheet Composition panel.

- Changes you make to elements when a view is activated also display in the original view.

**Enhanced**
in 2017

- If you are unsure which sheet a view is on, right-click on the view in the Project Browser and select **Open Sheet**. This item is grayed out if the view has not been placed on a sheet and is not available for schedules and legends which can be placed on more than one sheet.

## Resizing Views on Sheets

Each view displays the extents of the model or the elements contained in the crop region. If the view does not fit on a sheet (as shown in Figure 5–65), you might need to crop the view or move the elevation markers closer to the building.

© 2016, ASCENT - Center for Technical Knowledge®

*If the extents of the view change dramatically based on a scale change or a crop region, it is easier to delete the view on the sheet and drag it over again.*

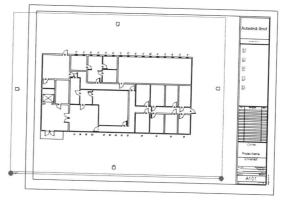

**Figure 5–65**

---

**Hint: Add an Image to a Sheet**

Company logos and renderings saved to image files (such as .JPG and .PNG) can be added directly on a sheet or in a view.

1. In the *Insert* tab>Import panel, click  (Image).
2. In the Import Image dialog box, select and open the image file. The extents of the image display as shown in Figure 5–66.

**Figure 5–66**

3. Place the image where you want it.
4. The image is displayed. Pick one of the grips and extend it to modify the size of the image.

- In Properties, you can adjust the height and width and also set the *Draw Layer* to either **Background** or **Foreground**, as shown in Figure 5–67.

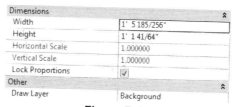

**Figure 5–67**

- You can select more than one image at a time and move them as a group to the background or foreground.

---

# Practice 5e

# Manage View Position on Sheets

### Practice Objectives

- Set up project properties.
- Create sheets individually and use placeholder sheets.
- Modify views to prepare them to be placed on sheets.
- Place views on sheets.

*Estimated time for completion: 20 minutes*

In this practice you will complete the project information, add new sheets and use placeholder sheets to add sheets to the project. You will fill in title block information. You will then add views to sheets, such as the Wall Sections sheet shown in Figure 5–68. Complete as many sheets as you have time for.

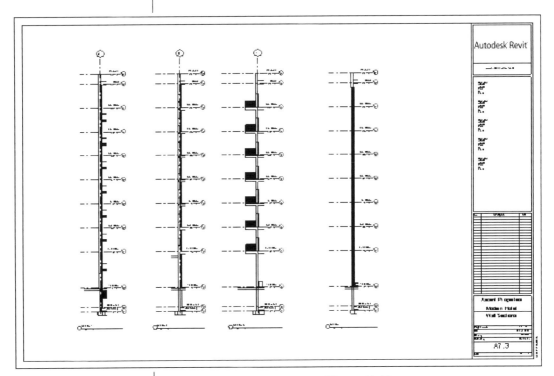

Figure 5–68

© 2016, ASCENT - Center for Technical Knowledge®

### Task 1 - Complete the project information.

1. Open the project **Modern-Hotel-Sheets.rvt**. This file contains some additional elements that are required for the practice.

2. In the *Manage* tab>Settings panel, click ⬚ (Project Information).

3. In the Project Properties dialog box, in the *Other* area, set the following parameters:

*These properties are used across the entire sheet set and do not need to be entered on each sheet.*

   - Project Issue Date: **Issue Date**
   - Project Status: **Design Development**
   - Client Name: **Ascent Properties**
   - Project Address: Click **Edit...** and enter your address
   - Project Name: **Modern Hotel**
   - Project Number: **1234-567**

4. Click **OK**.

5. Save the project.

### Task 2 - Create sheets.

1. In the *View* tab>Sheet Composition panel, click ⬚ (Sheet).

2. In the New Sheet dialog box click **Load...**.

3. In the Load Family dialog box, navigate to the *Titlesblocks* folder and select **D 22 x 34 Horizontal**. Click **Open**.

4. In the *Select placeholder sheets:* area, **New** is selected by default. Click **OK**.

5. Zoom in on the lower right corner of the title block. The Project Properties filled out earlier are automatically added to the sheet.

6. Continue filling out the title block, as shown in Figure 5–69. Changing the sheet number and sheet name also changes the name in the Project Browser. Certain labels can be entered on a per sheet basis, such as the *Sheet Name*, *Sheet Number*, *Drawn by*, and *Checked by*. Leave the *Issue Date* as is.

*The Scale is automatically entered when a view is inserted onto a sheet. If a sheet has multiple views with different scales, the scale displays **As Indicated**.*

Figure 5–69

7. In the Sheet Composition panel, click (Sheet). Using the D-sized title block, create the following new sheets:

- A2.1 - 1st Floor Plan Overall
- A2.2 - 1st Floor Plan
- A2.3 - 2nd-8th Floor Plan (Typical)

8. Click (Sheet). This time, in the *Select placeholder sheets:* area, select one of the placeholder sheets and click **OK**.

9. In the Project Browser, expand *Sheets (all)*. Note that the selected placeholder sheet and the other sheets that you created are displayed.

10. Click (Sheet) again. Select all of the other placeholder sheets (use <Ctrl> or <Shift> to select multiple sheets) and click **OK**.

© 2016, ASCENT - Center for Technical Knowledge®

The rest of the sheets are placed in the project, as shown in Figure 5–70.

*Having typical placeholder sheets created in the company template is a timesaver. Another option is having the sheets already in the template project.*

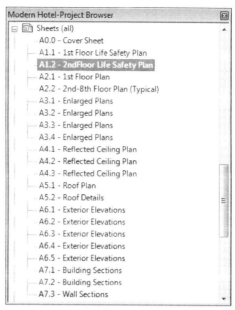

**Figure 5–70**

## Task 3 - Set up and add views to sheets.

1. Duplicate (no detailing) the **Floor Plans: Floor 1** and **Floor 2** views and name them **1st Floor-Life Safety Plan** and **2nd-8th Floor-Life Safety Plan**.

2. Open the new views and do the following:

   *The crop region defines the extent of the view on the sheet.*

   - Hide all elements except the actual building elements.
   - Turn on the crop region and ensure it is tight up against the building.
   - Turn the crop region off.

3. Open the appropriate sheet and drag and drop the corresponding Life Safety Plans onto it.

4. Rename sheet **2nd Floor Life Safety Plan** as **2nd-8th Floor Life Safety Plan**.

5. Repeat the process of adding views to sheets using the views you have available.

- Modify crop regions and hide unnecessary elements in the views, as shown in Figure 5–71. Turn off crop regions after you have modified them.

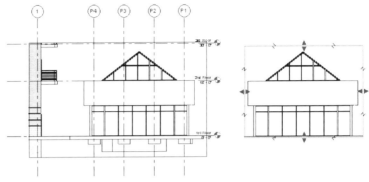

Figure 5–71

- Verify the scale of a view in Properties before placing it on a sheet.
- Use alignment lines to help place multiple views on one sheet, as shown in Figure 5–72.

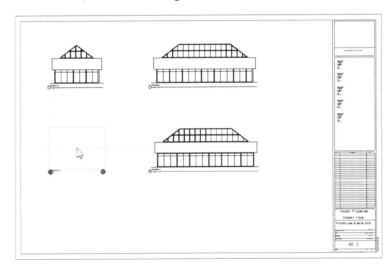

Figure 5–72

- Change the view title, if required, to more accurately describe what is on the sheet.

- To make minor changes to a view once it is on a sheet, double-click inside the viewport to activate the view. To return to the sheet, double-click outside the viewport to deactivate the view.

6. Once you have added callout, section, or elevation views to sheets, switch back to the **Floor Plans: Floor 1** view. Zoom in on one of the markers. Note that it has now been automatically assigned a detail and sheet number, as shown in Figure 5–73.

*Your numbers might not exactly match the numbers in the example.*

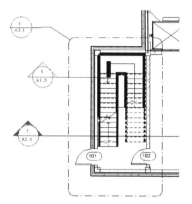

**Figure 5–73**

7. Save the project.

# 5.7 Organize and Sort Items in a Schedule

A Building Component schedule is a table view of selected parameters of an element such as air terminals, structural foundations or doors, as shown in Figure 5–74. They can include instance parameters that are automatically filled in (such as the **Height** and **Width**) and type parameters (such as the **Fire Rating** and **Frame**) which need to be added.

| | | | | | | | |
|---|---|---|---|---|---|---|---|
| | | | | <Door Schedule> | | | |
| A | B | C | D | E | F | G | H |
| Mark | Height | Width | Fire Rating | Frame Type | Frame Material | Finish | Function |
| 2 | 7' - 0" | 10' - 0" | A | A | Steel | Brushed | Exterior |
| 3 | 6' - 8" | 3' - 0" | B | B | Wood | Paint | Interior |
| 4 | 6' - 8" | 3' - 0" | B | B | Wood | Paint | Interior |
| 5 | 6' - 8" | 3' - 0" | B | B | Wood | Paint | Interior |
| 6 | 6' - 8" | 3' - 0" | B | B | Wood | Paint | Interior |

**Figure 5–74**

## How To: Create a Building Component Schedule

1. In the *View* tab>Create panel, expand ⊞ (Schedules) and click ⊞ (Schedule/Quantities) or in the Project Browser, right-click on the Schedule/Quantities node and select **New Schedule/Quantities**.
2. In the New Schedule dialog box, select the type of schedule you want to create (e.g., Doors) from the *Category* list, as shown in Figure 5–75.

*In the Filter list drop-down list, you can specify the discipline(s) to show only the categories that you want to display.*

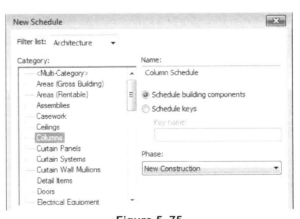

**Figure 5–75**

© 2016, ASCENT - Center for Technical Knowledge®

3. Type a new *Name*, if the default does not suit.
4. Select **Schedule building components.**
5. Specify the *Phase* as required.
6. Click **OK**.
7. Fill out the information in the Schedule Properties dialog box. This includes the information in the *Fields*, *Filter*, *Sorting/Grouping*, *Formatting*, and *Appearance* tabs.
8. Once you have entering the schedule properties, click **OK**. A schedule report is created in its own view.

## Fields Tab

In the *Fields* tab, you can select from a list of available fields and organize them in the order in which you want them to display in the schedule, as shown in Figure 5–76.

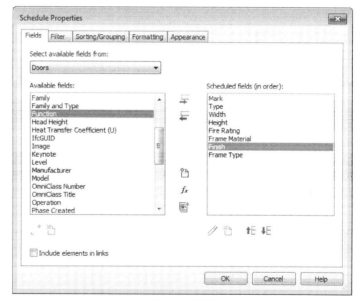

Figure 5–76

## How To: Fill out the Fields Tab

1. In the *Available fields* area, select one or more fields you want to add to the schedule and click ⇥ (Add parameter(s)). The field(s) are placed in the *Scheduled fields (in order)* area.
2. Continue adding fields, as required.

   • Click ⇤ (Remove parameter(s)) to move a field from the *Scheduled fields* area back to the *Available fields* area.

   • Use ⬆E (Move parameter up) and ⬇E (Move parameter down) to change the order of the scheduled fields.

*You can also double-click on a field to move it from the Available fields to the Scheduled fields list.*

## Other Fields Tab Options

| | |
|---|---|
| **Select available fields from** | Enables you to select additional category fields for the specified schedule. The available list of fields depends on the original category of the schedule. Typically, they include room information. |
| **Include elements in links** | Includes elements that are in files linked to the current project, so that their elements can be included in the schedule. |
| **(New parameter)** | Adds a new field according to your specification. New fields can be placed by instance or by type. |
| $f_x$ **(Add Calculated parameter)** | Enables you to create a field that uses a formula based on other fields. |
| **(Combine parameters)** | Enables you to combine two or more parameters in one column. You can put any fields together even if they are used in another column. |
| **(Edit parameter)** | Enables you to edit custom fields. This is grayed out if you select a standard field. |
| **(Delete parameter)** | Deletes selected custom fields. This is grayed out if you select a standard field. |

**New**  in **2017**

## Filter Tab

In the *Filter* tab, you can set up filters so that only elements meeting specific criteria are included in the schedule. For example, you might only want to show information for one level, as shown in Figure 5–77. You can create filters for up to eight values. All values must be satisfied for the elements to display.

**Figure 5–77**

© 2016, ASCENT - Center for Technical Knowledge®

- The parameter you want to use as a filter must be included in the schedule. You can hide the parameter once you have completed the schedule, if required.

| | |
|---|---|
| **Filter by** | Specifies the field to filter. Not all fields are available to be filtered. |
| **Condition** | Specifies the condition that must be met. This includes options such as **equal**, **not equal**, **greater than**, and **less than**. |
| **Value** | Specifies the value of the element to be filtered. You can select from a drop-down list of appropriate values. For example, if you set *Filter By* to **Level**, it displays the list of levels in the project. |

## Sorting/ Grouping Tab

In the *Sorting/Grouping* tab, you can set how you want the information to be sorted, as shown in Figure 5–78. For example, you can sort by **Mark** (number) and then **Type**.

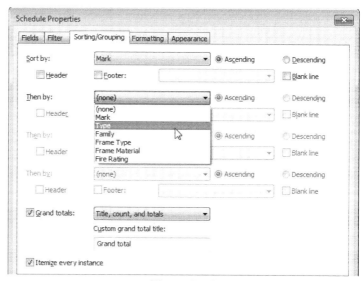

**Figure 5–78**

| | |
|---|---|
| **Sort by** | Enables you to select the field(s) you want to sort by. You can select up to four levels of sorting. |
| **Ascending/ Descending** | Sorts fields in **Ascending** or **Descending** order. |
| **Header/ Footer** | Enables you to group similar information and separate it by a **Header** with a title and/or a **Footer** with quantity information. |
| **Blank line** | Adds a blank line between groups. |
| **Grand totals** | Selects which totals to display for the entire schedule. You can specify a name to display in the schedule for the Grand total. |
| **Itemize every instance** | If selected, displays each instance of the element in the schedule. If not selected, displays only one instance of each type, as shown in Figure 5–79. |

| <Window Schedule> | | | | | | |
|---|---|---|---|---|---|---|
| A | B | C | D | E | F | G |
| Type | Count | Height | Width | Manufacturer | Model | Comments |
| 36 x 36 | 6 | 3' 0" | 3' - 0" | Anderson | FX3636 | |
| 36" x 48" | 7 | 4' - 0" | 3' - 0" | Anderson | FX3648 | |
| Grand total: 13 | | | | | | |

**Figure 5–79**

## Formatting Tab

In the *Formatting* tab, you can control how the headers of each field display, as shown in Figure 5–80.

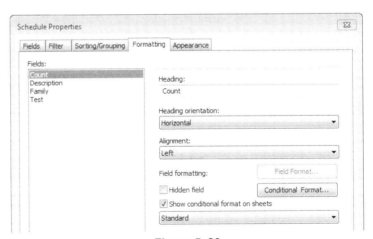

**Figure 5–80**

© 2016, ASCENT - Center for Technical Knowledge®

| | |
|---|---|
| **Fields** | Enables you to select the field for which you want to modify the formatting. |
| **Heading** | Enables you to change the heading of the field if you want it to be different from the field name. For example, you might want to replace **Mark** (a generic name) with the more specific **Door Number** in a door schedule. |
| **Heading orientation** | Enables you to set the heading on sheets to **Horizontal** or **Vertical**. This does not impact the schedule view. |
| **Alignment** | Aligns the text in rows under the heading to be **Left**, **Right**, or **Center**. |
| **Field Format...** | Sets the units format for the length, area, volume, angle, or number field. By default, this is set to use the project settings. |
| **Conditional Format...** | Sets up the schedule to display visual feedback based on the conditions listed. |
| **Hidden field** | Enables you to hide a field. For example, you might want to use a field for sorting purposes, but not have it display in the schedule. You can also modify this option in the schedule view later. |
| **Show conditional format on sheets** | Select if you want the color code set up in the Conditional Format dialog box to display on sheets. |
| **Calculation options** | Select the type of calculation you want to use. All values in a field are:<br>• **Standard** - Calculated separately.<br>• **Calculate totals** - Added together.<br>• **Calculate minimum** - Reviewed and only the smallest amount is displayed.<br>• **Calculate maximum** - Reviewed and only the largest amount is displayed.<br>• **Calculate minimum and maximum** - Reviewed and both the smallest and largest amounts are displayed.<br>• This is often used with rebar sets. |

**Enhanced**
in 2017

## Appearance Tab

In the *Appearance* tab, you can set the text style and grid options for a schedule, as shown in Figure 5–81.

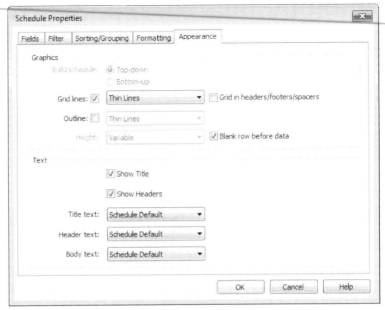

**Figure 5–81**

| | |
|---|---|
| **Grid lines** | Displays lines between each instance listed and around the outside of the schedule. Select the style of lines from the drop-down list; this controls all lines for the schedule, unless modified. |
| **Grid in headers/ footers/spacers** | Extends the vertical grid lines between the columns. |
| **Outline** | Specify a different line type for the outline of the schedule. |
| **Blank row before data** | Select this option if you want a blank row to be displayed before the data begins in the schedule. |
| **Show Title/Show Headers** | Select these options to include the text in the schedule. |
| **Title text/Header text/Body Text** | Select the text style for the title, header, and body text. |

© 2016, ASCENT - Center for Technical Knowledge®

## Schedule Properties

Schedule views have properties including the *View Template, View Name, Phases* and methods of returning to the Schedule Properties dialog box as shown in Figure 5–82. In the *Other* area, select the button next to the tab that you want to open in the Schedule Properties dialog box. In the dialog box, you can switch from tab to tab and make any required changes to the overall schedule.

Figure 5–82

Figure 5–83

**Enhanced** in 2017

Just like other views, schedules can have View Templates applied. When you specify a view template directly in the view, as shown in Figure 5–83, none of the schedule properties can be modified.

- Schedule view templates are type-specific. If you apply one to a different type of element, only the *Appearance* information is applied.

- If you apply a schedule view template to a schedule of the same type, it overrides everything in the existing schedule including the fields.

- If you have a complicated schedule, you might want to create a view template for it to avoid losing that organization.

- To create schedule view templates, you need to create at least one from an existing view. Then, you can modify it and duplicate it in the View Templates dialog box.

## Filtering Elements from Schedules

When you create schedules based on a category you might need to filter out some of the element types in that category. For example, in the Autodesk Revit software, doors (and windows) in curtain walls are automatically added to a door schedule, as shown at the top in Figure 5–84, but are typically estimated as part of the curtain wall rather than as a separate door. To remove them from the schedule, as shown at the bottom in Figure 5–84, assign a parameter that identifies them and then use that parameter to filter them out of the schedule.

Door Schedule- 1st

| Door Type | Door Size | | | Frame | | |
|---|---|---|---|---|---|---|
| | Width | Height | Thickness | Frame Type | Frame Material | Head Detail |
| 8' - 3 1/2" | 9 - 4 1/4" | | | | | |
| | 3' - 0" | 7' - 0" | 0' - 2" | A | Aluminum | |
| | 3' - 0" | 7' - 0" | 0' - 2" | B | Aluminum | |
| | 3' - 0" | 6' - 8" | 0' - 2" | C | Aluminum | |

Door Schedule- 1st

| Door Type | Door Size | | | Frame | | |
|---|---|---|---|---|---|---|
| | Width | Height | Thickness | Frame Type | Frame Material | Head Detail |
| | 3' - 0" | 7' - 0" | 0' - 2" | A | Aluminum | |
| | 3' - 0" | 7' - 0" | 0' - 2" | B | Aluminum | |
| | 3' - 0" | 6' - 8" | 0' - 2" | C | Aluminum | |
| | 3' - 0" | 6' - 8" | 0' - 2" | C | Aluminum | |

**Figure 5–84**

- This type of filtering can be used for any schedule in any discipline.

### How To: Filter Elements in a Schedule

*Create a type specifically for this if you are using one that is also used elsewhere.*

1. Select an element (such as a door used in curtain walls) and modify the Type Parameters. Add a value to one of the parameters that you are not otherwise using in your schedule. For example, set *Construction Type* to **CW**, as shown Figure 5–85

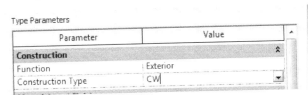

Type Parameters

| Parameter | Value |
|---|---|
| **Construction** | |
| Function | Exterior |
| Construction Type | CW |

**Figure 5–85**

© 2016, ASCENT - Center for Technical Knowledge®

2. Create a schedule and include the field, such as *Construction Type*.

3. Modify the *Filter* of the schedule so the parameter does not equal the specified value. In the example shown in Figure 5–86, *Construction Type* **does not equal CW**. Any types that match this filter are excluded from the schedule.

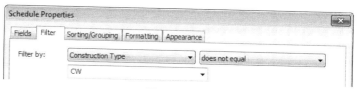

**Figure 5–86**

4. In the final schedule, the elements display with the specified value. Right-click on the column header and select **Hide Column(s)**, as shown in Figure 5–87. It is just used as a filter and not part of the final schedule.

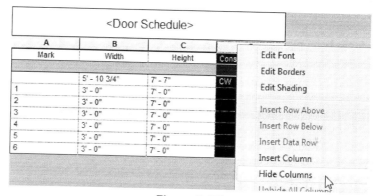

**Figure 5–87**

| Practice 5f | # Organize and Sort Items in a Schedule |
|---|---|

## Practice Objectives

- Create building component schedules.
- Apply filters.
- Enter information.
- Place schedules on a sheet.

*Estimated time for completion: 15 minutes*

In this practice, you will create Door and Window schedules, filter out curtain wall doors, and add information to cells in the door schedule. You will also place the schedules on a sheet, as shown in Figure 5–88.

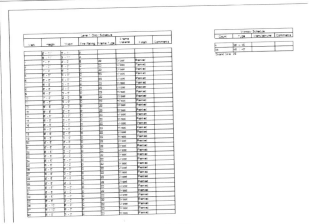

**Figure 5–88**

## Task 1 - Create a Door schedule.

1.  In the practice files folder, open **Clark-Hall-Schedules-Create-A.rvt**.

2.  In the *View* tab>Create panel, expand (Schedules) and click (Schedule/Quantities).

3.  In the New Schedule dialog box, set the *Filter List* to **Architecture** only to limit the number of categories and then set the *Category* to **Doors.**

4.  Name the schedule **Door Schedule-Level 1**. Click **OK.**

© 2016, ASCENT - Center for Technical Knowledge®

5. In the Schedule Properties dialog box, in the *Fields* tab, add the following fields, as shown in Figure 5–89:

- *Level*
- *Mark*
- *Height*
- *Width*
- *Fire Rating*

- *Frame Type*
- *Frame Material*
- *Finish*
- *Comments*
- *Construction Type*

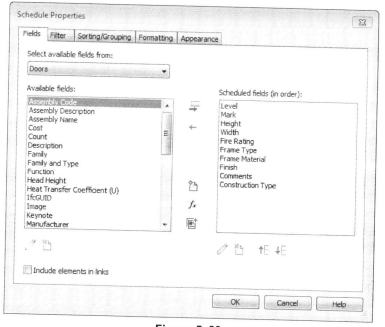

**Figure 5–89**

6. Click **OK** to create the schedule. Note that Level 1, Level 2, and Level 3 doors are included.

7. In Properties, in the *Other* category, next to **Filter**, click **Edit....** The Schedule Properties dialog box opens with the *Filter* tab selected. Set *Filter by* to **Level - equals - Level 1**.

8. In the dialog box, in the *Sorting/Grouping* tab, sort the doors by **Mark**, and click **OK** to update the schedule.

9. Save the project.

## Task 2 - Remove the Curtain Wall Doors from the schedule.

1. Continue working in the new **Door Schedule-Level 1** view, The doors in the curtain walls do not display with a **Mark**, as shown in Figure 5–90. Additionally, they are not included in door schedules and need to be removed.

| A | B | C | D |
|---|---|---|---|
| Level | Mark | Height | Width |
| Level 1 | | 6' - 11" | 5' - 11" |
| Level 1 | | 6' - 11" | 5' - 11" |
| Level 1 | 1 | 7' - 0" | 3' - 0" |
| Level 1 | 2 | 7' - 0" | 6' - 0" |
| Level 1 | 3 | 7' - 0" | 6' - 0" |
| Level 1 | 4 | 6' - 8" | 3' - 0" |
| Level 1 | 5 | 6' - 8" | 3' - 0" |

Figure 5–90

2. In Properties, in the *Other* category, next to **Filter**, click **Edit...**.

*You need to type **CW** because the option does not yet exist in the project.*

3. In the Schedule Properties dialog box, in the *Filter* tab, add the additional Filter: **Construction Type - does not equal - CW**, as shown in Figure 5–91, and click **OK**.

Schedule Properties

| Fields | Filter | Sorting/Grouping | Formatting | Appearance |

| Filter by: | Level | equals | Level 1 |
| And: | Construction Type | does not equal | CW |
| And: | (none) | | |

Figure 5–91

4. In the Schedule, next to one of the curtain wall doors, in the *Construction Type* column, type **CW**. An alert displays prompting you that this is a type property. Click **OK** and the curtain wall doors are no longer included in the schedule, as shown in Figure 5–92.

| A | B | C | D |
|---|---|---|---|
| Level | Mark | Height | Width |
| Level 1 | 1 | 7' - 0" | 3' - 0" |
| Level 1 | 2 | 7' - 0" | 6' - 0" |
| Level 1 | 3 | 7' - 0" | 6' - 0" |
| Level 1 | 4 | 6' - 8" | 3' - 0" |

Figure 5–92

5. Save the project

© 2016, ASCENT - Center for Technical Knowledge®

## Task 3 - Fill in additional information in the Door Schedule

1. Continue working in the **Door Schedule-Level 1** view,

2. In the *Fire Rating* column, type a letter for one of the door types. Because the door type controls the **Fire Rating** parameter, an alert box opens, as shown in Figure 5–93. Click **OK**.

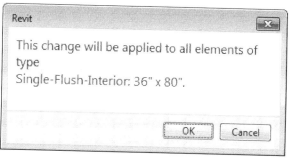

**Figure 5–93**

3. Repeat with the other doors until they all have a fire rating.

4. Open the **Floor Plans: Level 1** view and select one of the interior single doors.

5. Right-click and select **Select All Instances>In Entire Project** in Properties. Set the following parameters:

   - *Frame Type:* **22**
   - *Frame Material:* **Wood**
   - *Finish:* **Stained**

6. Switch back to the schedule to verify that it has updated with the new information.

7. In the schedule view, set the rest of the doors to the following parameters:

   - *Frame Type:* **21**
   - *Frame Material:* **Aluminum**
   - *Finish:* **Brushed**

8. Right-click on the *Level* header and select **Hide Columns**. Repeat the procedure with the *Construction Type* header. This removes the columns from the schedule, as shown in Figure 5–94, while still enabling you to use the fields as filters.

| | | | | | | | |
|---|---|---|---|---|---|---|---|
| **A** | **B** | **C** | **D** | **E** | **F** | **G** | **H** |
| Mark | Height | Width | Fire Rating | Frame Type | Frame Material | Finish | Comments |
| 1 | 7' - 0" | 3' - 0" | A | 21 | Aluminum | Brushed | |
| 2 | 7' - 0" | 6' - 0" | A | 21 | Aluminum | Brushed | |
| 3 | 7' - 0" | 6' - 0" | A | 21 | Aluminum | Brushed | |
| 4 | 6' - 8" | 3' - 0" | B | 22 | Wood | Stained | |
| 5 | 6' - 8" | 3' - 0" | B | 22 | Wood | Stained | |
| 6 | 6' - 8" | 3' - 0" | B | 22 | Wood | Stained | |
| 7 | 6' - 8" | 3' - 0" | B | 22 | Wood | Stained | |
| 8 | 6' - 8" | 3' - 0" | B | 22 | Wood | Stained | |

<Door Schedule-Level 1>

**Figure 5–94**

9. Save the project.

## Task 4 - Create a Window schedule.

1. Create a new window schedule with the following fields: **Count**, **Type**, **Manufacturer**, and **Comments**.

2. In the *Sorting/Grouping* tab, sort the windows by **Type**. Toggle on **Grand totals** and toggle off **Itemize every instance**.

3. Click **OK** to create the schedule. It lists the total count for a single type (only one type is used in the project), as shown in Figure 5–95.

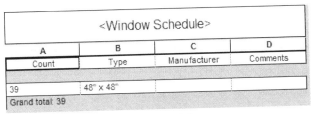

**Figure 5–95**

© 2016, ASCENT - Center for Technical Knowledge®

4. In the **Floor Plans: Level 1** view, select the three windows in the Conference Room in the office wing. In Properties change the type to **Fixed with Trim: 36" x 72"**.

5. Switch back to the schedule view. A change should display in the schedule that reflects the new window type, as shown in Figure 5–96.

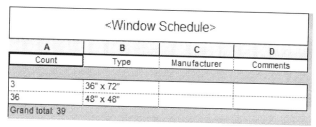

| <Window Schedule> | | | |
|---|---|---|---|
| **A** | **B** | **C** | **D** |
| Count | Type | Manufacturer | Comments |
| 3 | 36" x 72" | | |
| 36 | 48" x 48" | | |
| Grand total: 39 | | | |

**Figure 5–96**

6. Open the **A601- Schedules** sheet. Drag and drop the schedules to this sheet. Modify the width of each field as required.

7. Save the project.

© 2016, ASCENT - Center for Technical Knowledge®

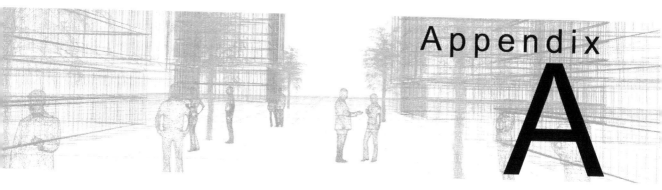

# Review Questions

The following review questions are provided to help you to self-evaluate your understanding and retention of the topics presented in *Autodesk® Revit® 2017 (R1) Architecture: Review for Certification*. They are not intended to represent the types of questions found in the Autodesk Revit Architecture Certified Professional exam. Answers are provided at the end of each topic.

## Collaboration

1. Which of the following elements, as shown in Figure A–1, can be copied and monitored? (Select all that apply.)

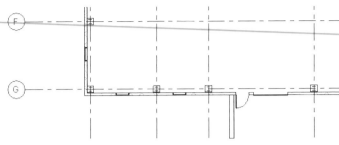

**Figure A–1**

   a. Grids

   b. Walls

   c. Columns

   d. Doors

2. Where should a central file be located?

   a. On your computer.

   b. On the company server.

   c. On each of the computers used by the team.

3. When you want to update the work that you have done and receive any changes others have made, but you do not want to change anything else, which command do you use?

   a. (Synchronize and Modify Settings)

   b. (Synchronize Now)

   c. (Relinquish All Mine)

   d. (Reload Latest)

4. Where should a local file be located?

   a. On the project manager's computer.

   b. On the company server.

   c. On each team member's computer.

© 2016, ASCENT - Center for Technical Knowledge®

5.  What do you need to do so that any new elements you add are placed in a particular workset, as shown in Figure A–2?

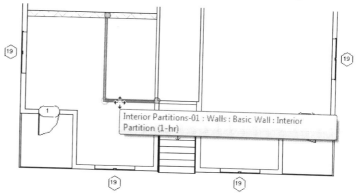

**Figure A–2**

a.  Gray out inactive worksets so you know not to work in them.

b.  Make the workset editable.

c.  Set the workset active.

d.  Create a new workset.

6.  When selecting an element to edit, the icon shown in Figure A–3 displays. What do you need to do?

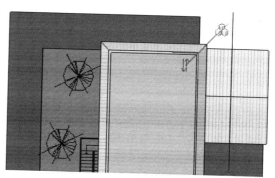

**Figure A–3**

a.  Nothing, you can edit the element without checking it out.

b.  Click the icon and an error dialog box displays indicating that you cannot edit the element.

c.  Click the icon and an error dialog box displays indicating that you cannot edit the element but you can request permission to edit it.

d.  Click the icon and a dialog box displays granting you permission to edit the element.

© 2016, ASCENT - Center for Technical Knowledge®

7. You have the most recent updates from the central file but some elements in a workset are not displaying, as shown in Figure A–4. Which of the following should you check? (Select all that apply.)

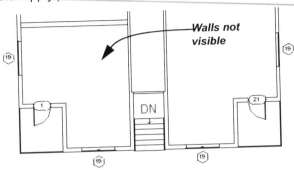

**Figure A–4**

a. In the Visibility/Graphics Overrides dialog box, change the Visibility Setting of the workset to **Visible**.

b. In the Worksets dialog box, request permission to edit.

c. Set the workset as active.

d. On the Status Bar, change the Worksharing Display.

e. In the Worksets dialog box, verify if the workset is open.

8. Which of the following types of vector files can you import into the Autodesk Revit software? (Select all that apply.)

a. DGN

b. DWG

c. DOC

d. DXF

© 2016, ASCENT - Center for Technical Knowledge®

9. Which of the following can you use to modify a raster image, such as the one shown in Figure A–5? (Select all that apply.)

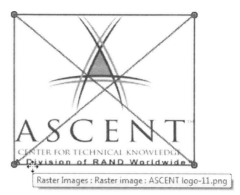

**Figure A–5**

a. Delete portions of the graphic.

b. Resize it by dragging the corners.

c. Query the information inside the graphic.

d. Change the foreground/background status.

**Answers:** 1a,b,c, 2b, 3b, 4c, 5c, 6a,c, 7a,e, 8a,b,d, 9b,d

# Documentation

1. Which command do you use to add a pattern (such as concrete or earth as shown in Figure A–6) to part of a detail?

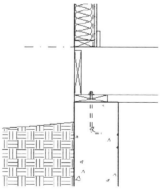

**Figure A–6**

a. Region

b. Filled Region

c. Masking Region

d. Pattern Region

2.  Which of the following describes detail components?

    a.  3D models created in a family file.

    b.  2D drawings made with detail sketch lines created in a
        family file.

    c.  2D drawings made with detail sketch lines and then
        grouped together using the **Create Group** command.

3.  Which of the following elements cannot be tagged using **Tag
    by Category**?

    a.  Rooms

    b.  Floors

    c.  Walls

    d.  Doors

4.  When a wall is moved (as shown in Figure A–7), how do you
    update the dimension?

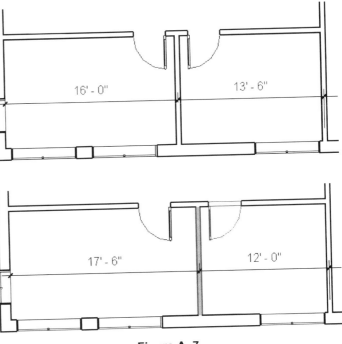

**Figure A–7**

    a.  Edit the dimension and move it over.

    b.  Select the dimension and then click the **Update** button in
        the Options Bar.

    c.  The dimension automatically updates.

    d.  Delete the existing dimension and add a new one.

© 2016, ASCENT - Center for Technical Knowledge®

5. If you want to have more than one color scheme that uses the same level and rooms, you need to create a view for each scheme.

   a. True

   b. False

6. If you are creating a color scheme to display the individual area of each room, as shown in Figure A–8, which of the following do you use?

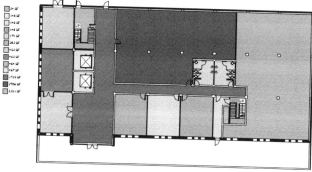

**Figure A–8**

   a. By Value

   b. By Range

7. When you want to demolish some elements, as shown in Figure A–9, in what phase should the elements be?

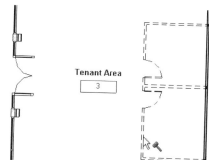

**Figure A–9**

   a. New Construction

   b. Existing

   c. Demolition

8. When creating a view that displays the *Phase* **New Construction** along with the existing and demolished elements, as shown in Figure A–10, which of the Phase Filters do you use?

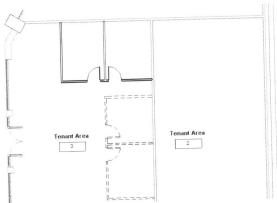

**Figure A–10**

a. Show All

b. Show Complete

c. Show Previous + New

d. Show Previous Phase

**Answers:**   1b, 2b, 3a, 4c, 5a, 6a, 7b, 8a

© 2016, ASCENT - Center for Technical Knowledge®

## Elements and Families

1. You are placing a curtain grid and it keeps snapping to one dimension, such as the TWO-THIRDS OF CURTAIN PANEL shown in Figure A–11, when you want it to be another. What should you do?

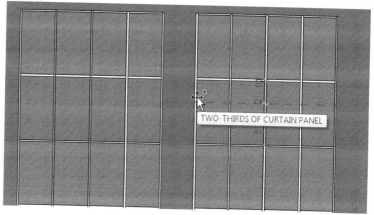

**Figure A–11**

a. Change the snap settings.

b. Edit the Curtain Wall Type to permit manual grid placement.

c. Use a Non-Uniform Curtain Wall Type instead of a Uniform one.

d. Place the curtain grid anyway, select the temporary dimension, and change it to the required value.

2. How do you select one panel to modify it?

a. Select the middle of the panel.

b. Point to the edge of the panel and press <Tab> until it is identified.

c. Select the curtain wall, right-click and select **Panel Select**.

d. In the Selection Priority drop-down list, select **Curtain Panel**.

3. How do you change the way in which two mullions intersect, as shown in Figure A–12? (Select all that apply.)

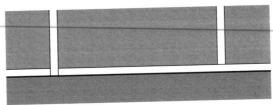

**Figure A–12**

a. Select one of the mullions and press <Tab> until the correct intersection displays.

b. Select one of the mullions and click the **Make Continuous** or **Break at Join** icons in the contextual tab.

c. Select one of the mullions and click the **Toggle Mullion Join** control.

d. Select both mullions and select the **Intersect** box in the Options Bar.

4. When creating a compound wall, you assign a Function for each layer. The numbers after the function names is the priority of the layers when they are joined together with other walls, as shown in Figure A–13. Which of the following function connects first?

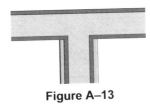

**Figure A–13**

a. Membrane Layer

b. Substrate

c. Structure

d. Thermal/Air Layer

e. Finish

© 2016, ASCENT - Center for Technical Knowledge®

5. How do you create a wall type that has more than one finish material on the vertical plane in the one type, as shown for stone and stucco in Figure A–14?

**Figure A–14**

a. Create separate wall types for the stone and stucco. Duplicate an existing Stacked Wall type and set the wall types to stone and stucco.

b. Draw two walls on top of each other and use  (Join Geometry) to link them.

c. Duplicate an existing Basic Wall type and use **Split Region** and **Assign Layers** to apply the stone and stucco materials to separate parts of the wall.

d. Draw the first wall, draw the other wall on top of the first, and use (Cut Geometry) to cut the second wall out of the first wall.

6. Which of the following is created when you label a dimension?

a. Family

b. Type

c. Parameter

d. Value

7. Which of the following are component families? (Select all that apply.)

a. Desks

b. Trees

c. Roofs

d. Columns

8. Which of the following commands, shown in Figure A–15, require profiles instead of sketches? (Select all that apply.)

Figure A–15

a. **Extrusion**

b. **Blend**

c. **Revolve**

d. **Sweep**

e. **Swept Blend**

9. Which of the following commands creates the element shown in Figure A–16?

Figure A–16

a. **Extrusion**

b. **Blend**

c. **Revolve**

d. **Sweep**

e. **Swept Blend**

© 2016, ASCENT - Center for Technical Knowledge®

10. In which dialog box do you specify sizes for component types?

 a. Family Editor

 b. Family Types

 c. Family Categories

 d. Family Properties

**Answers**: 1d, 2b, 3b,c, 4c, 5a, 6c, 7a,b,d, 8d,e, 9b, 10b

## Modeling

1. In which of the following ways can you NOT create topographical surfaces, such as that shown in Figure A–17?

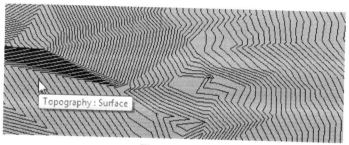

**Figure A–17**

 a. From an imported drawing that was creating using the AutoCAD® software.

 b. By sketching.

 c. From an imported drawing that was created using the AutoCAD® Civil 3D® software.

 d. From a points file.

2. Which of the following best describes the difference between a building pad and a floor?

 a. A pad affects the surrounding surface and a floor element does not.

 b. A pad must be placed at a level and a floor can be placed above or below a level.

 c. A pad must line up with walls and a floor can also be sketched.

 d. A pad cannot be sloped and a floor can be sloped.

3. What must be in place before you can add a floor to a mass element, as shown in Figure A–18?

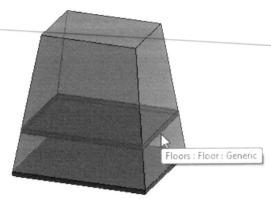

Floors : Floor : Generic

**Figure A–18**

   a. Additional mass elements at each floor.

   b. Sketches for each floor.

   c. An additional floor parameter in Properties.

   d. Mass floor elements at each floor.

4. Which of the following is NOT a stair component?

   a. Runs

   b. Landings

   c. Treads

   d. Supports

5. When do you need to use the (Railing) command? (Select all that apply.)

   a. When you want an extra railing in the middle of very wide stairs.

   b. When you create a stair or ramp.

   c. When you create railings that are not attached to stairs or ramps.

   d. When you use the **Stair by Sketch** command.

6. When creating a floor, ceiling, or roof by footprint the boundary sketch must be…

   a. Open

   b. Closed

   c. It does not matter.

© 2016, ASCENT - Center for Technical Knowledge®

7. How do you change the thickness of a floor, such as those shown in Figure A–19?

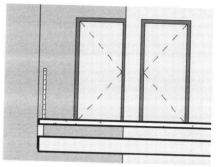

**Figure A–19**

a. In the Type Selector, change the Floor Type.

b. In the Options Bar, change the Floor Thickness.

c. In Properties, change the Floor Thickness.

d. In the contextual ribbon, change the Offset.

8. To create a roof sloping in one direction only (as shown on the front of the building in Figure A–20), you would create a roof...

**Figure A–20**

a. By extrusion and rotate the roof to the correct angle.

b. By footprint and specify the slope along one side.

c. By extrusion and use the Slope Arrow to define the overall slope of the roof.

d. By footprint and use the **Shape Editing** tools to create the slope.

© 2016, ASCENT - Center for Technical Knowledge®

9. To create a flat roof, which of the following commands would you use to draw a sketch of the boundary of the roof and to set its thickness?

   a. **Roof by Footprint** with the thickness set by the roof type.

   b. **Roof by Extrusion** with the thickness extruded from the sketch.

10. Which of the following methods makes a wall touch the underside of a roof?

    a. Select the wall and use ⬚ (Attach Top/Base).

    b. Select the roof and use ⬚ (Attach Top/Base).

    c. Select the wall and edit the profile.

    d. Select the roof and use the **By Face** option.

11. Which roof type and view should you use to create a curved roof as shown in Figure A–21?

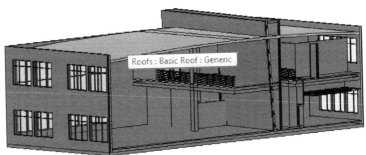

Roofs : Basic Roof : Generic

**Figure A–21**

   a. Roof by Footprint, Plan View

   b. Roof by Footprint, Elevation or Section view

   c. Roof by Extrusion, Plan View

   d. Roof by Extrusion, Elevation or Section view

**Answers:** 1c, 2a, 3d, 4c, 5a,c, 6b, 7a, 8b, 9a, 10a, 11d

## Views

1. In a schedule, if you change type information (such as a Type Mark) all instances of that type update with the new information.

   a. True

   b. False

© 2016, ASCENT - Center for Technical Knowledge®

2. Which of the following is true about the Visibility Graphic Overrides dialog box? (Select all that apply.)

   a. Changes made in the dialog box only affect the current view.

   b. It can be used to turn categories on and off.

   c. It can be used to turn individual elements on and off.

   d. It can be used to change the color of individual elements.

3. What type of view do you need to be in to add a level to your project?

   a. Any non-plan view.

   b. As this is done using a dialog box, the view does not matter.

   c. Any view except for 3D.

   d. Any section or elevation view.

4. Which of the following commands shown in Figure A–22, creates a view that results in an independent view displaying the same model geometry and containing a copy of the annotation?

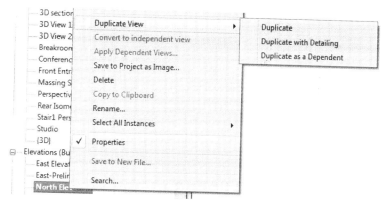

**Figure A–22**

   a. Duplicate

   b. Duplicate with Detailing

   c. Duplicate as a Dependent

5. When creating a Legend, which of the following elements cannot be added?

   a. Legend Components

   b. Tags

   c. Rooms

   d. Symbols

6. On how many sheets can a view be placed?

   a. 1

   b. 2-5

   c. 6+

   d. As many as you want.

7. Which of the following is the best method to use if the size of a view is too large for a sheet, as shown in Figure A–23?

**Figure A–23**

   a. Delete the view, change the scale and place the view back on the sheet.

   b. Activate the view and change the View Scale.

© 2016, ASCENT - Center for Technical Knowledge®

8. In the Schedule Properties dialog box (shown in Figure A–24), in which tab do you define the order of the list of elements?

Schedule Properties

| Fields | Filter | Sorting/Grouping | Formatting | Appearance |

**Figure A–24**

a. *Fields*

b. *Filter*

c. *Sorting/Grouping*

d. *Formatting*

e. *Appearance*

**Answers:** 1a, 2a,b, 3d, 4b, 5c, 6a, 7a, 8a

© 2016, ASCENT - Center for Technical Knowledge®

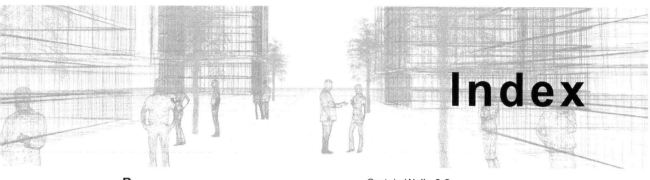

# Index

---

© 2016, ASCENT - Center for Technical Knowledge®

© 2016, ASCENT - Center for Technical Knowledge®